TEACH YOURSELF BOOKS

COARSE ANGLING

Cliff Parker's fishing career started in Manchester during World War II, in waters which are still waiting to be listed in an anglers' guide: Jackson's Clay Pit, Platt Fields boating lake, the pint-sized reservoir near Longsight Station (Trespassers Will Be Prosecuted), and some stretches of canal that changed colour every day.

He was about to give it all up when his father was demobilised, and started teaching young Clifford how to use a rod in waters where the fish didn't cough.

Since then Cliff has fished all over the country and in foreign parts, ranging from Yorkshire to the Sudan. For more than twenty years he has been writing about what to him is a great sport, a great philosophy and a lot of fun.

From fishing trips with his teenage son and daughter and his protesting but patient wife (she loves it, really), Parker gets much of his material for his laughter columns in the angling press.

Coarse Angling will, he hopes, get beginners very quickly into the business of catching fish. All other delights of the sport will follow . . . and those nobody can teach you.

COARSE ANGLING

Cliff Parker

**Illustrated by
Graham Allen**

TEACH YOURSELF BOOKS
Hodder and Stoughton

First printed 1976
Copyright © 1976
Cliff Parker

All rights reserved. No part of this publication may be reproduced or transmitted in any form or by any means, electronic or mechanical, including photocopy, recording, or any information storage and retrieval system, without permission in writing from the publisher.

ISBN 0 340 20381 1

Printed and bound in Great Britain for Teach Yourself Books, Hodder and Stoughton, London, by Cox & Wyman Ltd, London, Fakenham and Reading

Contents

	Introduction	*page* vii
1	How, When and Where?	1
2	A Who's Who of Coarse Fish	3
3	Tackle	14
4	Baits	40
5	Starting To Fish	64
6	Float Fishing	75
7	Legering	85
8	Spinning	94
9	Fly Fishing	100
10	Barbel	104
11	Bream	114
12	Common Carp	122
13	Crucian Carp	135
14	Catfish	139
15	Chub	141
16	Dace	151
17	Eel	154
18	Grayling	162
19	Gudgeon	166
20	Perch	169
21	Pike	178
22	Roach	195
23	Rudd	208
24	Tench	216
25	Zander	225

vi Contents

26	Wading and Boating	228
27	Fishing Floodwater	232
28	Care of Your Catch	234
29	Care of Your Tackle	239
30	Tackle You Can Make	245
31	Some Useful Knots	251
32	Logging and Mapping	254
33	Anglers' Manners	258
34	Is This a Record?	261
35	Some Useful Addresses	264
	Index	267

Introduction

Three things seem obligatory in the introduction to a book on coarse fishing: an explanation of the word 'coarse', an account of the popularity of coarse fishing; and a lyrical exposition of the joys of angling. Here they come, then, but briefly. An introduction is no excuse for an author to wallow.

'Coarse' is an unfortunate word, but there is no other. It has been around for a long time and it has stuck. It means all *freshwater* fish except those of the salmon family, and apparently derives from the old phrase 'in course', meaning ordinary. There is certainly nothing coarse about the tackle, the techniques or the fish.

The popularity of coarse fishing is undisputed. It is now well-known that more people *go* fishing than *watch* professional football. There are just under three million anglers in Britain, and of these almost two million are coarse fishermen (the rest being game and sea). More than a million coarse anglers fish at least once a week during the season, almost twice the crowds at Saturday's professional football matches.

One feature of coarse fishing is match angling—competition fishing for prize money—which is not dealt with specifically in this book. Match anglers use techniques which are refinements of basic coarse angling techniques. The techniques, bait and tackle change almost monthly as one development—or fad—follows another. This is not to decry match fishing but to explain why the best source of information on it is the weekly angling press.

The joys of angling are many, and each angler has his own special delights. Some enjoy the hunt, the outwitting of an invisible creature in another element. Some enjoy the thrill of the fight, the landing of a big fish on what seems incredibly fragile tackle. Some enjoy the sheer numbers of the catch. Some enjoy the hush and freshness of the early morning. Some enjoy the solitude. Some enjoy the acceptance of the angler by the wild creatures of the waterside.

The really lucky anglers enjoy it all. And you will enjoy it the sooner if I make this full stop the last.

Cliff Parker

1

How, When and Where?

In England and Wales, coarse fishing is not allowed all the year round. There is a statutory close season from 15 March to 15 June inclusive, imposed by the old River Authorities and continued by the Regional Water Authorities which replaced them in 1974. The close season, which is to allow the fish to spawn undisturbed, varies in certain parts of the country, and on many waters pike fishing is prohibited until 1 October. There is no close season for coarse fish in Scotland or Ireland.

The fishing rights on most waters belong either to the owner of the bank or to an angling club which pays a rent for these rights. So to fish, you usually have to buy a licence, which can be anything from a day ticket to a yearly subscription to a club. In some areas, a rod licence from the appropriate Regional Water Authority is also needed.

The easiest way to find out how and where to start fishing is to ask at the local library or tackle dealer for the names and addresses of the local angling clubs. Tackle dealers are often agents for clubs and can provide membership proposal forms.

Membership of a club brings many benefits. The most obvious is access to a number of waters for a modest membership fee. The club may be affiliated to larger angling societies, which means an even greater number of waters open to you. Clubs also organise coach outings to distant waters.

Another benefit of club membership is that you can meet experienced anglers who are more than glad to share their knowledge of angling in general and the club waters in particular. The techniques in this book must of necessity be general techniques, known to catch fish in the places you are likely to find them. But on every water there is some special technique or bait which has proved extra-successful, and the old hands will let you into the secrets.

The two biggest national angling publications in the United Kingdom are *Angling Times* and *Angler's Mail*, both weeklies. In both you will find up-to-date news and feature articles on current angling techniques and catches, along with river reports and other useful information.

2

A Who's Who of Coarse Fish

The number, size and variety of British freshwater fish is always a surprise to the non-angler, and discovering them all is a great delight for the novice. In spite of pollution and water abstraction, in spite of there being fewer fishable waters every year—and more anglers wanting to share the remaining space—the freshwater fishing scene in Britain is still an exciting one.

The smallest and calmest-looking pond may hold carp

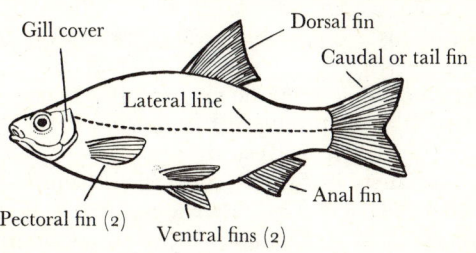

FIG. 1 Whatever the species, all fish have the same basic structure.

or tench of great size. The most tangled and overgrown 'jungle' swim of a narrow river may hold really big, rod-bending chub. The seemingly empty shallows near the bank may suddenly boil as a big pike slashes into its prey, or the surface water may part for the broad back of a cruising carp.

Coarse fish in Britain (anglers' fish, that is, excluding tiny nuisances like bleak, ruffe and minnow) are: barbel, bream, carp, chub, dace, eel, gudgeon, perch, pike, roach, rudd and tench.

The grayling is included in this book although it is strictly speaking a game fish, because it spawns with the coarse fish and is fished for by many coarse anglers lucky enough to live near a grayling water. Also included are two imported fish, the catfish and the zander. The zander has spread so rapidly over the past years that it will soon be in practically every river and canal system in Britain.

The following brief details on the fish will put you enough in the picture to follow the tackle and baits sections. The fish and the methods of catching them are discussed in greater detail later on.

With each fish is given the official record rod-caught weight. The record fish are freaks, by their very act of living longer and growing bigger. You are likely to catch fish very much below these weights but, by the same rule, there are fish in our waters very much bigger than the biggest yet caught. This is one of the great attractions of fishing—there are bigger fish in the waters than ever came out, and *you* may be the one to land the next record-breaker.

The records are reproduced by courtesy of the National Anglers' Council British Record (Rod-Caught) Fish Committee. The first British Record Fish Committee was established by *Angling Times* after a controversial claim for a record chub in 1955; it comprised two representatives from *Angling Times* and two scientists. In 1957 the Committee extended its representation, and from this time dates the Record Committee proper.

It revised the old record list, abandoning any which seemed doubtful. In 1968 the Committee handed over its work to the National Anglers' Council. After further revisions the NAC in 1969 produced a list which was greatly thinned down and substituted qualifying weights

A Who's Who of Coarse Fish

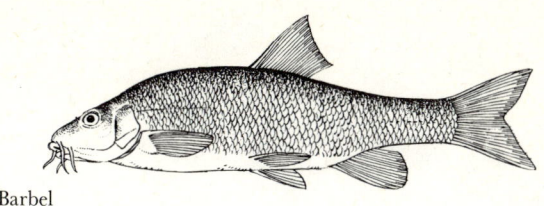

Barbel

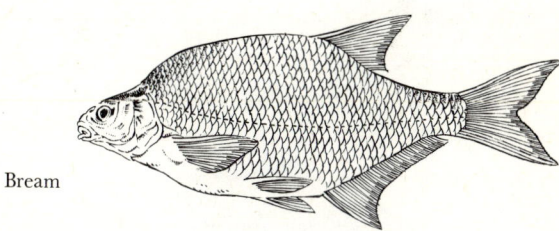

Bream

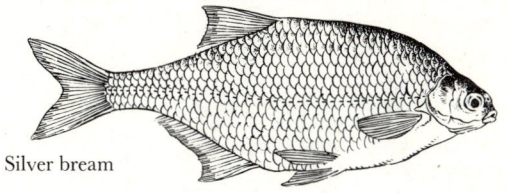

Silver bream

Carp

FIG. 2

6 *Coarse Angling*

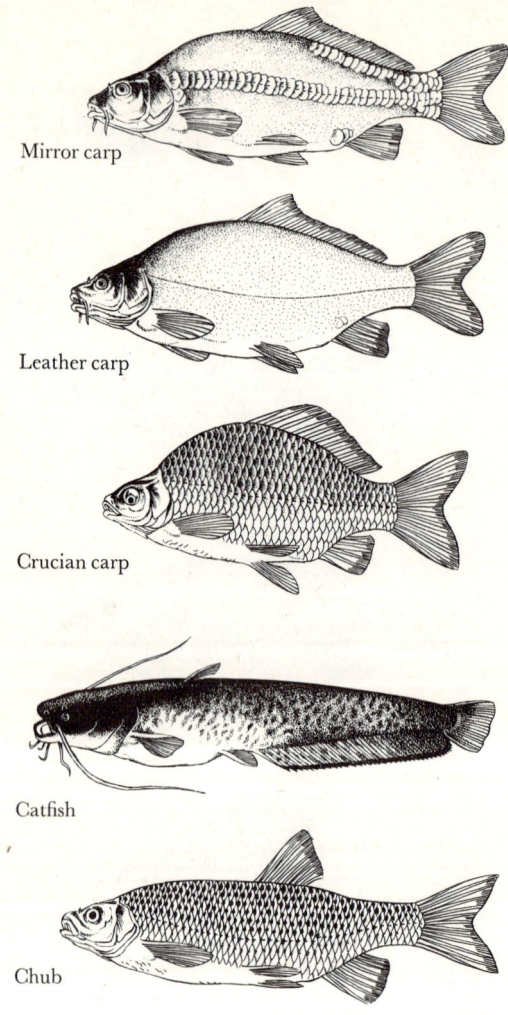

Mirror carp

Leather carp

Crucian carp

Catfish

Chub

FIG. 3

A Who's Who of Coarse Fish 7

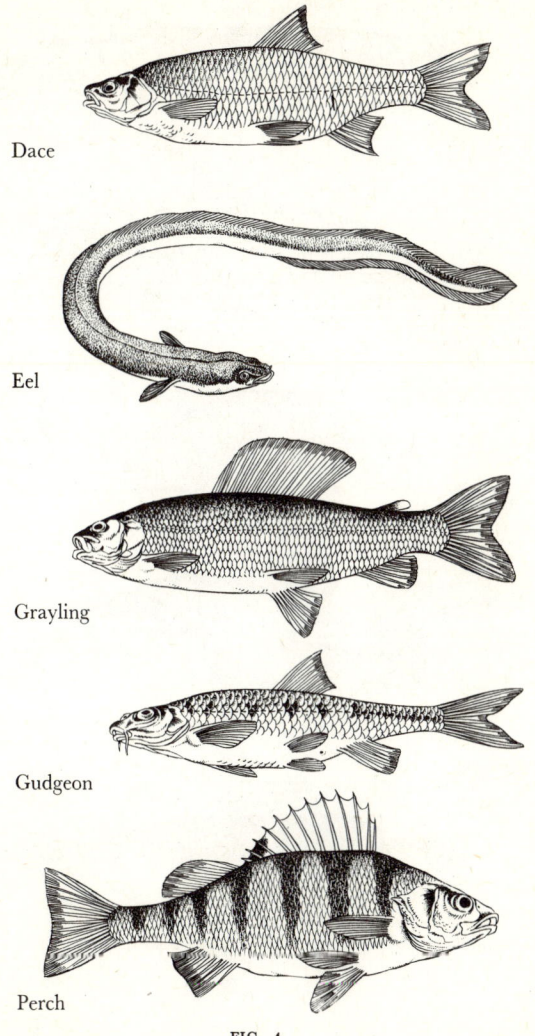

Dace

Eel

Grayling

Gudgeon

Perch

FIG. 4

8 *Coarse Angling*

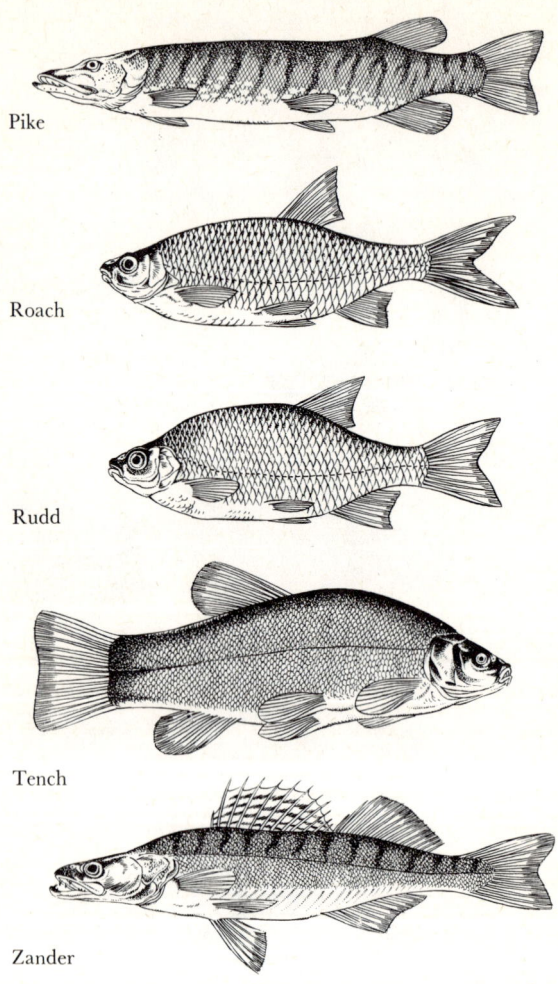

FIG. 5

for rejected records. The qualifying weights mean that no fish under that weight can be considered for the record, even if it is the biggest caught in the season.

Barbel
Record weight 13 lb 12 oz, taken in 1962 on the Royalty Fishery, Hampshire.

A powerful fish of fast water, built to hold the bottom against the current and equipped with barbules, or barbels, at the mouth to help search out food. Still a little localised in distribution, but having its range extended by stocking experiments.

Common or bronze bream
Record weight 12 lb 14 oz, taken in 1971 on the River Stour, Suffolk.

A grazing fish of still or gentle waters, where it moves around in shoals, often enormous ones. A slimy, deep-bodied fish, compressed laterally so that it looks huge from the side, but nothing much from the front.

It is often accused of having no fighting spirit, but a biggish bream can give a good account of itself, especially with some current to help it. Fighting fish or not, it is still a very popular one with anglers.

Silver bream
No record weight; qualifying weight 1 lb 8 oz. Any fish contending for this record must be produced, to make absolutely sure that it really is a silver bream, not a small bronze bream or a hybrid.

This fish is a small 'poor relation' of the bronze bream. The old record was only 4 lb 8 oz. Its habits are much the same as the bronze bream. Few anglers fish for it deliberately. The silver bream is also known as the bellows bream, white bream, tinplate bream or bream flat.

Coarse Angling

Common carp
Record weight 44 lb, taken in 1952 in Redmire Pool, Herefordshire.

The biggest British coarse fish, or at least the biggest so far caught on rod and line. A placid but powerful fish, living in every kind of water but mainly in lakes, pits and ponds. Eats heartily, and often noisily, in weedy shallows, using its barbels to help find food. For the angler, mainly a fish of summer and autumn.

Crucian carp
Record weight 4 lb 15 oz 8 drm, taken in 1972 at Johnson's Lake, New Hythe, Kent.

Nowhere near the size of its bigger cousin, it favours lakes and ponds and is commonest in southern England. Looked down on by carp specimen hunters, but a powerful little fighter on roach tackle and becoming more popular with every season.

Catfish
Record weight 43 lb 8 oz, taken in 1970 at Wilstone Reservoir, Tring, Hertfordshire.

The Danubian catfish, or *wels*, is an imported fish; its range is now spreading. Without doubt the ugliest fish in British waters, its name comes from the long 'whiskers' around its mouth. It likes still or slow water with plenty of mud. Not a determined fighter, but a heavy fish with a powerful first rush.

Chub
No record weight; qualifying weight 7 lb 3 oz; old record weight 10 lb 6 oz.

A chunky, brassy-scaled, wide-mouthed character who will take almost any bait offered, all the year round, once his natural caution has been overcome. Fond of medium-paced water in snaggy places: a run under overhanging trees and bushes is a typical chub haunt. Not a fighter of stamina, but his first rush can be quite spectacular.

Dace

Record weight 1 lb 4 oz 4 drm, taken in 1960 on the Little Ouse at Thetford, Norfolk.

The dace is a darting, silvery fish of no great weight, but a very game little fighter on light tackle. Feeds during the day and in strong sunlight, when most other fish are resting.

Eel

Record weight 8 lb 10 oz, taken in 1969 in Huntstrete Lake, Somerset.

The eel is found everywhere, in every kind of water. A fish of the summer and autumn, it hibernates in the winter. Very slimy and athletic, a great tangler and smasher of tackle, it used to be regarded as a pest. Nowadays a growing number of anglers are fishing for it deliberately.

Grayling

No record weight; qualifying weight 3 lb; old record weight 7 lb 2 oz.

A member of the salmon family, the grayling spawns with the coarse fish; it is often treated as one, and looked down on by game anglers. Probably the most beautiful British freshwater fish, with sail-like dorsal fin and iridescent colours. Its Latin name (*Thymallus thymallus*) comes from the supposition that it smells of thyme. It likes clean, fast water with a gravelly bottom.

Gudgeon

Record weight only 4 oz, taken in 1971 from Susworth Roach Ponds, Lincolnshire.

A small fish, looking like a miniature barbel. Would be classed as a nuisance if it were not for its fighting qualities. A shoal of gudgeon, fished for with the lightest of tackle, can liven up an otherwise dull day. A great encouragement to the beginner.

Perch
Record weight 4 lb 12 oz, taken in 1962 from Oulton Broad, Norfolk.

A flamboyant, piratical, spiky extrovert, with an unmistakable hump-backed shape and striped body. The perch hunts in packs and preys on smaller fish. Greedy and inquisitive, it usually turns up at some time or another during a day's fishing.

Pike
Record weight 43 lb, taken from Lockwood Reservoir, Walthamstow, London in 1974. One of 53 lb has been caught in Eire.

Long, lean and cruel-looking, the pike is the freshwater tiger. He lurks in places with plenty of cover, and prefers his prey to come to him, but will also roam featureless waters and patrol margins in search of food.

Feeds all season through, but on some waters pike-fishing is prohibited until 1 October. Sometimes all the pike in one location will come on the feed at once, making a real red-letter day in the angler's diary.

Roach
Record weight 4 lb 1 oz, taken from a Nottinghamshire gravel pit in 1975.

The roach is the commonest British freshwater fish, found in almost every quiet or medium-paced water. It is gentle and unassuming, a delicate biter, and loved by anglers. Known in Ireland as the rudd.

Rudd
Record weight 4 lb 8 oz, taken in 1933 at Thetford, Norfolk.

Looks like a beefier, more highly-coloured roach. A very pretty fish to look at and an exciting one to fish for. Its underslung jaw gives it a pugnacious look, unlike the timid, chinless, look of the roach. Will feed on bright, sunny days, when most other fish are resting.

Tench

Record weight 10 lb 1 oz 2 drm, taken from a Peterborough brick pit in 1975.

A solid, cautious and powerful fish which likes still water and plenty of mud and weed. Like the carp, it was once bred in stewponds for the table. The broad tail and muscular body of the tench guarantee a fight out of all proportion to its size.

Zander

Record weight 15 lb 5 oz, taken in 1971 in the Great Ouse Relief Channel.

Often known as the pike–perch, the zander is neither pike nor perch but an imported European predatory species which is spreading rapidly through the Great Ouse Relief System. Another species of pike–perch, the walleye, has a record weight of 11 lb 12 oz for a fish taken in 1934 from the Delph, Welney, Norfolk. The walleye, however, is a rarity. It is the zander which is undergoing a population explosion.

3

Tackle

Rods

Every angler eventually builds up a collection of rods for different fish, techniques and conditions, but the most important rod is the first one.

There is no such thing as a real all-purpose rod. You should start with one which will do *several* jobs reasonably well.

Hollow glass has now taken over from cane as the most popular rod-building material. A hollow glass rod does not have the same subtlety of action as built cane, but it will stand up to far more use—and misuse—without breaking or developing a permanent bend. It also needs far less maintenance.

Do not be tempted to buy a solid glass rod. It may not feel heavy in the shop, but after a morning's casting it will feel like a clothes prop, both in weight and action. Do not be tempted, either, to buy a flashy looking rod with gaudy whipping and a shiny finish. All the colour and flash will give the fish early warning that somebody is after them. Look for a dull finish and a neutral colour such as green or brown.

A length of 12 ft is a fair average for a first rod. Depending on your height and physique, however, you may prefer one as short as 10 ft or as long as 14 ft.

The longer rods are certainly better for casting over rushes or weeds by the bank, help you to keep yourself hidden from the fish, and mean you have less line out over the water. They also give more control over a hooked fish.

The shorter rods are useful for treed-up sections of bank or other situations where there is too little room to cast with a long rod.

The rod should be a three-piece and have a 'through action', meaning that it bends into the middle joint while the bottom joint, under normal conditions, stays rigid. (A tip-action rod, such as a match rod, is one in which only the

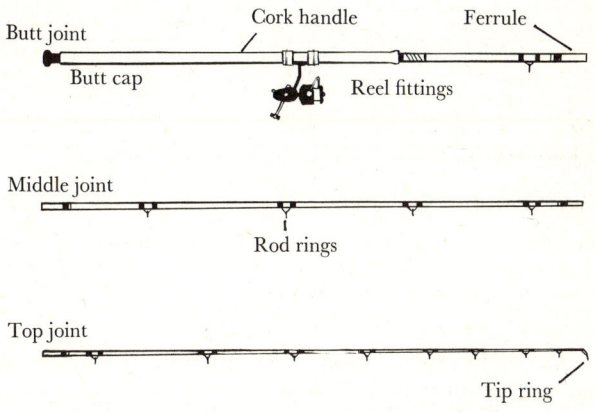

FIG. 6   The parts of a three-joint rod.

top joint bends, while the bottom two stay rigid.) This bending of the rod gives a flex which helps both in casting and in absorbing the lunges of a hooked fish, so taking some of the strain from the line.

It should have a test curve of between 1 and $1\frac{1}{4}$ lb. The test curve is a way of measuring the action of a rod, and is the weight needed to bend it until the tip is at right angles to the butt. (There is no need to take a spring balance along to the shop to measure the test curve: it should be included in the specification.)

This test curve tells you what lines you can safely use with

16 *Coarse Angling*

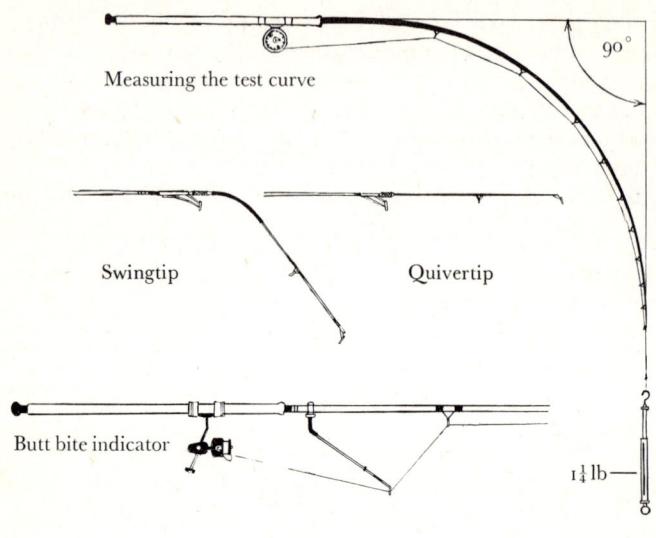

FIG. 7

the rod. The curve multiplied by eight gives you the maximum line strength. So with a test curve of 1 lb you could use a line of any strength up to 8 lb b.s. (breaking strain). With a curve of 1¼ lb, the strongest line is 10 lb b.s.

Test the rod in the shop for balance. To do this you fit a reel and hold the rod at a point about 3 in in front of the cork grip on the butt. The rod should then balance parallel to the ground. Most tackle dealers expect customers to test the rod for balance, and are glad to provide the reel for the operation.

Most rods have sliding winch fittings, so that the reel can be placed at any point on the cork grip which suits the angler. When balancing the rod, make sure that the reel is in the position you feel most at ease with. Some rods have a fixed screw winch fitting, so that the position of the reel cannot be altered.

Having found a rod with a test curve and balance which suits you, try a few practice casts (without line, of course) in the shop. This will help to choose the length which suits you and will give an idea of the rod's action. Again, most tackle dealers do not mind this a bit. If you are unlucky enough to hit on one who does, try another shop.

Now you will have a rod with which you can float fish and leger, which will operate with a range of line strengths, and which will cope with most of the fish you are likely to hook in ordinary conditions.

Some types of rod
Match rods are usually 12 to 14 ft long, in three sections. They have a tip action for a faster strike. Match rods are very light: the 12 ft rod is excellent for a long day's fishing. The longer rods are better for distance casting.

Many anglers prefer to use a match rod for their general fishing, rather than one with a through action. With a glass rod there is little risk of the tip 'setting' or breaking. But for a beginner, a through-action rod is best: the extra flex cuts down the risk of the line breaking with the fight of a lively fish.

Leger rods are between 8 and 10 ft long. Most have a through action and are normally two-piece. The 10-ft rods are necessary when using a swingtip.

Quivertip rods are 6 to 8 ft long including the quivertip spliced into the end.

Pike rods are about 9 to 10 ft long, in two sections, with a through action and generally with screw winch fittings.

Carp and/or specimen rods have a through action. They are either float rods and 12 or 13 ft long, or leger rods and usually 10 ft long.

Block-end rods are 6 to 7 ft long and have a very stiff action. They are used with a block-end feeder. When a fish bites it hooks itself.

Reels

There are two main types of reel: the *centre pin* and the *fixed spool*.

The centre pin is the older type of wheel-shaped reel, consisting of a drum on to which the line is wound, and operated by handles on the side. (It is older only in type: in materials and engineering methods used, it is every bit as up-to-date as the fixed spool.) The reel incorporates a ratchet mechanism which prevents line from being pulled off the drum when the check is applied. Most reels also have a drag

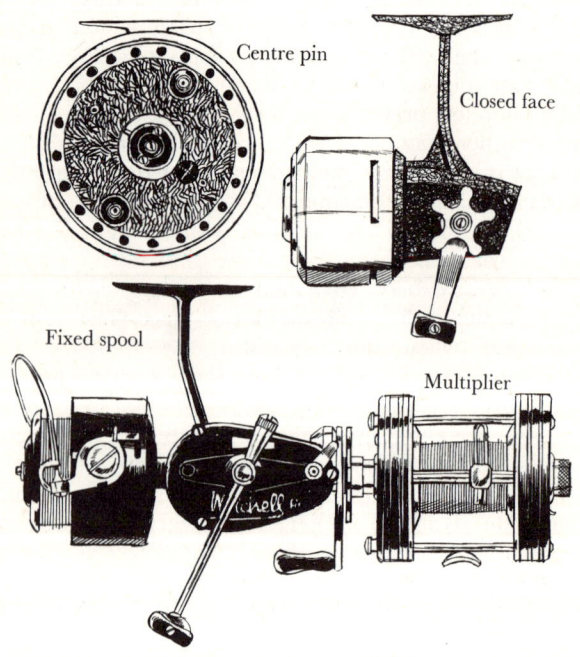

FIG. 8   Four types of reel.

mechanism which allows a fish to take line when it puts on pressure likely to break the line.

Angling purists still insist that a beginner learns to cast and play a fish on a centre pin before graduating to the fixed spool. This can be an expensive apprenticeship, however, as most anglers use the fixed spool for most types of fishing, reserving the centre pin for a few specialised techniques. The fixed-spool reel has several advantages over the centre pin. It is easier and quicker to cast with, does not overrun, allows a greater casting range, and is especially effective when light lines and baits are being used. (At one time it was considered *too* easy to use, and on some waters it was banned on the grounds that fish stocks were being depleted. That attitude towards it, however, has now disappeared.)

The fixed-spool reel has a stationary drum which faces up the rod. The line is wound on by a revolving pick-up, or bale, arm. The drum moves up and down as the line is wound on, to ensure even line distribution. The bale arm is moved back into the 'off' position to allow the line to run

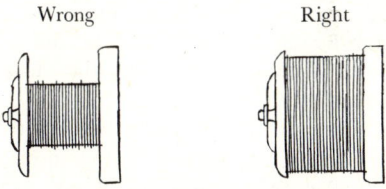

FIG. 9   Filling a spool.

free for casting, and flicked back on by a turn of the handle when the bait is in position. The fixed spool has a slipping clutch mechanism.

The spool must be filled with line almost to the lip, otherwise the friction of the lip on the line holds back the cast. Although shallow spools are now being made, most are too deep for the amount of line normally used. A backing of twine or old line can be wound on first to ensure that the spool is completely filled.

A spool can be removed and quickly replaced with another spool holding a line of different strength; this gives the angler a greater choice of tackle and techniques than with a centre pin. The centre pin, however, gives greater control over a fish and a better 'feel' when a fish is being played. Finger braking on the drum also makes for finer control in moving-bait techniques such as long trotting.

A variation of the centre pin is the *multiplying reel* which, through a system of gears, gives several turns of the drum for each turn of the handle. This fast retrieve is especially useful for spinning or for distance fishing. If the drum of a centre pin or multiplier—especially a multiplier—is allowed to keep revolving after the bait hits the water, the line will overrun and form a 'bird's-nest' tangle. This is easily checked, however, by finger pressure on the drum; overruns are caused by bad casting techniques rather than any inherent fault in the reel.

A variation of the fixed spool is the *closed-face reel* in which the spool is covered by a dome. The dome has a hole in the middle through which the line runs. This dome protects the spool and line from grit, but has the disadvantage of 'dampening' the feel of the fish.

Most anglers reel in with the left hand, so most fixed-spool reels have the handle on the left. Left-handed anglers can buy a fixed spool with a right-hand wind, and some fixed spools allow the handle to be fixed on either side. With a centre pin, there is no problem about left or right. A left-handed angler simply turns the reel round.

For care of reels, see p. 242; for casting techniques, see pp. 69–73.

Hooks

There are many bewildering combinations of sizes and patterns of hooks; the two basic patterns are *round bend* and *crystal*.

Round bend describes itself: the bend is a smooth, uninterrupted curve, giving the hook a large gape. This makes it an ideal hook for use with lobworms, crayfish, meat or any other large baits.

Crystal starts off as a round bend, and then the shank turns sharply upwards. This gives the hook a smaller gape and a longer straight length of wire to the point.

A patented variation of crystal, the *model perfect*, is different enough almost to be a third basic pattern. The arm of the hook leading to the point is set sideways at an angle to the shank. This offsetting of the point makes the hooking of a fish more certain because the point is not masked by the shank on the strike.

Hook sizes are confusing; it is best to stick to the Redditch or 'Old Scale' system of numbering.

Redditch was the centre of the needle-making industry, and the hooks made there were given a number which matched the gauge of needle wire used. The peculiar thing is that as the hook gets *bigger* the number gets *smaller*, until the numbers come down to 1. After that, the numbering starts again from 1, with the addition of the figure '0', and the order is reversed, i.e. the bigger the numbers, the bigger the hooks.

The full Redditch Scale, beginning with the smallest, is therefore: 26, 24, 22, 20, 18, 16, 14, 12, 10, 9, 8, 7, 6, 5, 4, 3, 2, 1; 1/0, 2/0, 3/0, 4/0, 5/0, 6/0, 7/0, 8/0, 9/0, 10/0.

In practice, few coarse anglers use hooks much smaller than 20 or bigger than 2/0. The really tiny ones are almost always used for match fishing, where a lot of 'tiddler-snatching' on very small baits has to be done.

Another scale, used by trout fishermen, is the Pennell or

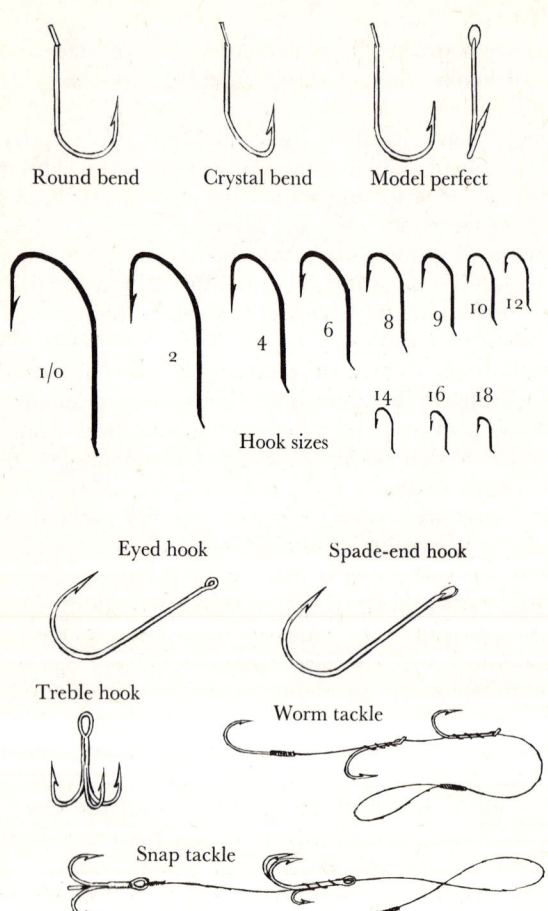

FIG. 10 Hooks and hook sizes.

'New' Scale. This starts at ooo for the smallest hook, the equivalent of a Redditch Scale No. 18, and the numbers increase with the size of the hook. Again beginning with the smallest, the scale is: ooo, oo, o, 1, 2, 3, 4, 5, 6, 7, 8, 9.

On the face of it, this is a simpler system. But because the Redditch Scale was so firmly established among coarse fishermen and in the trade, the New Scale just confused matters. Coarse anglers stick to the Redditch Scale and do not seem to have much trouble with it.

Most anglers use hooks ready-whipped to nylon. But for those who prefer to tie their own, there are *eyed hooks*, with an eye or ring at the end of the shank, and *spade-ended hooks* which, as the name suggests, have the end flattened like the head of the spade. Often the eyes or the spades are bent up or down. (See chapter 31, 'Some Useful Knots', for tying hooks.)

Tying your own hooks saves a lot of money: when you buy hooks you should pay for the quality of the hook, rather than the length of nylon.

Longshank hooks have a longer shank than normal. They are a help when using large baits such as lobworms, exert greater leverage on the strike, and make it easier for the hook to be removed with the fingers. The disadvantage, of course, is that there is more hook for the fish to notice.

Barbless hooks are being used more and more as anglers realise the need to harm fish as little as possible. If a fish is well-hooked, and the line is kept tight, a barbless hook will hold just as well as a barbed one. If, however, the hooking is less than good, or the line is allowed to slacken enough for the fish to jerk its head, the barbless hook is more likely to come away. More and more tackle shops are stocking these hooks now, but if you cannot get hold of them you can simply file the barb off ordinary hooks.

Treble hooks—three hooks set back to back at angles of 120° to each other—are used for spinning, livebaiting and deadbaiting. They can be used, also when fishing with a soft bait, such as silkweed or mussel, to hold the bait more securely.

Worm tackle is two or three round-bend hooks mounted one above the other, so there is a hook waiting wherever a fish bites. The advantages of this are offset by the unnatural presentation of the bait.

Snap tackle, two treble hooks whipped on to wire, is used for livebaiting and deadbaiting, mainly for pike.

The best hooks are forged hooks. These have a flat cross-section, not a round one like the ordinary wire hooks. There are many other refinements: hollow points, curved-in points, curved-out points, 'slices' (raised nicks) in the shank to help hold the bait. Anglers swear by one variation or another, and it will not be long before you have your own favourite. Whichever kind of hook you use, make sure its size matches the bait it carries, and always think small rather than big. A big fish can be held on a small hook: any fish, whatever its size, will be scared off by too hefty a piece of ironmongery.

And whatever the hook, it must be *sharp*—mass-produced hooks often are not. Rub it with fine emery paper or a sharpening stone before and after every use.

Lines

At one time fishing lines were made of silk, gut, cotton or flax. Today, the line used by practically every coarse angler is a monofilament of some man-made fibre, usually nylon or Terylene.

Artificial fibre is rot-proof, light, and very strong for its diameter. It is trickier to knot, however, than the old natural lines, loses some of its strength in water, and stretches under strain. This last factor has to be taken into account on a long-distance strike.

The breaking strain (b.s.) of a line is the deadweight needed to break it, and bears no relation to the weight of the fish the line will hold. Because the fish is supported by water, and because the spring of the rod absorbs some of its pull, even a big fish can be held on a seemingly inadequate line.

A hook length is usually of a lower breaking strain than the reel line, so that if it is caught in a snag the hook length will break first, losing only the hook.

A fixed-spool reel allows you to carry several spools holding different strengths of line. One of 3 lb b.s., one of 6 lb b.s. and one of 10 lb b.s. should cope with almost all the fish and conditions you are likely to encounter.

Nylon line is weakened by knotting and by having shot pinched on to it, so at the end of every trip cut off the last foot or so.

The simplest way of grading line is the breaking strain system, but sometimes it is listed under its diameter, or by the old 'X' system used for the gut casts of fly fishing.

A comparative table of the three systems reads:

Breaking strain (lb)	Diameter (in)	X rating
$1\frac{1}{2}$	0.004	8X
$2\frac{1}{4}$	0.006	5X
4	0.008	2X
5	0.009	1X
6	0.010	X
11	0.014	—
14	0.016	—

Floats

A full description of every type and variation of float would fill most of this book, and even then the list would be out-of-date before it was printed. Almost every week a new type, or a new refinement of an old type, is designed and marketed. Some prove themselves and join the ranks of the 'standards'. Others enjoy a brief craze and then fade quietly away.

Floats are the angler's favourite toys. It is doubtful if any angler, however tidy and methodical, however ruthless in throwing away useless tackle, however light he prefers to travel, does not carry far more floats than he needs.

There is no shame at all in collecting floats and playing with them. But down at the water, remember that a float's important functions are to support the bait and weights, and to give warning of a bite. If it does not do these well, it is not a good float—however pretty it looks.

Whatever the float, always use the lightest possible for that particular job. Fishing in still or slow water needs smaller floats and fewer weights than fishing in fast water; light baits like maggots can be used on smaller floats than heavier baits like lobworm and lumps of paste.

The part of a float underwater should be dark, so as not to reflect the light and so scare the fish. The tip above the water should be a bright colour—yellow, red, orange—and preferably fluorescent so that it can be seen easily at dawn or dusk. A *black* tip can be seen more easily than bright colours when the sun is on the water. It is also useful in certain conditions at dusk.

A useful tip to save time on the bank is to mark each float with the number of shot needed to cock it. Paint on the size of the shot (e.g. BB, 2 or 3), and a dot for each shot needed. You can find out how many shot each float needs by testing in the bath or in a milk bottle.

The plastic rings with which shop-bought floats are fitted are often unsatisfactory; they tend to split or slip, and not to hold the line securely. If this happens, throw the rings away and buy a length of bicycle valve tubing which can be cut into rings of any length you wish.

Floats are made from many different materials and combinations of materials; the most usual are quills—of goose, swan, crow, porcupine and peacock—cork, wood, cane, celluloid and plastic.

Quills are still the most useful all-round float, though sometimes sneered at by trendy anglers as out-of-date. Sizes of quills range from the tiny crow to the bulky swan and the

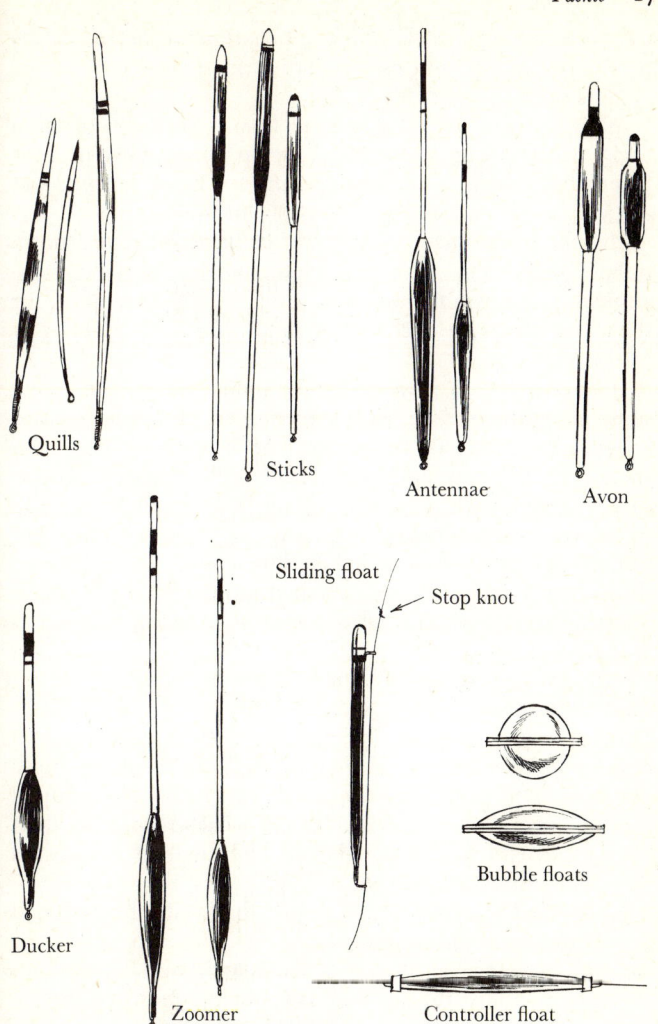

FIG. 11 A selection of floats.

long peacock. (Peacock quill can be cut into lengths.) Some quills are curved, but this is no handicap at all—in fact some anglers prefer curved ones.

Sticks are very useful all-round floats, with tops of balsa and bottoms of cane. Only the very tip shows above the surface. They cast well without needing too much weight, and are very sensitive to bites.

Antenna floats have a long, thin stem sticking up from a bulkier body. This allows the main part of the float to be sunken, leaving only the thin antenna sticking up above the water. They are excellent in windy conditions or choppy water.

Avons, duckers and zoomers are all basically floats with a long stem, generally of cane, with a body of cork or balsa—useful in wind and for distance fishing. The avon has a body near the top of the stem, and is attached top and bottom. It can carry plenty of weight and is useful in strong currents and upstream winds. The ducker, with the body near the bottom of the stem, is like an upside-down avon. It is used in a downstream wind, attached at the bottom only. The zoomer is a still- or slow-water float which looks like a ducker. It has lead incorporated into the body which helps in long-distance casting and also allows shotting on the line itself to be kept to the minimum.

Self-cocking floats stay upright, or cocked, without any weight on the line. It is a hollow float, often of celluloid, plastic or goose quill, with a removable cap. Shot are dropped into the float's hollow body to make it cock. A normal float can be turned into a self-cocker by clipping shot to the line on either side of the bottom ring.

Sliding floats are used where the depth of water being fished is greater than the length of the rod. The line runs free through two rings on the side of the float. When the line is in the water, it slips through the rings to the required depth, where it is stopped by a nylon stop knot or a rubber stopper (often a piece of valve tubing) tied on the line. When the line is reeled in, the stopper or stop knot passes through the rod rings and on to the reel, while the float slides down as far as the weights on the terminal tackle. (See chapter 31, 'Some Useful Knots', for the stop knot.)

Bubble floats are perspex or plastic bubbles which can be weighted by the insertion of shot, or by being partially filled with water. They enjoyed a boom in popularity some years ago and then fell out of favour, mainly because they were used for purposes for which they were never intended. The main functions of a bubble are to give weight for casting when no weight is used on the line, and for floating downstream to a wary fish such as a chub. (A bubble filled with water looks exactly like . . . a bubble.) Its drawbacks are the wash created by the slightest drag on the line, the resistance offered to a taking fish, and the plop made as the bubble leaves the water on the strike. The first two problems can be overcome by proper fishing: by making sure there is no drag, and by watching the line beyond the float—rather than the float itself—so that you strike before the float is affected. You can do nothing about the plop except to buy an oval, streamlined bubble.

Controller floats are short, stumpy wooden floats which are attached top and bottom. They are used, like bubbles, merely to give casting weight and to give an idea of where the bait is likely to be. They do not offer so much resistance to a taking fish as a bubble float but, of course, do not look anywhere near natural.

Float materials—reed, cane, cork and balsa are all common. You can buy bored balsa dowels for float bodies, and bored cork rings which can be glued on top of one another and shaped as necessary. Sarkandas reed started as a substitute for peacock quill, and is now preferred by many anglers because of its strength and ease of handling. It can be used in lengths on its own or, like cane, as the stem of a cork or balsa float.

Some floats you can make yourself (see pp. 249–50).

Weights

Weights have two main functions: to get the line *out* to the fish by giving sufficient impetus on the cast, and to get the bait *down* to the fish and keep it there. In float fishing they also keep the float upright in the water.

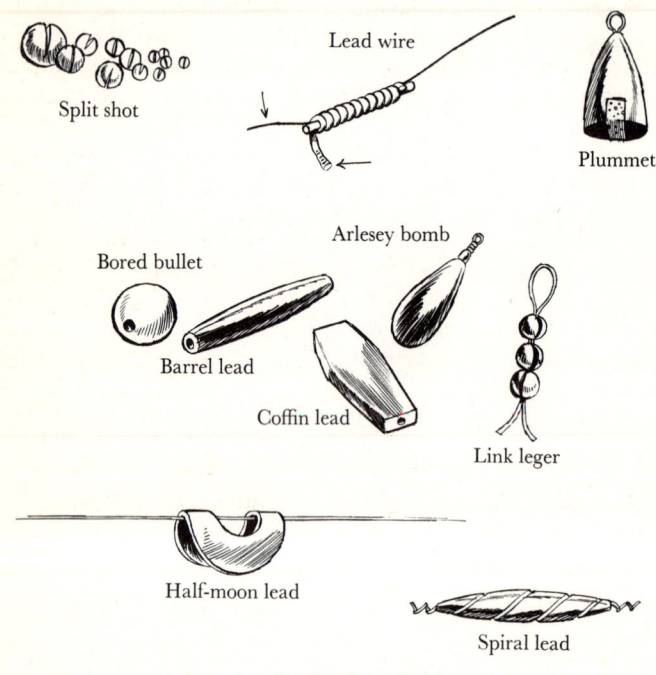

FIG. 12   A selection of weights.

The golden rule is never to use more weights than absolutely necessary. Lots of lead certainly makes casting easier, but it also helps to warn the fish that something strange is going on.

Split shot

These are the weights used most often, especially in float fishing. They are round lead pellets, like shotgun pellets, with a slot nicked halfway across each one. The line is placed in this slot and the pellet is squeezed on to grip tight.

Sizes of split shot, starting with the smallest and working up, are: 10 (known as micro), 8 (dust shot), 7, 6, 5, 4, 3, 2, 1, BB, AAA, SG, SSG (swan).

The most convenient way of buying shot is in plastic dispensers holding several different sizes in separate compartments.

The softer the shot, the easier it is to put on and take off, and the less likely to damage the line. Many anglers rely on their teeth or fingers to clip on the shot, but it is best to start by using pliers *very lightly*. Teeth can damage easily and fingers may not be able to squeeze tight enough to stop the shot sliding up or down the line.

A special oval form of split shot called a *mouse dropping* is used for hempseed fishing to avoid false bites, because fish mistake ordinary shot for hemp.

Swan shot can be clipped together in groups on a length of line to form a link leger.

Lead wire

This can be used for float fishing and for giving extra weight to spinners in fast water. It can be used in hemp fishing as another way of preventing false bites.

A short length of wire is laid against the line and the two are bound together tightly with another length of wire. The ends of the wire can be squeezed tight with pliers to hold it in position. If it still slides down the line, it can be held firmly with split shot clipped immediately above and below.

Leger leads

These take several forms, though all do the same job of holding the line on the bottom, while allowing it to run freely through a hole or eyelet. A split shot is pinched on below the leger weight to stop it running down to the hook.

In old types of leger lead, such as the *bored bullet*, *barrel* and *coffin* leads, the line runs in a hole drilled through them. These leads have the disadvantage of offering resistance to the line as a taking fish pulls it through, and of sinking into the bottom mud and taking the line with them.

Swivelled leads, such as the Arlesey bomb and the pyramidal 'Capta' leads, offer little resistance to the line. Because the swivel is at the top of the lead it is less likely to disappear in the mud. The shape of the pyramidal leads helps to keep them on top of the mud, but it also offers resistance when casting and reeling in.

Half-moon leads

These look like lead washers folded in half and are squeezed on to the line in the shape of a half-moon. The larger half-moons are used as anti-kink leads on spinning tackle. Fixed above a swivel, they stop any twisting from travelling further up the line.

Spiral leads

These are long oval leads with a 'corkscrew' at each end. The line goes through one corkscrew, is laid along the lead in a spiral groove, and comes out through the other corkscrew. Like lead wire, a spiral can give weight to a spinner, held in place by a simple loop knot on each corkscrew, or by stopping it at both ends with a split shot.

Plummets

A plummet is a conical lead with a piece of cork let into the bottom, which is used for testing the depth of the water. The line is threaded through the top ring and the hook pushed into the cork. A plummet will also do emergency duty as a leger lead.

Landing net and keepnet

The landing net is almost as important as the rod itself. Buy the best you can afford, and make sure it is a big one, with a long or telescopic handle, to make sure of coping with big fish and steep banks. A triangular frame is generally more effective than a round one. The net itself should be knotless, to avoid damaging the fish.

Get into the habit of setting up the landing net before you set up the rod. That way you will not forget it.

A keepnet is used to keep fish alive until the end of the day, when you may want to count them, weigh them, photograph them, or just gloat over them. Again, do get a knotless net, preferably micro-mesh, to avoid damage to the fishes' slime, scales or fins.

See chapter 28, 'Care of Your Catch', for the proper use of a keepnet. Remember that the proper place for a fish is . . . back in the water.

Rod rests and bank sticks

For a rod rest, you can at a pinch, simply use a forked stick. You can make one very easily too (see chapter 30, 'Tackle You Can Make'). There are many patterns of rests in the shops, running from simple stem-and-fork rests, to double-arm rests, and rests which assemble in different ways for different banks and conditions.

A rest must be strong and heavy enough for prolonged use (weak rests bend easily when pushed into heavy soil), and it must not catch the line when a strike is made. So make sure that the junction of the fork is a smooth curve and not a sharp angle, or that there is a hole at the junction to allow the line to hang free below the rod.

Bank sticks are like rod rests, except that instead of the fork they have a threaded socket which will take the screw attachment of a keepnet or bait tray. Buy a long one,

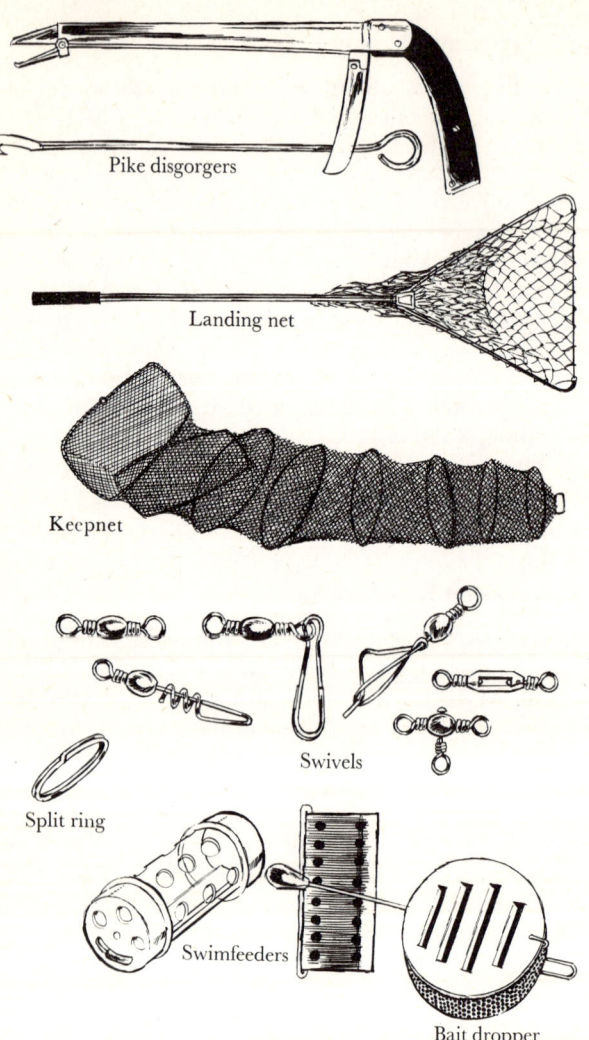

FIG. 13

preferably telescopic, to cope with different conditions and uses.

Disgorgers

A disgorger is used to take the hook out of the fish's mouth. The simplest kind is the *fish-tailed*, whose V-shaped end is used to push the hook out. The *ring-ended* disgorger, in which the ring is slid down the line and along the shank of the hook, gives more control over the unhooking and probably gives the fish less discomfort.

More and more anglers are using surgical forceps or needle-nosed pliers as disgorgers. The forceps are especially useful for taking out hooks which have gone home far back in the fish's gullet.

There are several plier-type disgorgers with extra-long handles for use on pike.

Gaff

A gaff is something you should do without. It is a big barbless hook on the end of a handle and is used by some pike anglers for landing large fish. Even a good gaffing, done properly through the skin behind the point of the lower jaw, hurts the fish. A bad gaffing is usually fatal. Better to spend your money on a large landing net.

Priest

A weighted cosh for killing fish. Buy a heavy one rather than a light one: someday you are bound to have a big fish which for some reason has to be killed.

Rod holdall

Not unlike a golfing bag, a holdall makes the carrying of

several rods a lot easier. The more expensive models have compartments for rod rests, reels and other tackle.

Umbrellas

The large angling umbrella makes angling more comfortable by keeping off rain, wind and sun. It can also be used to shade the keepnet. Some umbrellas can be fitted with canvas hangings to form a tent.

Baskets and tackle boxes

The roomiest and sturdiest fishing basket is the old-fashioned seat basket made from woven willow. It weighs more, however, than modern metal, plastic or fibreglass box seats. Several designs of metal, plastic or glass boxes incorporate pop-up compartments for easy access to floats, hooks, weights, etc.

Bite indicators

The most basic bite indicator is a dough bobbin squeezed on to the line. From there you can move on to swingtips, quivertips, butt indicators, right up to sophisticated electronic buzzer devices.

A *swingtip* looks like the end of a rod tip with a flexible plastic 'tail'. This tail is attached to the rod tip, leaving the swingtip hanging down limply towards the water. The line is threaded through the rings on the tip. When a fish takes, it moves the line and makes the tip—depending on whether the line was slack or taut—either swing out or drop back.

To help register bites on a swingtip, and to protect the tip from the wind, you can use a *target board*. This is a board with a simple pattern painted in contrasting colours. The board is placed as a background to the swingtip, so that when the tip moves, the angler can see by exactly how much. He is then better able to judge the strength of the bite, or whether it is a bite at all. The board can be useful in windy conditions, or when vegetation or moving water make a bad background for the tip, but it is a cumbersome piece of equipment to carry about.

A *quivertip* operates on much the same principle as a swingtip, except that it is a rigid attachment, not a flexible one, and quivers instead of swings. Many anglers prefer the quiver because it is less affected by wind and its movements show more clearly the difference between a real bite and an underwater snag.

Many rods are now sold with a threaded socket on the top joint to take a quiver- or swingtip. Accordingly, many tips are sold with a screw end to fit into this joint. Remember this when you buy; it is no use buying a tip with a screw end if your rod doesn't have a socket.

A *butt bite indicator* is a hinged arm which clips on to the bottom joint of the rod. The free end of the arm rests against the line. When a fish takes the bait and moves the line, the arm swings upwards to indicate it.

An *electric bite alarm* is like a rod rest with a battery-operated device in place of the fork. Two contact points in the device are separated by the line. When the line is pulled clear by a fish taking, the two contacts come together, a buzzer sounds and in some cases a light flashes. Electric bite alarms are fine for night fishing, when there is no light to follow the movements of ordinary indicators. But their use during the day can make the angler lazy.

Swivels

Swivels are used in spinning to prevent the twisting motion of the lure being transmitted to the main line. They are also used to cancel out the twisting fight of an eel. They are useful for attaching hook links and weights to the line, and are especially useful in legering and paternostering.

Snap link swivels, with a clip-on action, make the changing of links and weights even easier. Other types include barrel, snap link, buckle, box, corkscrew, and three-way swivels.

Split rings

These are like small key-rings, and are useful for joining lengths of dissimilar material such as wire and nylon. They can be used with swivels for attaching different kinds of terminal tackle.

Swimfeeders and bait droppers

A swimfeeder is a perforated plastic cone or cylinder filled with groundbait, or samples of the hookbait, and attached to the line like a leger weight (more often than not by a nylon link to cut down resistance to a taking fish).

Generally weighted by a strip of lead, the swimfeeder does duty as a leger weight and at the same time releases a steady stream of bait into the swim.

Open-ended swimfeeders can take almost any kind of hookbait or groundbait. The open ends have to be sealed with a stiff mixture of groundbait or mud. Block-end types are closed at each end, and are especially good for releasing maggots, which crawl out one by one through the holes. They can be bought, or can be made quite easily (see chapter 30, 'Tackle You Can Make').

A bait dropper is a closed metal container with a hinged side or bottom, operated by a weighted metal arm below the container. The dropper is swung out into the water on the end of your line. When the weight hits bottom, the arm is pushed up, allowing the container to open and the bait to fall out.

Unlike the swimfeeder, the bait dropper cannot be left on the line while you are fishing. You can use the rod you are fishing with, and retrieve the dropper immediately after use, or use a spare rod.

Spring balance

This is used to weigh fish at the waterside. It must be kept clean, oiled and free from dust or grit if the weights are to be accurate. Always weigh the fish in a plastic bag. *Never* stick the hook of the scales under the fish's gills.

4

Baits

Fish can be caught on everything, from a naked hook to a sausage, but naturally it helps to offer a fish something it is likely to be attracted to, in a size it can comfortably manage and in a way that will not arouse its suspicions.

This list of baits is by no means complete: almost every week fish are caught on new and sometimes bizarre baits. Some prove their effectiveness over a period and join the list of standard baits. Others enjoy a brief craze and are never heard of again. Others prove too effective (if there is such a thing) and are banned.

All the baits in this list have proved themselves. Groundbaits are looked at first, because they go in the water first. After that, hookbaits are presented in alphabetical order, not in order of effectiveness or popularity. (A list in order of popularity would probably run: maggots, casters, bread, worms. ... And then somebody would be bound to say, 'What about hemp, cheese and ... ?')

However revolting or messy the bait, the hands which prepare it and use it should be absolutely clean, with no taint of oil or nicotine—or soap—on them.

Groundbaits

Groundbait is thrown into a swim to attract the fish to the spot and keep them there. With a large shoal fish, such as bream, a good quantity must be used, but remember that the idea is to interest the fish—not to feed them so well that they ignore the hookbait.

As a general rule, use less groundbait rather than more, and feed it into the swim on the basis of little and often.

The simplest form of groundbait is just samples of the hookbait: a handful of maggots or casters, bits of cheese or soaked bread, whole worms or bits of worm.

A good all-purpose groundbait is made by taking out the inside of old loaves, soaking them in water, mashing them to pulp and then mixing the pulp with bran, chicken meal, sausage rusk or ground, dried breadcrumbs.

Samples of the hookbait can be added—and then the angler's secret ingredient. Every angler has a favourite additive which does or does not make a real difference to the appeal of the groundbait: flour, custard powder, sugar, honey, meat extracts, dried blood, fish oils . . . to name but a few. Whatever difference they make to the effectiveness of the bait—and many *do* work—they at least keep the angler happy, giving him that extra confidence which, in the end, may be all he needs.

Cloudbait is a mixture of finely crushed dried breadcrumbs and flour which hangs in suspension in the water, attracting the fish without feeding them. It can, of course, be used only in still or slow-moving water.

Groundbait must be fresh—it sours very quickly—and is best made up at the waterside. Tap water may often contain purifying chemicals which the fish can detect. Using water with which the fish is already familiar not only makes the groundbait mix more acceptable but also helps disguise any taints from the hands.

After every trip, throw surplus groundbait away—but *not* in the water. It can sour the water or spoil the fishing for somebody else. If other anglers on the bank do not want it, take it away.

Take care in moving water that the groundbait is reaching the fish and not being carried downstream over their heads.

Hookbaits

Artificial baits
Perch, pike, chub—and even grayling and rudd—are taken on artificial lures which imitate the action of a small fish or other underwater creature. Like floats, artificial baits are a great temptation to the fisherman. Most anglers finish up with more artificials than they need—some of which are not much use but look irresistible in the shop.

The basic divisions of artificial lures are: *spoons, bar spoons* or *spinners* and *plugs*. All are fitted with a swivel at one end and a treble hook at the other. Plugs may carry two or even three trebles.

The *spoons* are so called because their basic shape is like the bowl of a spoon. An interesting but unlikely story of their

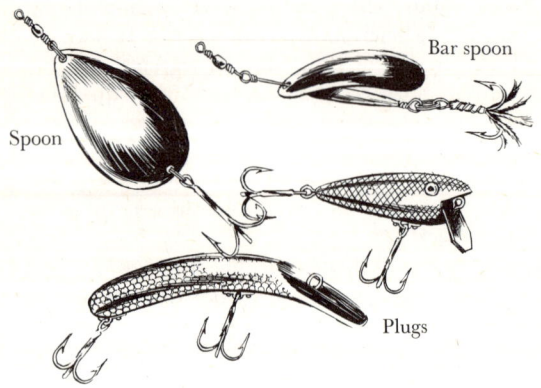

FIG. 14 Some artificial baits.

origin is that a silver spoon was dropped into a lake at a stately home tea party—and immediately seized by a rising pike. Spoons move through the water with an undulating motion and are often referred to as wobbling spoons. (This helps to distinguish them from bar spoons, which are also referred to as spinners.) The motion sends out flashes of light and vibrations which predators mistake for those of their prey. The action of a wobbling spoon is very attractive to pike.

A *bar spoon* has a spoon or blade which revolves around a weighted centre wire. The spoon revolves with a fluttering motion which sends out vibrations and flashes more urgent than those of the wobbling spoon. The smaller bar spoons, with blades only $\frac{1}{2}$ in long, are excellent for perch and chub.

A *plug* looks like a cartoon fish. They used to be made of wood, but today are almost all plastic. They do not revolve, but work through the water with a diving or wobbling motion, imitating a sick or injured fish. Plugs can be tiny and single jointed, or larger with one, two or even three joints. Different shapes are designed to work at different levels, so you will find them described as surface, shallow-diving and deep-diving. One type of plug has an adjustable vane at the nose. Changing the position of the vane determines the depth at which the plug will work.

Among the surface plugs is the 'popper'. Every time it is moved, it dives under the surface with a loud 'plop'! It can be deadly when the predators are feeding at the top of the water.

Methods of working the lures are described in chapter 8, 'Spinning'. For a home-made plug and spoon, see chapter 30, 'Tackle You Can Make'.

Beans, peas and sweetcorn

Beans of all varieties, peas and sweetcorn can be simmered until tender and used on appropriately sized hooks. They will take all coarse fish except pike, perch and eels. They can also, of course, be bought ready-canned, and are then soft enough.

Bloodworms

These tiny, thread-like red worms, only ½ in long, are the larvae of the yellow gnat. They are found in standing water, such as that in a water butt, in fine mud at the water's edge, and in the black ooze of drains and ditches. They can be sieved out with a fine-mesh net, or scraped off the surface of the mud with a special bloodworm rake (see chapter 30, 'Tackle You Can Make'). You can keep them at home in a dish of water and pack them for fishing in a tin of well-damped moss. Grubbing about in ditches can be messy, not to say smelly, so you may prefer to buy the bloodworms from an aquarists' suppliers.

They are excellent bait for most fish. Roach, dace, bream and tench are especially fond of them.

Their size makes them difficult to hook, and ordinary hooks tend to break them, so it is best to use them on special fine wire hooks with a small barb, on sizes from no. 16 down to a tiny no. 22. Lay them flat on the forefinger of the left hand, holding the tail down gently with the thumb, and insert the hook near the head.

Bread

Bread is an excellent bait for all but predatory fish, and can be used as *paste*, *crust*, *flake*, *cube*, or as a combination of crust and paste. It can also be used as small pellets, cut out with a bread punch.

Paste is made by scooping out the inside of an old loaf, wrapping it in a cloth, soaking it in water and squeezing the water out through the cloth. The soggy bread is then kneaded into a stiff dough.

Both the cloth and the hands must be scrupulously clean for this operation, to avoid tainting the paste. Many anglers prefer to make the paste at the waterside, in case the fish can

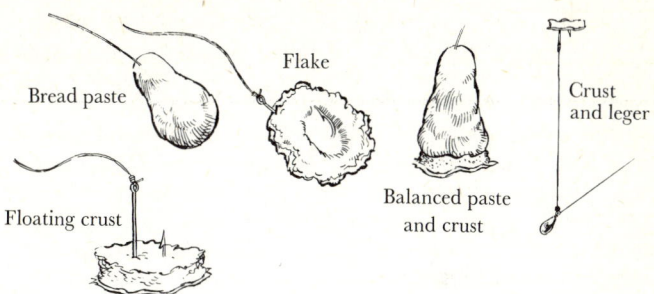

FIG. 15   Ways of using bread baits.

detect chemically treated tap water. This could be argued, but there can be no doubt that paste made at the waterside is absolutely fresh.

Paste can be stiffened by the addition of flour, or flavoured with honey, sugar, dried blood, cod liver oil—anything, in fact, which the angler believes will attract the fish. Every angler has his own 'secret' formula for flavouring paste and will swear by it. Blancmange powders will colour the paste as well as flavour it. Pastes can be coloured also by the dyes used for maggots.

Crust is at its simplest just a piece cut or torn from a loaf. It can be fished on the surface, as floating crust, in midwater from float or leger, or on the bottom.

Once in the water the crust swells and softens and is liable to come off the hook. This can be overcome by pressing the crust overnight. Cut the crust from the top of a loaf, leaving some of the white still attached. Wrap the crust in a damp cloth and press it overnight under a weight. It can then be cut into cubes or strips, torn off into irregular shapes, or made into neat little pellets with a bread punch.

A combination crust-and-paste bait can be made by cutting a circle of crust, pushing the hook through and back so that the crust is at right angles to the line—like a small platform—and then kneading paste into a dome on top of it. The right combination of the light crust and heavier paste makes for a slow-sinking bait which will rest on top of a weed bed.

Flake is simply a piece of bread torn from the inside of a new loaf. It is squeezed in the middle to make a waist and the hook put through the waist. It is very effective indeed, but comes off very easily in the water.

Cubes are cubes of bread, of a size appropriate to the quarry, cut from the firmer bread at the bottom of a loaf.

Caddis grubs

The caddis grub is the larva of the caddis fly. You can find it in early summer in shallow water, moving about, hiding under stones or clinging to reed stems. It has an unmistakable 'case' made from bits of twig, small stones, sand or shells. The grubs can be squeezed gently out of their cases or poked out with a matchstick or grass stalk. Hooked lightly through the skin near the tail on hooks nos. 8–16, they interest every fish except the pike.

As well as hunting the grubs in the shallows, you can try an old dodge: leave a weighted cabbage stalk or a gorse branch in the water for a while, and then pick off the grubs which have moved on to it.

The grubs can be kept lively in a tin of damp moss.

Casters

Casters are the chrysalises of maggots at a certain stage in their development. They are a very popular bait, and very expensive to buy. For a day's river fishing, you will need at least 2 pints.

To 'turn' your own casters, keep the maggots from the previous trip, if you are going fishing again within a week or so. Keep an *open* box of maggots in a dry place. They will turn into their chrysalis form very quickly. Once one maggot turns, keep an eye on the others.

Small riddles or sieves ($\frac{1}{8}$ in mesh—no larger) can be bought from tackle dealers and ironmongers. Once the maggots are 'turning' run the whole lot through the sieve. The lively maggots will wriggle through the mesh, leaving the chrysalises. Keep these chrysalises in a plastic bag in the fridge. They can be kept for a short while in a bowl of cold water, but the water must be changed every six hours.

The best casters are orange. Pick them out and place them in a separate tin for hookbait. At this stage the inside of the hard case is still full of solid matter, and the chrysalis will sink. Eventually the chrysalis changes colour from orange to dark red–black as the fly begins to form inside the case. It is no longer a caster, but a floater, and is useless. To sort floaters from casters, simply put them all in a bowl of water. The casters will sink, leaving the floaters on the surface to be scooped off and discarded.

Caterpillars

Groundbaiting is done for you all through the summer by caterpillars which fall off overhanging bushes to finish up inside the chub and dace waiting below. Ideally, pick your caterpillars at the waterside so they are the kind the fish are used to. Alternatively, comb through your flowerbed and vegetable patch. A squad of youngsters can collect enough in half an hour to have enough for groundbait as well as hookbait.

Cheese

Cheese is an excellent bait for roach, bream, carp—and especially for barbel and chub.

Providing it is not crumbly, it can be used in chunks broken from the pieces, or it can be worked together with some butter to make a soft but clinging paste. Dutch Edam cheese holds well on the hook, and can be cut into strips or cubes. The softer processed cheeses also hold well, and are handy to carry around in their individual foil wrappings.

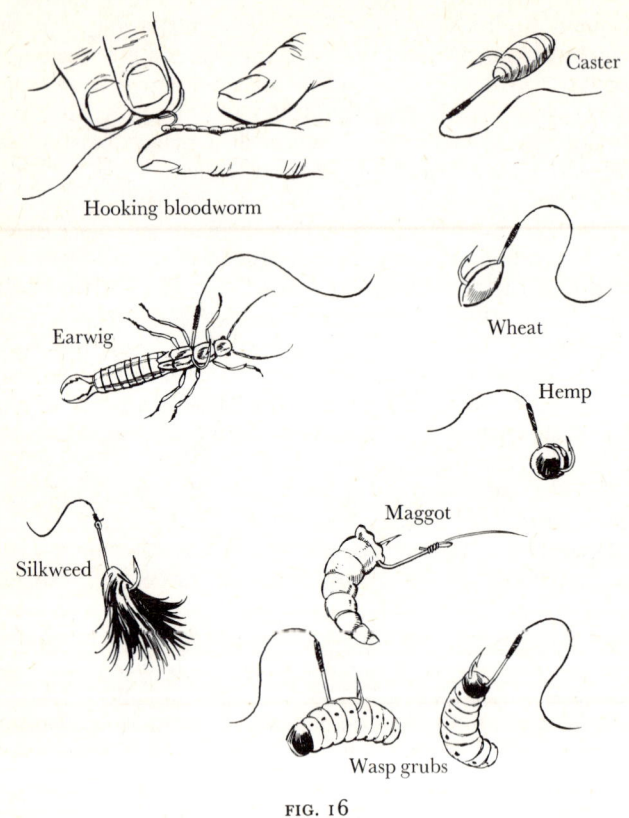

FIG. 16

Another kind of paste is made by mixing two parts of grated cheese with one part of breadcrumbs, wrapping them in a cloth and dipping the whole thing in boiling water. When the water has cooled, squeeze out the excess moisture through the cloth and knead into a paste. Flour can be added if it is still too soft.

Crayfish

The freshwater crayfish, which looks like a tiny dark-green lobster, is a deadly bait for barbel, chub and perch. Crayfish live only in clean water and their numbers have dwindled with increasing pollution in recent years, but they are well worth seeking out.

They live in holes in the bank under the waterline. You can catch them simply by putting in your hand and pressing down smartly as soon as you touch one. Now and again the crayfish get in first with a nip from the amazingly strong pincers, so you may prefer one of these slower, but less painful methods:

Dropnetting: A dropnet can be made from the end section of an old keepnet, or from any circle of stout wire and a piece of small-meshed net. It can be weighted with a plastic or netting bag filled with pebbles. Three or four pieces of line of equal length are tied to the rim an equal distance apart. The free ends are knotted together and tied to a single line. The dropnet is baited by tying a piece of bacon, meat or fish in the middle, and lowered into the water. After fifteen minutes or so it is hauled up, evenly and at a medium pace. With luck, there may be two or three crayfish busy with the bait.

Trapping: Crayfish can be taken overnight in a minnow trap made from a quart bottling jar. Make a funnel of wire gauze and place it over the mouth of the jar. Truss the jar firmly with a 'harness' of string and attach this harness to a length of line. Bait the trap, again with meat, bacon or fish, lower it into the water and retrieve it next morning.

Angling: This is hardly fishing, but it can be fun to catch crayfish in still water with a light rod and line. Bait the hook with a piece of meat, bacon or fish. Set the tiniest float so that the bait just touches bottom. When a crayfish gets to work on the bait, the float will tremble, dip very slightly, and move a little from side to side. The movements are so slight as to be unmistakably crayfish. Give the crayfish time to get a firm grip on the bait, then raise the rod gently and evenly. Slip a landing net under the cray as he reaches the surface.

In clear water, where you can see the crayfish holes, you won't need a float. Dangle the bait outside a hole until the crayfish appears, then inch the bait away from the hole until the cray is well clear. Now you can allow it to get hold of the bait. Haul up when it has a firm grip.

Forking: In clear shallow water where you can see crayfish, you can pin them down with the fork of a rod rest. If the water is too deep, either for the rest, or for you to retrieve the cray without a ducking, use a long bamboo cane, split at one end, and with the split held open in a fork by a matchstick. When you press down on the cray, the matchstick will break or come adrift. The fork will close over the cray's back and you will be able to lift it out.

Crayfish should be killed before use by a quick squeeze on the shell behind the head, and hooked through the second segment of the tail. Some anglers prefer to strip off the claws, but it is doubtful whether this makes much difference to a hungry chub who is used to eating crays fully-armed.

Crayfish can be freelined, or used with leger or float. Do not be in too much of a hurry to strike: the tail has to be in the fish's mouth before the hook can have any effect.

Currants and sultanas

Most fish will take these. They can be used dry, or softened by overnight soaking.

Dock grubs

Dock grubs, or docken grubs, are the larvae of the ghost moth, large white grubs with brown heads found in the roots of dock plants. They are excellent bait for roach, dace and chub, and should be hooked through the head, which is tougher than the soft body.

Earwigs

Earwigs are a summer and autumn bait, loved by dace. Collect them by hanging a folded sack from a stake in the middle of the flowerbed, or fill flowerpots with straw and up-end them on sticks among the flowers (preferably among dahlias, which earwigs love). They can also be had in numbers when you are elderberrying. Give the elderberry bunches a shake, and out will come the earwigs.

Use nos. 12–16 hooks. Hook through the thorax.

Fish baits

Deadbaits are strips of fish, preferably with a flash of silver skin still attached. These find several takers, as do the red gill fringes of fish such as perch which have had to be killed because of a deep hooking.

The use of fish *roe* is illegal. Fish oil—halibut or cod liver—can be used to flavour both hookbait and groundbait. A fish oil capsule can be pushed up the hook shank above the bait, so that the oil seeps out as an extra attraction.

Both salt and freshwater fish can be used, either whole or halved, as deadbait. Favourite saltwater fish are herring, mackerel and sprat. Freshwater fish can be roach, dace, rudd, chub or trout. Freshly-dead bait should be pierced through the middle of the body and squeezed to empty the air from the swim bladder; otherwise it will float.

Whole dead fish can be spun or wobbled in the same way as an artificial lure. Pike, perch, eels, barbel and chub will take fish deadbaits.

Livebaits mean live fish, either lip hooked or mounted on snap tackle, not the other live creatures used as bait. They mainly attract pike and perch, but chub, bream and even roach will take them.

Although livebaiting is practised extensively, a growing number of anglers look upon it as being unnecessarily cruel. I am one of that number, and do not propose to go into detail about livebaiting techniques. I prefer to use the space to explain why livebaits should *not* be used.

The first question, of course, is why, if an angler is prepared to use live maggots, worms and insects, should he not use live fish? The answer is in the degree of pain and distress involved. (It is a matter of degree, not principle: a maggot or worm undoubtedly feels some pain.)

Maggots, worms and insects are much further down the evolutionary scale. They are invertebrates. They have no bones, are soft-bodied, and do not have the pain receptivity of a fish. Much of the shock of being cast and of hitting the water is absorbed by their bodies' softness and elasticity. A fish, with its greater capacity to feel pain, its rigid body structure and its delicate balancing mechanism, suffers every time it is cast in.

Equally important—a fish *knows* when a predator is approaching and suffers fear as well as pain. Anyone who would deny this should watch the frantic darting of a pike float when the livebait senses approaching danger. The livebait suffers yet again on the strike, when the hooks are ripped out of its body; ripped out of flesh far tougher and more sensitive than that of a maggot or worm.

Livebaiters argue that a free-swimming fish is permanently in danger of attack by a predator, and that far more fish are killed naturally on any water than are killed as livebait. Leaving aside the obvious counter that a free fish has a chance to escape, this is undeniably true. But the angler has a straight choice: he may deliberately cause pain to a reasonably sensitive creature, or he may not. And he must accept that a refusal may result in his having a smaller bag on a particular water on a particular day.

In the end, it boils down to a squaring with your conscience: is your pleasure worth their pain?

Fruit
Many fruits can be used as bait. Elderberries on nos. 10–16

hooks are readily taken by roach, rudd and dace, especially where elder trees overhang the water. Chub and barbel will take stoned ripe cherries, ripe strawberries, and ½-in slices of banana. Roach, dace and rudd will go for raspberries, blackberries, redcurrants. Pieces or cubes of larger fruit such as apples and pears will also be taken.

Hips and haws
These should be used only when fully ripe. They will take most coarse fish except pike, perch and eel, and are especially effective where wild rose bushes overhang the bank.

Hempseed
Ever since its introduction into this country by Belgian refugees in the First World War, hemp has been a controversial bait. It is banned on many waters on several grounds—(a) it is too deadly, (b) it dopes the fish, (c) it sours the water, or (d) it takes only small fish.

The answers, as in all bait controversies, lie in its proper use. Taking the objections in order, (a) it certainly is a very effective bait, especially in summer and autumn used in streamy runs, but it is no cast-iron guarantee of fish. There is no evidence at all that (b) it dopes the fish. Any groundbait used to excess (c) remains on the bottom, eventually decomposes and sours the water. So why not ban bran or breadcrumbs? Why not ban groundbait altogether? If hemp is over-used, it is the fault of the angler, not the bait. The small fish argument (d) has been knocked on the head so many times by catches of big roach and dace that it is surprising to hear it still trotted out.

Hempseed for hookbait is prepared by simmering it gently in a saucepan of water until the husks split to show a fine white line. Seed for groundbait can be simmered longer until the white inside bursts out.

The traditional way of baiting with hemp is to push the bend of the hook into the split, so that the husk slips itself on to the bend and the point is left protruding. For the sake of a stronger hold, many anglers prefer to push the point in at one end of the white split and out at the other.

The trace should be weighted either with mouse-dropping shot, or with a coil of lead wire, stopped at each end with a mouse-dropping to stop it sliding up and down. If split shot is used, the fish will mistake it for hemp and keep you busy striking at false bites. This is not only frustrating for you, it is frightening for the fish and may result in a shoal clearing off.

So, on waters where you are still allowed to use hemp, groundbait sparingly. Try it on hooks nos. 10–16 for roach, dace, rudd, bream—and even barbel. Strike as soon as the float dips. Once the fish are biting, an $\frac{1}{8}$ in piece of black cycle valve tubing can be used on the hook in place of the hemp.

Grasshoppers

When you can catch them—and a landing net swished through long grass is as good a method as any—they make a beautiful surface bait for chub. Hook them through the back.

Greaves

The waste pieces of tallow left over from candle-making, are a traditional bait, mentioned only for old times' sake. The number of anglers who use it today could be counted on the fingers of a boxing glove. The greaves 'cake' was boiled and the most appetising pieces of fat used as hookbait, the rest as groundbait. Its passing is mourned by barbel and chub.

Macaroni

Macaroni is boiled in milk just long enough to soften it. It is used on the hook in lengths of up to $1\frac{1}{2}$ in. Excellent bait for chub.

Maggots

Maggots, or gentles, are the larvae of bluebottles and other flies and are the most popular coarse-fishing bait. They are perhaps too popular, because anglers stick to them through thick and thin when other baits might be far better.

Maggots are the bait most likely to make the non-angler exclaim, 'Ugh!' Properly kept, however, they are quite clean and do not smell—not very much, anyway. You will soon get used to them.

There are four common kinds of maggot. *Liver maggots*, the biggest, are the larvae of the bluebottle; *pinkies* come from the greenbottle; *specials* come from a large housefly, and *squats* from the common housefly.

The chrysalis of that maggot is known as a *caster* (see p. 46). True casters are chrysalises at the stage in their development when they sink in water. Those which do not sink are known, obviously, as *floaters*.

Maggots will stay alive in the water much longer if they are hooked properly, that is through the frill of skin at the back where the 'eyes' are. (The 'eyes', of course, are not eyes.) Any maggot which dies on the hook, is mauled or sucked clean by a fish, should be replaced immediately. They can be used singly, in pairs or bunches, or as a 'cocktail' in tandem with a caster or a small red worm. Casters can be used likewise.

It is not advisable to keep maggots indoors, unless in an unheated room, because warmth makes them turn very quickly into chrysalises. In hot weather they are best kept in a plastic container in the salad drawer or bottom shelf of the refrigerator. Female members of the family are never very keen on this, but in a clean and properly secured container, there is no danger of their contaminating any food.

Increasing prices and occasional scarcities of commercially bred maggots are encouraging more anglers to breed their own. This is an operation which, again, is never popular with the women of the house. It is, indeed, a smelly process, and should be done as far away from the house as possible (but not too close to the neighbours).

A piece of liver or raw meat laid in a pan of clean damp sand, bran or sawdust, and put in a cool, shady place—a shelf in the garage or under the foliage in the garden—will attract bluebottles and greenbottles. Do not use sawdust which may be tainted with turpentine, as it often is. If in doubt, stick to sand or bran.

Within twenty-four hours there should be enough 'blows'—clusters of little white eggs—on the meat. Cover the container to prevent any more flies getting in.

Within three or four days the maggots—livers and pinkies—will hatch, and feed voraciously on the meat. After a further week or ten days they will be fully grown, and should be transferred to a fresh pan of damp sand to clean themselves.

At this stage you will find that sand is the most convenient 'nursery' medium: the maggots can be separated from it simply by sieving. With bran or sawdust, tip the lot into a bucket of cold water. The maggots will sink to the bottom and you can pour off the floating bran or sawdust. Dry the maggots on a soft cloth before putting them on to the new damp sand. When they have wriggled into the sand, scrape the top clean of any dead maggots, skins or chrysalises.

After a few days in the sand, the maggots will be free of grease and smell and ready to use.

If you want a higher proportion of pinkies among the maggots, use fish instead of the meat.

Specials can be bred in sour bran. For this you need a plastic container, enough bran to fill it three-quarters full, and some sour milk. Scald the bran and, when it has cooled, squeeze it dry. Add enough sour milk to give it a stiff, porridge-like consistency. Place the mash into the container and leave it in a cool, dark place. It takes longer for the blows to appear on sour bran, perhaps three to five days.

Some amateur breeders place small pieces of fish in the bran to help attract the flies.

When the maggots are fully grown, they can be separated from the mash by putting the mixture in a fine sieve and putting the sieve under the tap. The running water will soon separate the bran from the specials, which will remain at the bottom of the sieve. They can then be cleaned in damp sand.

Squats—if you want them, that is: their small size fits them for use only as groundbait—can be bred on either the meat or the fish. Some will appear anyway—it is impossible for the amateur breeder to ensure that only one kind of fly blows on the stuff.

Mealworms

Mealworms live in meal and meal bins. As grain merchants are seldom kindly disposed to any anglers who infer that there are any on the premises, it is better to buy them from the pet shop, where they are sold as food for birds and small mammals. They can be kept in meal and do not smell. Most fish like them, especially roach, dace and chub. Use hook sizes nos. 10–16.

Meat and fat

Pieces of raw meat will take perch, chub and barbel. Offal or chicken guts will take eels. Chub and barbel are particularly attracted by slices of luncheon meat and pieces of raw, or lightly boiled, sausage. Other meat baits worth trying are strips of bacon and bacon fat.

A traditional bait which is not always easy to come by these days is bullock's pith. This is the white pith from inside the spinal cord of a bullock. When the outer skin is removed, the pith should be washed to bring out the whiteness. It is used in acorn-sized pieces on large hooks (nos. 6–8) for chub.

Mussels

The freshwater or swan mussel, hooked through the relatively harder 'tongue' is excellent bait for all fish—even pike will take it. Use on hooks nos. 6–12. Tie it on with wool if you find the tongue too soft to hold. Give the fish a little time before striking.

You can collect mussels in clear water with the help of a pair of waders and a landing net. Take extra care in running water—they often lie deeper than they appear to be.

Potatoes

A classic carp bait is a parboiled (lightly boiled) potato. This should be lightly hooked to allow the hook to come out on the strike. Smaller parboiled whole potatoes, or pieces of potato, can be used for other bottom-feeders such as tench, bream and barbel.

Potatoes can also be used completely boiled, and threaded on to the hook with a baiting needle. A pad of crust in the bend of the hook will help stop the soft potato flying off on the cast.

Slices of raw potato are useful for fishing on top of weed. Raw or parboiled potatoes can be used in pellet form, using a bread punch to take out pellets. Or a narrow metal tube can be pushed through a potato, the cylinder of potato pushed out with a pencil and cut into appropriately-sized pieces.

Shrimps

Saltwater shrimps, either peeled or whole, will take barbel, perch, roach, rudd, bream, chub, dace. So will freshwater shrimps, either alive or boiled—but first you have to catch them. Live shrimps should be hooked lightly through the back.

Silkweed

This is the delicate, light green weed which grows on weirs, lock gates, underwater masonry, etc. The best way of attach-

Wheat, barley and tares

Soak wheat grains in water overnight, rinse, and then simmer in a saucepan until the grains split to reveal the white inside. Some anglers add sugar to the water: as well as sweetening the wheat, this helps to turn the husk brown. Small quantities can be placed in a thermos flask of boiling water and left overnight. By morning they will have split. For both methods, some anglers prefer to use milk instead of water. The point of the hook—nos. 12–16 can be used—is pushed in at one end of the white split and out at the other. Ready stewed wheat can be bought at tackle shops.

Barley is prepared and used in the same way.

After soaking overnight tares are simmered in milk or water, with sugar or without, until they are soft, but not until the skin splits.

All three baits will take roach, rudd, dace and bream.

Woodlice

These little, armoured garden pests can be found in damp corners, under stones, under the bark of dead wood and in compost heaps. They can be trapped, like earwigs, with a piece of folded sacking hung on a stick in the garden, or simply laid on the flowerbed. For collecting them in quantity, a dustpan and soft handbrush are very useful.

Use on hooks nos. 12–16 for roach and dace.

Worms

The worm is the old-fashioned, all-purpose, all-year-round bait, not to be sniffed at because it is associated with bent pins and pieces of string. Every fish will take it—even the mighty pike will lunge at a bunch being worked sink-and-draw, and will even strike at a single lob being worked for perch.

There are about fifty species of worms in British soil, but the angler is happy to work on three basic divisions: the lob, the small red worm and the brandling.

ing it is to draw the hook through the growth until a decent-sized, straggly-ended cluster—complete with insect life—is attached. For fishing away from the source of the weeds, keep a handful in a closed tin.

Silkweed is fished on hooks nos. 10–12, and will claim roach, rudd, dace and barbel. Some anglers prefer to use small treble hooks because of their better hold on the weed.

Slugs

Chub love the big black or orange slugs. Roach, tench, bream, carp will all take the small grey slugs.

Catch them at night with a torch, or before the dew has evaporated in the morning. 'Trap' them by leaving out, overnight, halves of raw potato or the skins of halved oranges or grapefruit laid as 'domes' on the flowerbeds. A sharp stick pushed through the skin and into the ground will prevent the dome being blown over during the night.

Wasp grubs

Found during the summer, obviously and unfortunately, in wasps' nests. Take the nest only after killing off all the adult wasps with a proprietary wasp killer. (Make sure it is a wasp killer safe for an amateur to use: some are highly poisonous to animals and humans and are intended for use only by experts. And stick strictly to the manufacturer's instructions.)

Wasp grubs are soft and come off the hook easily, so many anglers bake them lightly or boil them to toughen the skins. Others prefer to leave them as they are and chance losing a few. The young grubs—those without wings or legs—are best for hookbait. The older grubs, and the crumbled 'cake' of the nest, can be used as groundbait.

Do not keep a nest for too long unless you are especially fond of adult wasps. Try the grubs singly or in pairs on hooks nos. 8–14 and expect to do well, especially with roach, dace and chub. Strikes should be quick.

The lob is the big, fat garden worm. Red worms and brandlings can be found in dozens in compost heaps and manure heaps. The name 'small red' is self-explanatory. The brandling is a smelly, yellow-striped worm which many anglers believe—because of its scent—to be deadly on coloured waters.

A fourth kind of worm, the bluehead, is like a big, tough lob with a cream body and a 'blue' head. It has a reputation for staying alive longer in water than an ordinary lob.

Red worms and brandlings, obviously, can be had by turning over a compost or manure heap. Lobs and blueheads can be had by digging in the flowerbeds, or by 'stalking' them at night with a torch. Worms are very sensitive to vibration, so the stalking must be done with a light tread. They keep their tails tucked into the holes, ready for a quick retreat. As they will not stay around for long in the glare of a torch, you have to be quick. Obviously, the tail end is the best place to grab them, but don't waste any time making your mind up which is which.

Worms in a lawn will come to the surface if the lawn is watered with a strong solution of salt and water. This is recommended only for a quick collection in an emergency: repeated use of the salt will do the lawn not a bit of good.

Hunting worms before each fishing trip can be inconvenient, time-consuming and, in dry or frosty weather, fruitless. The answer is either to make a patch in the garden to which worms will be attracted, or to build your own wormery where they can live and breed.

The most basic form of worm patch is simply an area on to which the teapot is emptied regularly, so keeping the soil damp and providing a regular supply of food for the worms. The patch can be improved by digging in garden and kitchen refuse—grass cuttings, leaves, peelings—or soaked and shredded newspapers.

One useful dodge is to dig in soaked pieces of corrugated

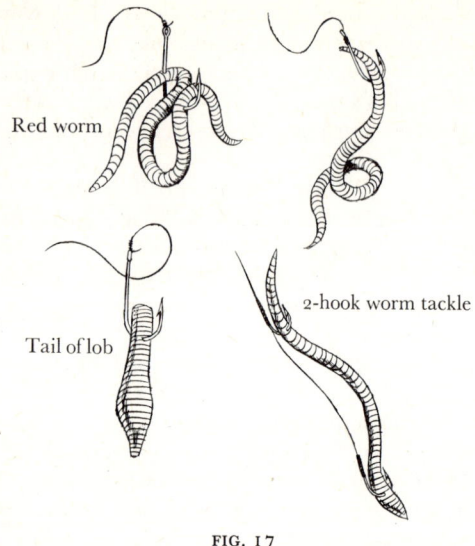

FIG. 17

cardboard, about three inches square. The red worms crawl into the corrugations, using them as ready-made holes. When collecting time comes, all you need do is turn up the pieces of cardboard and throw them in your bait tin. The worms will be inside like bullets in a bandolier.

For a self-contained, escape-proof wormery, you need a large box, water butt or plastic bin. The contents can be built up in layers over a period as you do with a compost heap: a layer of earth, then a layer of refuse—garden refuse, kitchen refuse, shredded paper, etc. A canful of worms can be tipped on in between each layer as the contents grow. Keep the wormery damp, but keep it covered so that heavy rain will not leave it waterlogged. Eventually, the worms will breed, so that in time the wormery will provide all the worms you need without having to be re-stocked.

Worms dug from heavy clay soil should be tough enough to stand a lot of wear and tear on the hook. Those from lighter soils, or from wormeries or compost heaps where the living has been easy, will benefit from a toughening-up course—'scouring'—in an airholed tin filled with florist's moss. Put the worms in the tin several days before they are needed, and up-end the tin every twelve hours. The worms will keep burrowing through the moss to the bottom, and in so doing will clean themselves and toughen their skins.

Small worms can be used singly or in pairs or bunches, on round bend or small treble hooks. Lobs can be used whole or halved. A much-favoured traditional bait is the tail of a lob, but it is doubtful whether a hungry perch or chub cares which end it eats.

Large lobs can be fished on special worm tackle—two or three round-bend hooks mounted one above the other. The worm tackle has the advantage of holding the worm securely, of displaying it well, and of having a hook at whichever end the fish bites. It has the disadvantages, however, of being more obvious to the fish and of increasing the risk of a gut-hooking.

A good tip for holding a worm, incidentally, especially in cold weather when one's fingers are stiff and insensitive, is to roll it first in dry sand or soil.

5

Starting To Fish

The first golden rule for using tackle is—make sure you have it. It sounds silly, but the combination of sleepiness and excitement in the early morning often leads to equipment being left behind. Try to have it all checked, packed and ready the night before. Don't be tempted to take odd bits out again to play with them. It is worth drawing up a check list so that the individual items can be ticked off as they are packed.

Don't let the early morning excitement make you forget about possible cold and hunger later on. You may not feel in the mood for food—but you will when the first thrills have worn off. As well as sandwiches—or chocolate and raisins if you want to travel light—pack a flask of hot soup, tea or coffee.

Remember that the waterside in the early morning can be *very* cold and *very* damp. Wear waterproof outer clothing and Wellington boots with a couple of pairs of socks. Under the outer garments, wear several layers of thin clothing rather than one thick one. This keeps you warmer and makes it easier to peel off as the day warms up. Find room somewhere for a spare pair of socks: it is not always the other fellow who falls in, or finds the shallows not as shallow as they look.

Wear a hood or some form of headgear which protects the ears as well as the head. Wind is a great chiller.

The approach to the water

The difference between passive fishing, such as bottom fishing, and active fishing, such as fly fishing or spinning, has been described as the difference between trapping and hunting.

The bottom fisherman tries to entice the fish to his hook-bait in a likely spot, whereas the fly fisher or spinner seeks out the fish and pursues them with his bait.

Like all generalisations, however, this is an oversimplification. There is a fair amount of hunting involved even in so-called passive fishing. You first need to scan the water, as the hunter scans the land, for the likely locations of your quarry. And you begin, as he does, by *stalking* it... by getting within range undetected.

Fish are scared away by the unusual: by vibrations, by shadows which ought not to be there, and by light reflected from shiny, white, or brightly coloured surfaces. So the first essential is to blend into the surroundings, to keep the fish unaware of anything unusual on the bank. It begins with camouflage.

All fishing clothes should be drab in colour: brown or dark green for preference. *All* clothes. It is no use wearing a camouflaged jacket which opens to reveal a flash of white shirt, or being encased in drab from top to toe and then blowing your nose on a brilliant white handkerchief.

All tackle—except of course for intentionally bright lures—should be dark and have a matt or dull surface. However exciting a shiny, varnished rod or a bright red tackle box may look in the shop, leave it there.

When the fish are known to be really shy, it is not carrying things too far to rub your spectacle lenses with anti-flash liquid (from gunshops and some army surplus stores). Really keen anglers have been known to even rub their faces with burnt cork.

66   *Coarse Angling*

Look before you leap

Unless you are familiar with the water, choose a vantage point away from the bank and there decide where you are going to fish. It must, of course, be a spot likely to hold fish, but it should also have plenty of cover, either in front or behind (we come to that later), and at the same time allow you plenty of room to cast.

Unless you will be moving through trees of tangled growth likely to make carrying a rod awkward, tackle up away from the bank. Now *stalk* down to the water, treading softly and crouching low.

Tread softly because fish are much more sensitive to vibrations transmitted from the ground through the water, than to air-borne sounds. Fish pick up vibrations through

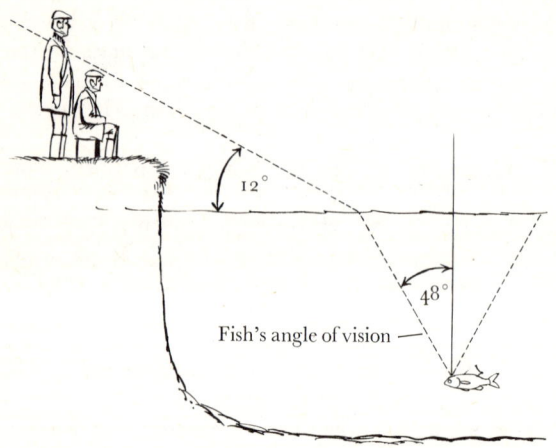

FIG. 18   Refraction. Because of the bending of the light rays at the surface of the water, the fish can see 'through' the bank between it and the angler. This illustrates, too, why a seated angler is less likely to be spotted than a standing one.

their lateral lines, using natural vibrations to help find their food or to give warning of the approach of a predator. Any unnatural vibrations will alert the fish straight away—and those caused by a heavy footfall are surprisingly strong.

Crouch low so that the fish will be less likely to see you. Firstly, you should be below the line of any cover behind you, blending into what to the fish is a large, dark mass. Secondly, you should be below the skyline. Even a fish, which is not the brightest of creatures, knows the difference between a tree on the skyline and a two-legged moving object. Thirdly, you will defeat the effect of *refraction* on the fish's eyesight.

Refraction is the name given to the bending of light rays when they pass from one medium to another of a different density, in this case from air to water.

The illustration shows how the principle affects what a fish can see above the surface: the fish is less likely to see a seated or crouching angler than a standing one—and it can see an angler even when the bank is between them.

Shadows, especially moving or sudden ones, frighten fish. A shadow on the water could be that of a heron, poised to strike, and the fish's instinctive reaction is to get clear as quickly as possible.

Once you are at the water, no matter how excited you feel—and there are few anglers who do not get butterflies in their stomachs at the prospect of catches to come—take things slowly. Make all the necessary preparations before even thinking about your first cast.

Put the keepnet gently into the water in a suitable place (see pp. 236–7, 'Care of Your Catch'). Make up the landing net if you haven't done so already. There are few things more saddening than hooking a fish and being unable to land it because the net was not made up. Push the rod rest firmly into the bank.

Set out your hookbait and groundbait containers where you can reach them without moving from the spot. Have the disgorger in your pocket. Test the depth of the water with the plummet, making as little disturbance as possible. Throw in some groundbait and/or samples of hookbait. Now, and only now, are you ready to bait up and cast out.

Assembling the rod

Assemble the rod from the top joint downwards. At the end of the day, when you unship it, do it from the bottom joint upwards. The reason is that you are always immediately handling the heavier sections, leaving the lighter sections waving free. If you do it the other way around, you will find it more difficult to hold the rod and you may be putting a strain on the slimmer sections.

As you add each section, 'sight' along the rod to make sure that the rings are in line. A set of rings offset from the others can lead to difficulty in casting, tangles and wear on the line.

Make sure that the reel is attached firmly, whether it is gripped by sliding winch fittings or seated in a screw-up clamp. Loosely held reels have a nasty habit of falling off on the strike, or coming adrift during a hard fight. Not only could you lose a fish like that, but possibly the reel as well.

Thread the line through the rings. With a fixed-spool reel, remember to make sure that the bale arm is in the 'off' position before you draw off any line. If it is left in the 'on' position, the line will be on the wrong side of it, and it will

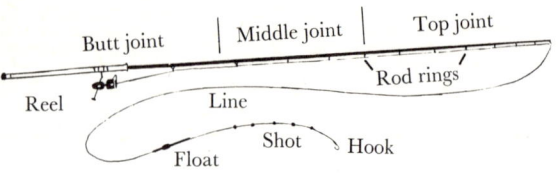

FIG. 19 The rod assembled and ready for action.

Starting To Fish 69

fail to pick up line when the handle is turned. (Not only will the arm fail to pick up the line but also it will allow any amount of it to be stripped off the reel—something else which often becomes evident only when a fish is on the end of the line.)

Fit on the float and shot, or leger weight (see chapters on 'Float Fishing' and 'Legering') and you are ready to cast.

Casting

The first thing to do before you cast is to look around and make sure there are no snags—trees, bushes, stonework, animals or people—in which your hook might fix itself.

For *overhead* casting with a fixed-spool reel, press the line against the butt of the rod with the right forefinger. With the left hand, move the bale arm of the reel into the 'off' position.

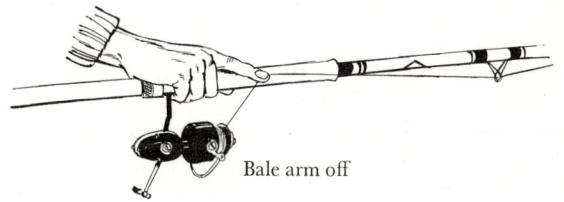
Bale arm off

FIG. 20 Ready for the cast with a fixed-spool reel: the bale arm is off and the line is held against the butt with the forefinger. At the end of the casting swing the finger is lifted.

Imagine you are facing to the right of this page and standing against a giant clock face. Take the rod over your right shoulder until it reaches ten o'clock.

With a smart movement of your wrist, bring the rod over your shoulder to two o'clock. As the weight shoots out in front of the rod, 'follow through' with the rod tip so that the line runs smoothly through the rings.

The first forward movement of the wrist, though smart, should be smooth. You are throwing a bait, not cracking a whip and you first have to overcome the inertia of the line. A jerky movement will not only result in a short cast, but may flick the bait off the hook.

At the top of the wrist movement, while the bait is still gaining momentum from the pull of the line, finish off with a smart flick, as if you were flicking a blob of mud off the rod tip.

After the cast, don't forget to put the bale arm back in the 'on' position with a turn of the handle.

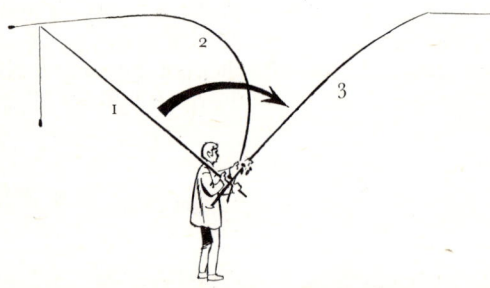

FIG. 21   Overhead cast: 1 Start with the rod over your shoulder at ten o'clock. 2 Bring the rod forward smartly. 3 As the weight shoots out, take your finger off the line. 'Follow through' the flight with your rod tip.

With a centre-pin reel, you need two hands for the cast. Take the check off the reel. Draw off several large loops of line and hold them in the left hand. As the line shoots forward and starts to straighten out, let go of the loops. The length of the cast here will depend on the amount of line you have pulled off. Put the check back on the reel as soon as the bait is in the water.

If you are fishing under trees, or with snags behind you, or from a cramped position, try an *underhand* cast.

Starting To Fish 71

With a fixed-spool reel, hold the line against the butt with the right forefinger, take off the bale arm, and take the weights in the left hand, holding the line taut.

Start with the rod pointing to two o'clock. Lift the rod tip and at the same time let the weights go so that they swing outwards like a pendulum. At the highest point of their swing, drop the rod tip and take your forefinger off the line. The reel line will now be stripped off to follow the weights across the water.

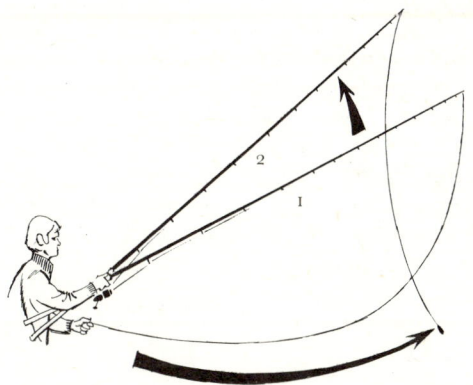

FIG. 22 Underhand cast: 1 Hold rod at two o'clock, weight in left hand. 2 Lift rod and release weight. When weight is at highest point of swing, drop rod tip back to first position.

For an underhand cast with a centre-pin reel, take off the check and draw off several loops of line into the left hand. Use the rod exactly as you did with the fixed spool. This time let the loops of line go when the weights reach the highest point of their swing. Don't forget to put the check back on the reel.

Casting practice on the lawn or in an open space increases

both range and accuracy. You can lay down handkerchiefs or pieces of paper at varying distances, and keep score of how many times you can drop the weights right on them. For home practice, incidentally, don't use hooks. You may find yourself carrying realism a bit too far by hooking some passing friend or neighbour.

Practice will give you the chance to concentrate on the action, which should be confined to the wrist and forearm. There is no need to use the shoulders or the trunk. By treating the rod as an extension of the arm, you will achieve an easy, graceful and effortless movement which will drop the bait far away and accurately. Keeping the effort to a minimum is important: at the waterside you will be casting for eight hours or more at a stretch, and that can be *tiring*.

Don't confine your casting exercises purely to distance and accuracy. Try casting from all kinds of positions— standing up, sitting down and kneeling. Try casting from under trees, behind bushes, or any other cramped spots. Try it in different directions relative to the wind.

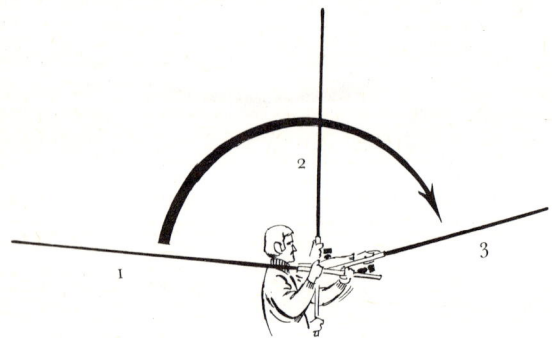

FIG. 23 Two-handed overhead cast: 1 Hold rod over shoulder, parallel to ground. 2 Bring rod forward smartly. When weight has shot out to fullest extent, release line. 3 'Follow through' with rod.

For casting really long distances, you may need to use a two-handed overhead cast. You can forget the centre pin for this: a fixed spool is essential for distance.

Left hand at the bottom of the butt, right hand at the top. Right forefinger holding line to butt. Bale arm off. Hold the rod over your shoulder, parallel to the ground. Now bring the rod forward over your shoulder, s–m–o–o–t–h–l–y, speeding up as the rod gains momentum and finishing with a flick of the rod tip. When the weights have shot out to their fullest extent, take your finger off the line and follow through with the rod.

Striking and playing a fish

Striking a fish is making the movement with the rod which sets the hook in the fish's mouth. The moment of striking, and the strength and manner of the strike, depend on the fish, the distance, the current, and other factors discussed in the chapters on individual fish.

The main thing to remember is that the purpose of the strike is to set the hook. Nothing more. A strike at close range in still water need be a mere turn of the wrist. A strike at long range may involve running back one or two paces and laying the rod right back over your shoulder, but even then bear in mind that on the other end of the line is a modest-sized fish, not a blue whale.

Playing the fish is the most exciting part of the whole operation. At last you are into your quarry, and you are still not sure how big it might be. It is up to you now not to lose the fish through clumsiness or over-excitement.

Rule one, as in so many other things, is *don't panic*.

Use your wrist to do the playing. Keep the rod tip *up* and the line taut. However violently the rod tip wags, it is absorbing the lunges of the fish and so taking the strain off the line. Whatever you do, don't allow the fish any slack: if it gets any slack it will run and smash the line.

There is a difference between allowing slack and giving line. If the fish threatens to break the line, give it line—but do it in a controlled and calm manner. Give it slowly. And keep it taut.

Recover the line as soon as you can turn the fish, but do not be in too much of a hurry to get the fish to the bank. Let it do the pulling and tire itself to the point where you have it completely under control. On the other hand, do not play it to the point of exhaustion just for the fun of it.

Keep the fish away from snags by using *sidestrain* to turn it. All this means is lowering the rod and pulling it sideways, and it is a very effective method of controlling a fish.

Do not *reel in* directly against the fish's pull. This strains the line, wraps it too tightly around the spool, causes snarl-ups on later casts, and has been known to crack a plastic spool. Start reeling with the rod tip high, or back over your shoulder, and let it move towards the fish as you reel. When you have reeled in a little line, lift the rod tip back to its original position.

Pumping is a more exaggerated version of the normal reeling and playing action. It is used for getting big fish out of deep water or away from snags. You reel in quickly, allowing the rod tip to move down towards the fish and then lift the rod to haul the fish towards you, repeating the operation for as long as necessary.

When the fish is under control, bring it to the bank and over the landing net. Have the net submerged before the fish gets near. And always bring the fish to the net, never jab the net at the fish.

Once the fish is over the net, lift the net and drop the rod tip at the same time. Until then, keep the line taut. And do not trust the fish an inch. Even a seemingly exhausted fish can give an unexpected jerk or leap which may break the line or throw the hook.

6

Float Fishing

A float has two main functions: to support the bait and the necessary weights in the water, and to warn the angler that a fish is biting.

It can hold the bait at any desired depth. The depth is adjusted simply by sliding the float up or down the line. In moving water it carries the bait at that depth at the speed of the current. In still water it holds the bait stationary at that depth or, if the weight is on the bottom, acts purely as a bite indicator.

The different kinds of float and their uses have already been discussed (pp. 25–9). Here we look at different float-fishing techniques.

It is simplest to start with a float in gently moving water, holding the bait just off the bottom. This is one of the commonest techniques and takes most kinds of fish.

Fishing the swim

Fishing the swim, also known as swimming the stream, starts with the choice of a good swim.

A swim is a stretch of moving water fished by an angler. Its extent can be determined by physical features which bring it to an end—rocks, trees, jutting out banks or piling, bends, or swifter currents which cut across it. Or the extent can be simply the distance from his pitch which the angler wants to fish.

A good swim offers plenty of cover to the angler, but also room to cast. It holds cover and food for the fish, in the form of weed, roots or rocks, but also has clear spaces between them where the bait can be deployed. It flows steadily, but not too fast, and has one or two eddies where the bait can linger temptingly for a while.

The plummet tells us the depth of the swim. We fix the float so that the bait is just off the bottom. And we cast in upstream, allowing the float to drift back down towards us, and to carry on downstream away from us for as far as is practicable.

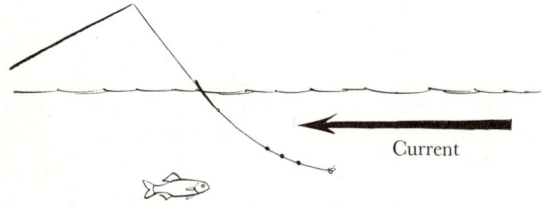

FIG. 24   Upstream fishing.

Surface currents travel faster than those on the bottom. So on its way downstream towards us, the bait is behind the float and we can do nothing about it. This does not matter too much, because the fish will be facing upstream and away from us. When a fish bites we shall be striking backwards from the fish's head, and stand a fair chance of driving the hook home in the side of its mouth. We are also striking in the direction in which the float is travelling so that the line is almost straight between the rod tip and the fish. Of course, as the float has been drifting down towards us, we have been reeling in the slack line from the surface.

When the float is downstream from us, it is a different matter. If the bait lags behind the float now, there will be a sharp angle between the line above and below the float. Instead of the float being between us and the fish, it will be *beyond* the fish. All this extra line has to be taken up on the strike, giving the fish more chance to let go. As we are striking *away* from the fish, all it has to do is open its mouth, and we do the rest by pulling out the bait.

So as the float drifts downstream away from us, we check the float gently now and again to allow the bait to swing out in front. Not only does the occasional check get the bait back out in front, but it gives it an attractive little swing upwards and then a slow downward drift.

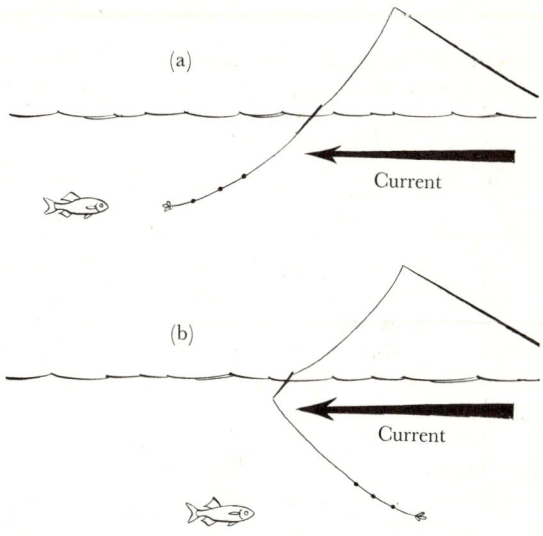

FIG. 25 Downstream fishing: (a) right; (b) wrong.

When the float reaches the end of the swim, give a gentle strike—just in case a fish is mouthing the bait—and reel in again. Try to reel in with as little disturbance as possible, raising the rod high to lift the terminal tackle from the water, rather than reeling it all the way back through the swim and possibly frightening the fish.

In a moving swim, the float should be always on the move. A float which stops could be responding to the bite of a roach or rudd—the signal for a quick strike—or the bait may simply have hit a snag.

A bait which comes to a standstill in slack water should not be allowed to remain too long, or it could become hidden by debris or nibbled away by fry or crayfish. In any case, fish are more attracted to a moving bait. Many bites come on the drop—that is, as the bait drifts down in the water after a cast.

As well as the length of the swim, explore as much of its width as your casts can reach. Investigate particularly the runs between the weedbeds, the edges of the bank which may have been undercut to form a shelf, under which the fish may be lurking. Get the bait into eddies, which are often the sign of a hole in which fish lay in wait for food sinking through the slacker water. Try under overhanging trees, which provide a steady supply of falling insects. Go for the slack water behind a rock, or behind stonework or piling, where fish gather to feed on the weed, or on food released by the slowing down of the current.

Work out the effects of the current on groundbait. If you want to get the groundbait into a hole, for instance, it is useless dropping the ball smack on top of it. The current will take it away downstream before it has a chance to sink. Throw in the groundbait upstream and let the current wash it naturally into the hole. Experiment with the groundbait and see how fast it sinks. If it is sinking too slowly, squeeze it more tightly, or add some clay or sand to stiffen it. If you have a spare rod, you can use a bait dropper or a swimfeeder to make sure the groundbait is going exactly where you want it.

In absolutely still water such as a lake, do not allow the bait just to lie indefinitely. Again, it may be nibbled away

The lift method

A very sensitive method, ideal for tench, bream or shy roach. A length of peacock quill or sarkandas reed is attached by the bottom only. An AA or swan shot is clipped about 2 or 3 in from the hook to rest on the bottom. The float is set over-depth.

With the weight on the bottom, the line is drawn taut to cock the float. A taking fish moves the weight and causes the float to lift and lay flat. A rest must be used for this method, because even the steadiest hand causes vibrations which affect the float.

Trotting

Trotting, sometimes called long trotting, is used for fishing downstream in moving water and is effective even in quite fast currents. The float needs to be fairly hefty and the weights heavier than would normally be used for fishing the swim. The depth at which the bait is presented can be adjusted by altering the number and grouping of the weights.

A free-running centre-pin reel is used, with the check off when the bait is moving. The rod is pointed directly at the float, so that the current can pull line off the reel. This is normally the only check needed to keep the bait moving ahead of the float. Finger pressure on the reel, lifting the rod tip, or moving it to either side, can be used to guide the float into likely places on either side of the main run.

Stret pegging

Again used for fishing downstream in moving water, stret pegging is like a cross between laying on and rolling leger. (Many anglers prefer rolling leger, as stret pegging can sometimes be clumsy.)

The float is set well over-depth. Several heavy shot or a drilled bullet are fixed to the line about 15 in above the hook. (The bullet is stopped with a split shot above and below.)

Float Fishing 81

For gentler rivers, open out the bulk shot, keeping the end one about 18 in from the hook and spacing out the rest of the shot up the line. This allows the bait to swing about naturally in the current.

So much for the general approach to float fishing. Let's look now at some techniques of float and bait presentation.

Float and bait presentation

Laying on
A great favourite in still or gently moving water. A single shot is set to lie on the bottom, with the hook trail lying free beyond it. A dust shot can be used midway to cock the float if necessary. A small quill float is used. In windy weather it can be attached by the bottom only.

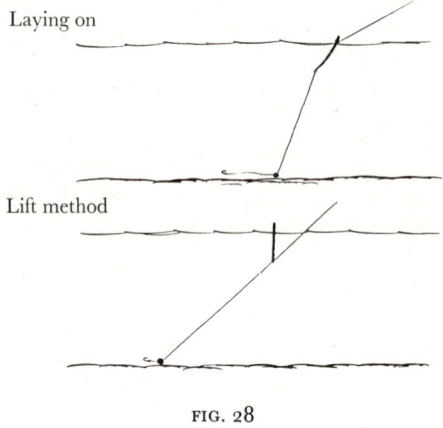

FIG. 28

A taking fish moves the bait, lifts the shot, and causes the float to lie flat, to run along the surface, to go under . . . or all three in succession.

each float, each angler. It depends also on how far you want to cast, how fast you want the bait to sink, how much wind there is and in which direction it is blowing.

So there are no hard and fast rules about shotting. All this book can offer is a few generalisations which will be modified by particular conditions, by your own preferences, and by chats with local anglers and tackle dealers.

For close-in work on canals or stillwater lakes, the tiniest float and a few small shot should be enough. For a slow-sinking bait, clip one shot just below the float, and another about halfway down the line. If another shot is needed to give weight for the cast, clip it on about halfway between the second shot and the hook. For a faster sink, clip all three shot about 9 in from the hook.

For longer-range work on still water, try the bulk of the shot halfway between float and hook, and one shot between the bulk shot and the hook. For a slow sink, move up the bulk shot a little nearer the float, and make the single shot nearest the hook a small one.

For powerful rivers bulk the shot together about 9 in from the hook. This is necessary to keep the bait down in the current.

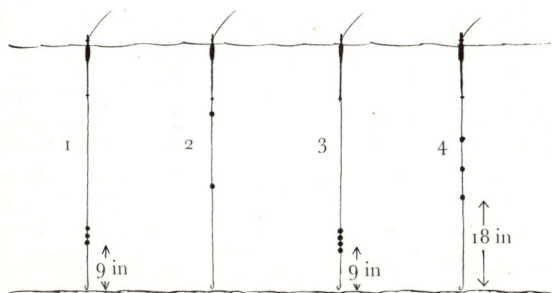

FIG. 27 Shotting patterns. 1 Slow water for fast sink. 2 Slow water—for slow sink. 3 For powerful rivers. 4 For gentler rivers.

Float Fishing 79

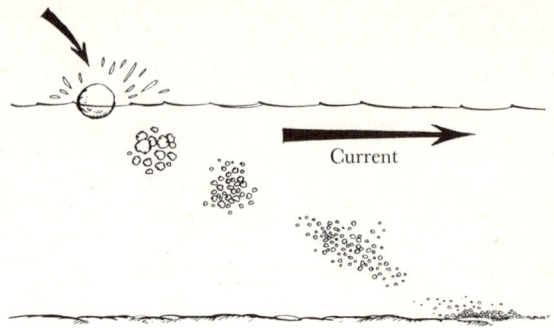

FIG. 26 Groundbaiting. In moving water, groundbait will settle some distance from the point at which it hits the surface.

by fry or other small creatures, without a tremble on the float. Or it may disappear into weed or mud.

In any kind of water, do not be mean with your baits. Examine them after every retrieval. A maggot may have been 'blown' by a fish without your noticing, leaving just an empty skin. Or it may simply have died, and be hanging there with no movement to attract the fish. A worm may have died, or could have lost half its length in a bite which did not register. Paste, flake or crust may have fallen off. Cheese, sausage or luncheon meat may have had all the colour and flavour washed out of it.

Do not be content to sit at the same swim for hours without a bite. If you have tried every likely spot and nothing has come along, ring the changes on bait. Switch from maggot to worm, bread or cheese. If nothing happens on the new baits after a while, move to another swim.

Shotting patterns for fishing the swim

The arrangement of shot on the line varies with each water,

Float Fishing 83

The line to the bait is kept taut, with the float lying well back on the surface. When the weight hits bottom, the hook length travels out in front of it. Line is given out to allow the bullet to bump along downstream. The bait can be allowed to travel in an unobstructed run, or the line can be checked now and then and the bait held in one place for a while before being allowed to continue.

Like rolling leger, this useful method allows the bait to be dropped into any holes along the swim.

Bubble floats and controller floats

Plastic bubble floats and wooden controller floats give casting weight to surface-fished baits and are useful if light or distance make it difficult to see the bait or the line on the surface. The controller floats, fastened at each end, lie flat on the surface. Only the smallest of bubble floats should be used. The weight of a bubble can be varied by the amount of water sealed into it.

Sink and draw

Sink and draw is a technique normally associated with spinning, but it can be used with a bait float-fished off the bottom. It is often a way of livening up a quiet swim.

The bait is allowed to sink after the cast, is lifted up, and allowed to sink again. The process is repeated at intervals,

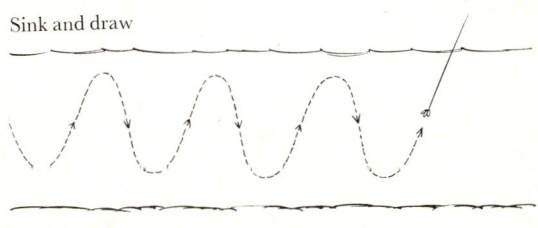

FIG. 29

with a couple of turns on the reel each time to take up the slack line.

It can add life to a worm, maggot or deadbait. As the reel is turned with every lift, the method covers quite a stretch of water.

7

Legering

Legering is a method of fishing on the bottom, often—but not always—with the bait static. It has grown tremendously popular in recent years and has accounted for many of the bigger fish.

The line is threaded through a special leger lead, either through a hole in the lead or through a ring attached to the lead. A split shot is pinched on the line at a predetermined distance from the hook. This stops the hook and bait being pulled back to the weight, but allows the line to run out freely through the weight when a fish moves off with the bait. A good general distance from the hook to the weight is about 18 in.

Legering is especially useful in fast water, where float tackle would be swept away, and for casting long distances. It has the added advantage of offering the fish almost no resistance as it turns away with the bait.

The origin of the word (in its alternative spelling, *ledger*) seems to be the Old English *licgan*, to lie, or *lecgan*, to lay. These suggest that the technique is a stationary one in which the weight, line and bait lie in one place, waiting for the fish to come along. This was, indeed, the old concept of legering, using a heavy weight to anchor the bait in one spot and leaving it there, often until the angler became bored, packed up and went home.

It is better to approach legering from its less likely derivation, the French word *léger*, meaning light. This is a reminder to use only enough weight to achieve the necessary length of cast and to hold the bait against the current. In the rolling leger technique, you use *less* weight than will hold the current, so that both weight and bait go rolling along the bottom to search a wider area.

Of recent years, and especially since the invention of the swingtip and quivertip, legering has progressed from a primitive and often clumsy technique to a very sensitive and specialised one. Many former float anglers who would have scorned the very thought of legering twenty years ago now think of it first. Until the 1950s match fishermen invariably used floats, but now legering is one of the major techniques of match fishing.

Leger rigs

The simplest leger rig of all is a *shot leger*. It is simply a large split shot pinched on to the line about 18 in from the hook. It will not, of course, stay put if there is much current or

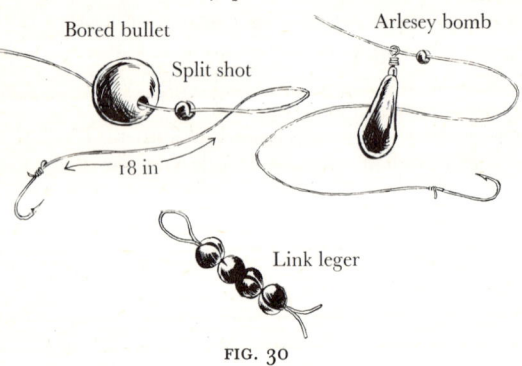

FIG. 30

wind, but it is simple, sensitive, and works well as a light rolling leger.

'True' leger rigs use a pierced lead—a bullet, barrel or coffin—or one with a ring or swivel attachment such as an

Legering 87

Weed fishing with link leger

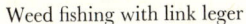

Running paternoster

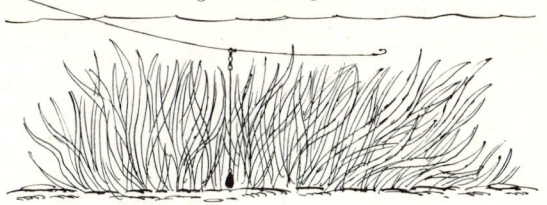

For bottom bait Off the bottom bait For surface bait

Float leger

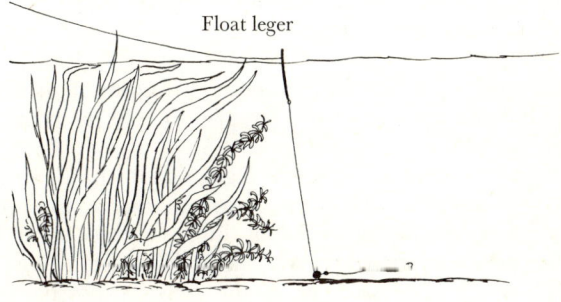

FIG. 31

Arlesey bomb or the pyramidal Capta (see chapter 3, 'Tackle').

Some anglers use a split ring as a stop instead of the split shot, which means that the fish has less weight to move when it picks up the bait and is therefore less likely to take fright.

The *link leger*, invented by Fred J. Taylor, is a simple but significant variation on the basic leger rig. It is adaptable to all sorts of conditions and does away with the need for carrying a number of leads of different weights. It consists simply of a length of nylon with several swan shot clipped to it. The nylon is either folded over the reel line, so that the shot are clipped to a doubled length, or attached by a split ring or swivel. The link is stopped in the normal way by a split shot on the reel line. The link can take any number of swan shot, so that the weight can be as heavy or as light as you wish, varied by the addition or subtraction of shot.

Ordinary leger weights can be converted to link legers by adding a length of nylon and a split ring or swivel to clip on to the reel line. The nylon link can be any length which suits the purpose. This extra length of nylon cuts down resistance to the fish by giving more 'play' when the bait is taken away. It is also a great help when fishing on a weeded bottom. The weight sinks through the weeds, but the bait is allowed to remain on top of them.

Swanshot links are an aid to accurate groundbaiting. The knobbly line of shot enables a 'sausage' of groundbait to be squeezed on it, and gives sufficient grip to hold the groundbait on the cast.

Running paternoster is a versatile leger rig which allows the bait to be fished at any level from bottom to surface. The hook length is tied, or attached by a split ring, to the free-spinning middle ring of a treble swivel. The reel line is threaded through the other two eyes of the swivel, allowing the swivel to be moved up and down the line to a predetermined depth.

Float leger

As the name suggests, this technique combines both float and leger fishing. The leger is rigged in the normal way, and a float attached at the point where the line breaks the surface of the water.

Because the weight is on the bottom, the float is not supporting anything, and acts purely as a bite indicator. This means that it can be really small and slim, offering almost no resistance to a taking fish. Attaching it only by the bottom ring makes it a more sensitive instrument and allows the float to ride upright in the water.

A float will allow a leger rig to be fished on the far side of an underwater obstruction—a ledge, say, or a bed of weeds. The float changes the direction of the line and holds it clear of the obstruction, avoiding snags.

The float may signal a bite in the normal way, by trembling and dipping. Or, if the fish has lifted both bait and weight off the bottom, by lying flat. If the float lies flat, remember that this indicates slack line, so make sure that the strike is good and firm.

Some anglers use float leger because of its sensitive bite indication; others because they feel they are getting the best of both techniques. And there are many who will always be float fishers at heart, and who like something to look at while they are waiting.

Legering techniques and bite indication

Static leger
A static leger is an ideal technique for fishing a specific location such as a chub or perch hole, a clear patch in a bed of weeds or a known bream hole.

The best bite indicators of all are your fingers. Hold the rod with the butt under your right arm, and take the line between the thumb and forefinger of your left. Hold the line taut with the rod parallel to the water. Bites will be felt as a pluck, a thrum, or as a strange 'sawing' sensation. This last is difficult to describe, but you will recognise it when it happens. As well as the sensation in your fingers, there may also be a twitching or a thrumming of the rod tip. This is *touch-legering*. As well as being an exciting way of registering bites, it also tells you much more about what is going on underwater than the other methods.

This said, holding the rod throughout a day's fishing can be tiring, not to say boring if nothing happens for a while. So until the fish are actually on the feed, you may prefer to use a rod rest. Two rests, or an adjustable combination rest, are best. The rod can then be pointed in different directions and the tip lowered or raised according to the conditions, the method of bite indication used, and the different parts of the location which are to be tried.

In still water on a windless day, you can allow the line to slacken so that it forms a bow between the rod tip and the surface of the water. When a fish takes, this bow will either tighten or fall even slacker.

Another still-water technique is to pull off several loops of line below the bottom ring and lay them on a piece of paper at your feet. When a fish moves off with the bait the loops will uncoil and follow the rest of the line through the rings.

For still or slow-moving water, a *dough bobbin* can be used. This is a ball of breadpaste which is squeezed around the line, either about a foot below the rod tip or between the first and second butt rings. Though the bobbin must be small—not much bigger than a sparrow's egg or a large pea—its weight will be enough to form an angle in the line. When a fish takes, this angle will either straighten out or become more acute as the bobbin either rises or falls.

An alternative to the dough bobbin, and especially useful in night fishing or when the fish is to be allowed to move off with the bait, is a cylinder of silver paper or aluminium foil placed around the line between the reel and the first butt ring. For this technique, the bale arm of the reel is left in the off position. When the fish takes, the cylinder will be lifted and carried towards the ring as the line moves off. Because it has virtually no weight, the fish will feel no resistance. And because the line can run smoothly through the cylinder, there will be no friction or jamming against the ring.

Two other simple forms of bite indication are the paper-and-pebble and nylon spool techniques. In each case, line is drawn from below the first butt ring. For the first, a piece of paper is folded over the line, laid on the ground and weighted down with a small pebble. A bite will lift the line and dislodge the pebble. For the second, the line is wound once around an empty nylon spool. A take will lift the spool, which will then fall off the line.

Pointing the rod tip directly at the bait, so that there is no friction set up by the angle in the line, helps enormously with these methods of bite detection. On windy days the rod tip should be sunk beneath the surface of the water.

Watching the tip of the rod for bites has not been mentioned because by the time the rod tip is twitching, the fish is fully aware that something is amiss. And nowadays anglers prefer to watch a quivertip or a swingtip (see pp. 36–7).

With a swingtip, the rod is placed in a rest so that it lies parallel to the water. When a fish takes, the tip either lifts or drops back. It is often used in conjunction with a target board, which helps to show bites more clearly and acts as a windbreak.

The quivertip, of course, quivers. It gives a more exaggerated indication of a bite than the rod tip and does not offer so much resistance to the fish.

Despite the widespread use of the swingtip, many anglers do not like it at all. As it flops about on the end of the rod, it gives the appearance of a broken rod tip, and this gives some anglers an uneasy feeling. Since the introduction of the quivertip, its popularity has increased enormously at the expense of the swingtip.

Finally, we have the electric bite alarms, which have been discussed (p. 37). These are especially useful for night fishing.

Rolling leger

Rolling leger is a roving technique which enables a swim to be covered as thoroughly as with a float. The lead—and Arlesey bomb or a swivelled bullet—is light enough to be rolled by the current along the bottom.

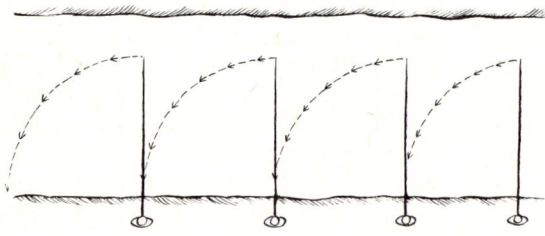

FIG. 32   Covering the swim with rolling leger.

A swim can be searched by casting out and then tightening the line, so that the push of the current and the pull of the line combine to bring the leger back in an arc to the near bank. By moving further downstream for each successive cast, the swim is covered very thoroughly indeed. A rolling leger can also be trotted straight downstream, and can be checked to linger a while in any likely hole or lie.

Bite detection is by touch. The bumping around of the lead makes it confusing at first, but you will soon learn what the different sensations indicate.

Freelining

The most uncomplicated technique of all, using neither float nor weights. All you need is rod, fixed-spool reel, line, hook and bait.

Freelining can be used to present floating baits—crust or chrysalis—to rudd. It can hang a worm over a lily pad to attract rudd, tench and carp, or send the worm down a swim to a chub hole. It can be used right on the bottom with any bait which sinks, including deadbait.

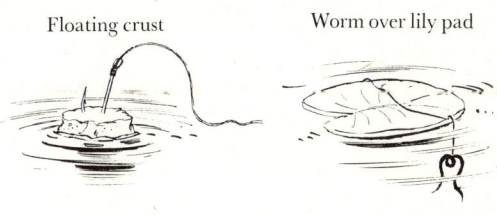

FIG. 33

The advantage of freelining is that the bait is presented completely naturally, with no float or ironmongery to alert the fish. The disadvantage is that the casting distance is limited by the small weight of the bait.

8

Spinning

In chapter 4, 'Baits', we looked at the three main types of artificial lure: the spoon, the spinner or bar spoon and the plug. We also looked at natural spinning baits such as dead gudgeon, dace and minnow.

Mention spinning and most anglers think of pike, with perch running a close second. It is surprising how few of them think of chub, though many excellent chub fall every season to spinners.

Spinners for perch or chub can be used on a nylon trace, with a swivel at each end. The swivel at the top end of the trace can be attached to the reel line by means of either a split ring or another swivel. As a further precaution against kinking, you can use an anti-kink lead or vane on the trace, just in front of the swivel which joins it to the reel line.

If there are likely to be pike about, you can use a wire trace instead of a nylon one, although this 'dampens' the action of small lures. For pike spinning, the trace must always be wire.

Spinning can be done with either a multiplier or a fixed-spool reel, using either a spinning rod or a hollow glass Avon rod. Don't buy a spinning rod which is too short. You ought to have a length of about 10 ft to give you the necessary control over the lure and to clear any obstacles on the bank.

Before you buy any artificial lures, check that the wire

used for the hooks is strong in relation to its thickness and that the hooks are sharp. With plugs, check also that no two hooks can overlap and so foul each other on the strike.

Lures take a lot of punishment underwater, from bumping over rocks, sand and gravel, and from snagging on roots, weed stems, piling and other obstacles. So sharpen the hooks every time you use them.

Although, in theory, a predatory fish can home in on prey by vibration alone, it does prefer to see it as well. So you will find that as a general rule, spinning in coloured, soupy water does not produce much. Unless the lure happens to pass right in front of the nose of a perch or a pike, they are likely to ignore it and concentrate on the search for worms and carrion.

Some anglers swear by summer spinning. Others wait until the autumn when the weeds are starting to clear. Others will wait for the cold, clear waters of winter. Whatever the time of year, if you have reasonably clear water and good light, you can spin with a fair chance of success. The basic rule for all artificials is to use brightly coloured ones on dull days and ones with duller finishes on bright days.

Most anglers soon learn to use artificial lures properly, if only because they are not cheap. Leaving a few on the river bed costs a lot more than do ordinary hooks and split shot. It pays to get in some dry-land practice with a new lure, either on the lawn or in a field by the water, to get some idea of its weight and 'feel'.

The cast with a spinner is made in the same way as for float fishing. Avoid spinning where there are likely to be snags: keep clear of those you can see by varying the speed of the retrieve and guiding the lure with the rod (once you have tried this you will see why a short spinning rod cannot give you the control of a longer one).

As a general rule, pike like a slow-moving bait with an uneven action. Perch like one which moves a little faster and which changes direction and speed now and again. Chub like a fast-moving lure cast upstream in front and to the side of a shoal and wound back at an even pace.

Perch and pike are often intrigued by a lure which behaves like a sick or crippled fish. Remember that the idea is to let the predator catch up the lure, not to outpace or outmanoeuvre it. Imagine what the action is like underwater. You are imitating a fish whose movements will be wobbly, uncertain, fluttering, rising and falling as it struggles to get along, pausing every so often to realign itself for another spurt of movement. It is so full if its own troubles that it fails to notice how close is the pike in the reeds, or how the pack of hungry perch is closing in. . . .

Covering the water

If you cannot see your quarry, search a water systematically. Find a likely hole or swim and make every cast a foot or so to one side of the last. A lazy pike may not stir for a bait which wobbles past 3 or 4 ft away, no matter how many times it does it. But if that bait gets nearer and nearer every time it appears, the pike will be unable to resist it, when it wobbles under his nose.

Recovering a snagged lure

When a lure hits a snag, you will be reluctant simply to walk backwards until the line snaps. It may be your favourite plug; in any event it has cost enough to make attempts at recovery worthwhile.

Remember the first, and familiar, rule of ordinary terminal rig recovery—*don't panic*. Tugging at the lure will only drive the hooks in further.

Let the line go slack and wait for a couple of minutes. The current may do the job for you and carry the lure out of the snag. If it does not, walk down the bank to a position behind the plug and pull gently and firmly on the line. Don't jerk.

Small bait on single hook
Large shot

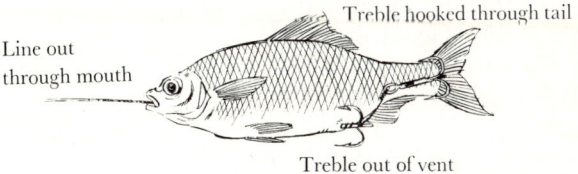
Treble hooked through tail
Line out through mouth
Treble out of vent

Wobble tackle

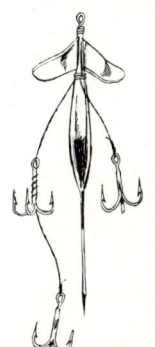
Deadbait spinning flight

FIG. 34

If you can get close enough, you may be able to reach the lure with a landing net. Or cut a long pliable twig, make a noose of the end of it around your line, and slide the noose down to the lure.

No luck? Try tying a split ring or a snap link swivel to a length of strong line. Clip a plummet or leger lead to the split ring and clip the ring to the reel line. The ring will slide down the line to the lure, carried by the weight of the plummet. If you now move opposite or downstream of the lure, and pull on the cord, you stand a very good chance of success. If all else fails and the water is not too deep or swift, don't be afraid to ask the help of any angler wearing waders. He will have lost lures himself in the past and will almost certainly be glad to retrieve yours.

Spinning with deadbaits

Deadbaits—minnows, roach, rudd, gudgeon, sprats—can be used as spinners. With freshly killed baits, the fish should be punctured at about the middle of its body, and squeezed, to deflate the swim bladder.

The simplest form of deadbait spinning rig is a single hook through both lips or eye sockets of the bait, attached to a wire trace which in turn is attached to the reel line by a swivel. A large shot is nipped on the trace 3 or 4 in from the hook to pull the bait downwards. The bait can then be worked with a sink-and-draw action simply by raising and lowering the rod tip and reeling in the slack line as you do so. A fish worked like this wobbles rather than spins.

Another way of preparing a deadbait is to thread the trace with a baiting needle from the vent to the mouth of the fish. Two trebles are mounted close together at the end of the trace. One is left sticking out of the fish's vent, while the other is hooked through the tail fin, or tied to the 'wrist' of the tail with thread or wire, or simply left to trail alongside or a little way behind the fish.

Wobble tackle gives a deadbait an attractive undulating motion in the water. There are several different forms of the tackle. One is a snap consisting of two traces, three treble hooks and a single. Another has a spike which is pushed into the fish's innards. (This can also be bought with vanes attached as a spinning flight for deadbaits.) A simpler rig is a large single hook which goes through the bait's lips, and a treble a little further down the trace which goes into the bait's side. In each case, the body of the bait is curved by the rig, giving the fish the wobble in the water.

Spinning with worms

Lobworms and blueheads can be spun, either on a single hook about an inch behind the head, on two-hook Pennell tackle or three-hook Stewart tackle. Sink-and-draw is the best motion.

9

Fly Fishing

Because fly fishing needs special tackle, and because its application to coarse fish is limited, I do not deal with it at length. (See *Fly Fishing*, by Maurice Wiggin, Teach Yourself Books.)

You may, however, acquire a fly rod or get the chance to use one, so it is worthwhile looking briefly at basic fly-fishing techniques which could land you roach, rudd, chub, perch, pike, dace or grayling.

FIG. 35

There are two main kinds of fly—dry and wet. Dry flies imitate spend flies or duns (flies newly emerged from the water) and are fished on the surface in smooth water. Wet flies imitate nymphs (fly larvae) or drowned flies and are fished below the surface in broken water. Fancy wet flies imitate shrimps or small fish.

Tackle

A fly rod should have a springy, but not floppy, action right down to the butt. The reel should be a light and smooth-running centre pin.

To a coarse fisherman used to fine monofilament, a fly line looks impossibly thick. It needs that thickness, however, to give it the necessary casting weight. There are three kinds

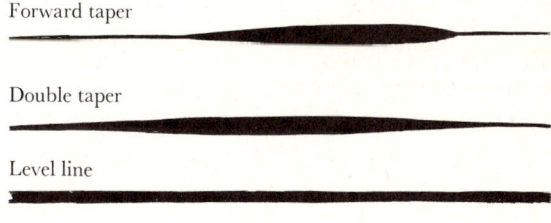

FIG. 36   Fly lines.

of line: *forward taper*, *double taper* and *level*. The forward taper is thicker at the hook end than at the reel end, making the line very accurate on a short cast and giving an extra few feet of distance on a long one. The double taper is thick in the middle and tapers towards both ends. This enables the angler to reverse the line when one end is worn. The level line, used for wet fly fishing, is the same thickness throughout its length.

The fly is tied to the line on a nylon cast.

Dry fly lines should be treated with floatant before use.

Fishing with the fly

The fly itself has little or no weight—all the weight is in the line. So casting with a fly rod is different from casting with a bottom rod.

The rod is held in the right hand, with the thumb laid

against the back of the butt for better control. All the action is from the wrist.

Before casting, strip off several coils of line with the left hand. Imagine you are facing to the right and standing against a large clock face. Hold the rod at two o'clock and raise it smartly to twelve o'clock.

Pause until the line has reached its full extent behind you. Then bring the rod smartly forward so that the line shoots out in front of you. When it reaches its fullest extent, allow the coils in your left hand to follow the rest of the line.

By repeating the movement, and pulling off more line each time you do so, you can keep quite a length of line in the air. To hit your target, aim at a spot about 3 ft above it and then drop the rod tip.

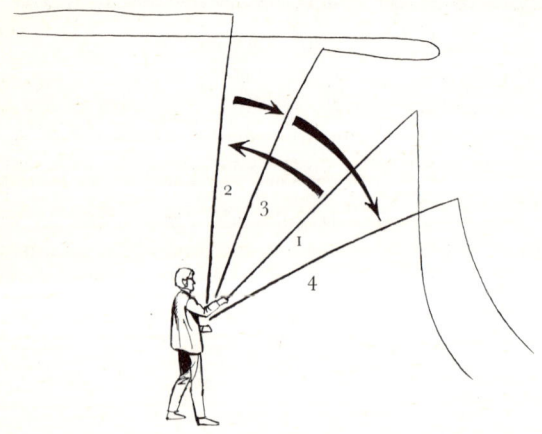

FIG. 37 Casting a fly. 1 Hold the rod at two o'clock. 2 Raise the rod smartly to twelve o'clock. Allow line to fly backwards to full extent. 3 Bring rod smartly forward to one o'clock. 4 When the fly is 3 ft above the target, drop the rod tip.

Fly Fishing 103

Dry flies are cast upstream to land beyond the rises of a feeding fish. The fly floats back towards you, over the fish, and you take in the slack line as it does so. Pause momentarily after a take before striking.

Wet flies are fished underwater and downstream. If you do not know the exact location of the fish, you can try casting across to the opposite bank and retrieving the line in short tugs, taking in just a few inches at a time. The current will swing the fly in an arc back to your own bank.

Keep your eye on the cast where it meets the water to watch for the tell-tale dimpling or straightening which signals a bite.

Practically any big trout fly, wet or dry, will take chub. Perch and pike go for big wet flies such as Teal and Yellow, or Butcher. Grayling go for small flashy flies with a touch of yellow or red, such as Orange Quill, Wickham's Fancy, Red Tag or Yellow Tag. Dace, roach and rudd can be taken on small flies which resemble the insects active at that particular time and place.

10

Barbel

Barbus barbus

Not even its most ardent admirer would call the barbel a pretty fish. Two of its nicknames—pigfish and leatherchops—are a guide both to its habits and appearance. But as a fighter there is no other fish to match it. Pound for pound it puts up a better scrap than a salmon.

It is a fish of fast water and its shape is designed to help it hold its position on the bottom against the current. Its underside is almost flat. Its cross-section is triangular. Its head is wedge-shaped and its body streamlined. These features mean that the faster the current flows, the more firmly is the barbel pressed to the bottom of the swim.

The name pigfish refers to its habit of grubbing around the bottom and sucking anything edible into its underslung mouth. For preference it feeds on worms, shrimps, fry, elvers, crayfish, frogs, minnows and weed.

Leatherchops refers to its thick, tough lips. Its 'proper' name refers to its barbules or barbels, four sensitive feelers—two on the top lip and two more at the corners of the mouth—with which it searches for food.

Its other distinguishing feature is the tall dorsal fin, the longest ray of which is a strong, bony spine with a saw-like edge. This spine suffers in a keepnet, and barbel which have been caught several times often have a broken or frayed fin. The answer to this is to return the fish, after weighing and photographing if necessary, without keeping them in the net; or to use one of the new knotless nets which offer much less chance of snagging the fin.

The colour of the fish varies with the water from grey green, through bronze to golden brown, with orange coloured fins. Fish from clear water are generally lighter in colour than those from muddy or coloured water.

Small barbel look very much like gudgeon, but can be distinguished by the absence of spots on the fins (the flanks are lightly speckled, but not so strongly as the gudgeon). It also differs by having four barbels—though on small fish these may not be properly developed—against the gudgeon's two.

At one time the barbel was found in Britain only in rivers which flowed from west to east, such as the Thames, Trent and the rivers of the Yorkshire dales. It is not found at all in Scotland or Ireland. As it is found in the rivers of Germany, Belgium, Holland and France which flow from east to west into the North Sea, it is assumed that the fish lived in both the British and Continental rivers when they were all part of the same system.

In 1896, a hundred barbel were taken from the Kennet, a tributary of the Thames, and put into the Dorset Stour. These fish multiplied rapidly and spread to the Hampshire Avon. In the 1950s, barbel were introduced into the Bristol Avon, the Severn, the Great Ouse, Welland and Nene, and reintroduced into the Trent, whose barbel had been killed off by pollution. In all these rivers, to one degree or another, the fish have flourished—in the Severn to the point of a population explosion.

Barbel have been turning up recently in still waters, even pits and reservoirs. How they got there is a mystery, but it has added impetus to experiments in stocking still waters with barbel and in breeding the fish in hatcheries.

Although barbel can be, and are, caught in winter, they are essentially a fish of the summer and autumn and tend to go 'off' with the first frosts. They certainly dislike cold water, as has been proved on the Severn when cold water from Welsh reservoirs has been allowed into the river.

The classic barbel 'pitch' is a well-oxygenated, shallow run with a fast flow and a clean, gravelly bottom. The fish tend to lie out of the main current at points where the flow slows down and food tends to drop to make easy pickings. They will lie in pools at the tail end of fast runs, at the tail and in the eddies of mill runs and weir pools, behind boulders which cause the current to eddy and the food to drop. In very fast runs they like to lie in channels, out of the main current, or in the weedbeds alongside the run which not only hold their own stocks of food, but which trap food brought downstream.

Barbel are shoal fish, and the shoals are likely to be found where the three main conditions—gravel or hard bottom, the tail end of a fast run, shallow water—are all fulfilled.

They spawn between May and July, according to the summer temperatures, in fast gravelly runs in the shallows, often moving into tributaries to find the right conditions. After spawning they congregate in weir pools to clean themselves, to scour away the tubercles which develop on the scales during spawning and, presumably, any external parasites they have picked up at the same time. After scouring, which is over by August, they move back into their favourite lies . . . and wait for the food.

Baits

Groundbaits

Groundbait for barbel, whatever it is, must be a stiff, heavy mixture which will sink in the fast water before it starts breaking up. Mix it with sand or clay, or squeeze it round a stone.

Unless you are fishing a long way downstream, throw the bait into the swim *upstream* of your pitch to give it extra distance in which to sink, so ensuring that the bait does not overshoot the fish.

If a groundbait is packed into a hollow clay ball, it can be thrown in downstream. Press some samples into the outside of the clay to encourage the fish to start breaking it up.

In the old days, groundbaiting for barbel was done for days in advance with bucketfuls of lobworms or pounds of greaves, the waste from tallow candle manufacture. Those days are gone—in any case, most waters are fished so heavily now that the fish are getting a constant supply of groundbait.

Make a stiff base mixture of breadcrumbs, meal, cereal or sausage rusk—or any combination of these—and add plenty of hookbait samples. If you are going to try a selection of hookbaits—say, maggots, luncheon meat and sausage—put some of each into the groundbait. Start with four to six generous balls of bait to encourage a shoal to build up. Continue with smaller balls at regular and frequent intervals.

Hookbaits
True to its name of pigfish and its carpet-sweeper habits, the barbel eats heartily and will take all kinds of bait: worms, bread—cube, crust, flake, paste—cheese and cheese paste, maggots, casters, wasp grubs, luncheon meat, sausage, silkweed, dead elvers, lampreys, crayfish or gudgeon . . . and even hempseed.

The tastes of the fish, however, vary from river to river, even from stretch to stretch. So unless you are fishing a water regularly and are able to 'educate' the fish into a liking for a particular bait, it is best to find out what the locals are using and start with that. Find out if you can not only what bait is best, but how big it ought to be. Barbel in a particular swim can develop a taste for a ball of paste, piece of sausage or luncheon meat of a particular size, often because they have grown suspicious of successful baits of a different size.

The size of the bait determines the size of the hook, always bearing in mind that the barbel's big mouth and leather lips—not to mention its fighting strength—need a larger hook rather than a smaller one. Do not think smaller than a no. 12 hook, and be prepared to use as big as a no. 2.

Use worms—red worms, brandlings and lobs—either singly or in bunches, on hooks ranging from nos. 12 to 8. For cheese, paste, bread, luncheon meat or sausage, use nos. 8–4. Dead minnows can be hooked through both lips with a no. 8. Dead lampreys, elvers and gudgeon are hooked behind the head or in the centre of the body on a no. 6 or no. 8. Crayfish are hooked through the second tail segment on a no. 4 or no. 2. A treble hook will hold silkweed best in fast water, its size matched to the bunch of weed. For maggots and casters, go down to a no. 10. For wasp grubs, a no. 8. Hempseed—in spite of its size a real killer on some waters—can be fished on a no. 10 or no. 8.

Tackle

We have already discussed the hooks. Remember to sharpen them; a barbel's lips take some penetrating.

For float fishing use an 11-ft Avon rod with a $1\frac{1}{2}$-lb test curve, a 5-lb b.s. line—stepped up to 7 lb b.s. for weedy swims—and a fixed-spool reel. Some anglers insist on a 10-lb b.s. line even in clear swims, but this is a hangover from the old days when it was thought that barbel tackle had to be heavy. The slipping clutch on the reel—provided it is properly set and free from grit—should take care of any undue strain in the first stages of the fight.

For those who prefer it, a centre-pin reel is a great pleasure to use. The bait can be trotted down the swim with the ratchet off the reel, the line being pulled out by the current. The progress of the line can be checked at any time by light finger pressure on the edge of the drum, allowing the bait to swing out in front of the float.

Legering needs a stronger rod to take the strain of the

extra weights or swimfeeders, but it should still be about 11 ft long to control both bait and fish. Both float and leger rods should have a good through action to take the strain of the strike and the pull of the fish.

Floats should be big enough to carry plenty of weight, and long and slender rather than chubby to cut down the resistance to turbulent water. There should be plenty of tip showing above the water, especially if you are fishing at long range. If there is no wind, a good-sized cork or balsa float can be used, fastened top and bottom. In windy conditions, use a float with a long thin tip, such as a peacock quill or sarkandas reed with a cork or balsa body. For fishing in wind, fasten the float by the bottom ring only, using a shot clipped to the line on each side of the bottom ring, or by passing the line through the ring several times. (This last method has the disadvantage of making a change of depth a tedious business.)

Because of the barbel's tough lips, you will need surgical forceps or needle-nosed pliers to remove the hooks.

The keepnet should be big and knotless and should never be overcrowded. Two keepnets are better than one, if you can afford them.

Leger weights and swimfeeders are dealt with in the following pages.

Fishing for barbel

To find out the conditions on the bottom, put some petroleum jelly on your plummet. This will bring up samples of what lies underneath.

The barbel is a bottom feeder, so that is where the bait should be. Though it will occasionally feed in midwater, and sometimes even at the surface, it is not at home there. Because of its underslung mouth it has to turn upside down to feed anywhere off the bottom, and much prefers just sucking up food from the river bed.

The bait should be presented slowly, giving the fish a chance to locate it and time to suck it in. Though the barbel will pick up most of what comes its way, it will not exert itself to turn round and chase a bait downstream.

It is a very powerful fish, packed with muscle from head to tail, and its first rush is a shock to anyone not used to it—sometimes even to those who are. Do not panic, keep a steady pressure, give line when necessary and use sidestrain to turn the fish if it tries to dive into weed or other snags.

The strike must be hard, with the rod going well back—especially in distance fishing—to compensate for line stretch and to set the hook firmly.

Barbel fight with a characteristic 'thumping' action which can smash the line if any slack is allowed to develop. Even when giving line, keep a steady pressure so that the line is taut throughout its length.

The fish really has to be *played*. There is no question of trying to drag it in. If it dives to the bottom and uses the force of the current against its torpedo shape to hold it there, reduce the pressure on the line so that it can move downstream. Then put the pressure back on, with sidestrain if possible, to pull it clear.

Remember, when you reduce the pressure *keep the line taut*—whatever you do, don't let it just go slack.

A 'beaten' barbel will appear to give up, lying just beneath the surface with all the fight apparently gone. Don't let this fool you, and take special care with your netting technique. A touch of the net rim on a barbel's flank may trigger off a last powerful thrash which can throw the hook, break the line or smash the rod tip.

The fight does, however, exhaust the fish. If you can bear it, forget the keepnet and return the fish straightaway. Hold it in the water against the current—if necessary, 'walk' it—for a couple of minutes until you are sure it is fit to swim away. If you must use the keepnet, make sure there is a current flowing through it.

Float fishing

On a smooth, medium-paced swim, where the depth is even throughout the length, and there are no weeds or snags, the bait can be set to just trip the bottom. But even here the speed of the float has to be controlled so that the bait stays there. A float travelling ahead of the bait—remember that surface water travels faster than that at the river bed—will lift the bait, as will a float which is held back by wind blowing upstream. When this happens the bait will pass straight over the fish's head, or may even brush a fin or a flank and result in a foul hooking.

Most swims vary in depth throughout their length. There are hollows, eddy holes and narrow, deeper channels into which the bait must go: these could be the very places in which the barbel are lying.

The safest way to ensure that the bait gets to the bottom and stays there is to put a BB shot on the line just beyond the depth of the swim and have a length of about 18 in trailing below this shot.

Slow down the progress of the float so that the shot is rolling on the bottom a little in front of the float, and the trailing length to the hook moving in front of the shot.

When the wind is blowing, use a cork- or balsa-bodied peacock quill or reed float fastened by the bottom ring only. When the wind is blowing upstream, the extra length of trail will compensate for any dragging effect on the float. When the wind is blowing downstream, extra care must be taken that the float is not blown ahead of the bait.

Although most barbel bites on float tackle are quick and definite, there is always the chance that a fish will take the bait as it stops at the end of the swim, and be mouthing it when the times comes to reel in. So strike, as a matter of course, at the end of every run. And strike *expecting* a fish—if you strike absent-mindedly you may get the surprise of your life.

Legering and swimfeeding

Legering is the most popular method of barbel fishing. Although it is perhaps not so interesting as float fishing, at least you know where the bait is—on the bottom.

Because barbel waters tend to be fast, there is more temptation than usual to use too heavy a lead. Resist it. Put back the lead you first thought of and use the smallest one which will do the job. The barbel is not over-cautious, and certainly not bait-shy, but even he objects to great slabs of lead clunking about the bottom and will spit out a bait which offers too much resistance.

With a leger you can get three kinds of bite: the straightforward and more common 'bang' which will jerk the rod tip or snatch the line from between the fingers; the vibrating 'saw' bite; and the 'drop back'.

The saw bite happens when the barbel has taken the bait, but stays put instead of moving away. It can be detected by the trembling of the rod tip, but better still by the saw-like vibrations through a line held between finger and thumb. Once you have felt it, wait for the next 'saw' and strike.

The 'drop back' bite is caused by the fish lifting the bait and slackening the taut line to the rod tip, allowing the tip to spring up. Strike—if you wait for the line to get taut again it may be too late.

Depending on the swim and the bait, you can use one of the three basic leger techniques: static leger, rolling leger and swimfeeder leger, with or without sliding links.

The links have several advantages. The link itself can be weaker than the reel line, so that breaking away from a snag means only the loss of the link and weight. The link can be weighted with swan shot, whose numbers can be adjusted quickly to give exactly the weight needed. Or it can be attached by a link swivel for an easy change of conventional weights. Still another advantage is that a taking fish feels, initially, less resistance.

Use a static leger or swimfeeder to put the bait exactly

where you want it in a swim where you know barbel are likely to lie, or in a clear patch in a weedy swim. Static legering and swimfeeding is always done downstream.

For static legering you can use any of the weights: Arlesey bomb, drilled bullet, coffin lead or a swan shot link. Leave about 18 in between weight and hook.

Swimfeeders come into their own in the faster waters where the speed of the current makes normal groundbaiting difficult. The open-ended swimfeeders are the best to use. Cone-shaped feeders offer less resistance in faster water and are easier to reel in. Block the ends with stiff groundbait and use as small a feeder as you can. It does not take long to refill for each cast. If the current starts moving the feeder about, add swan shot to the link just above the feeder until there is enough weight to hold it in position.

A rolling leger is useful on a strange swim, or whenever you are uncertain of the fishes' likely position. The swim must be free of snags, however, and have a hard bottom. The leger is cast across the stream and allowed to roll back to the near bank in an arc, pushed by the current's pressure.

With static and swimfeeder leger, you can watch the rod tip for bites, but still by far the best method is to hold the line between finger and thumb. The more delicate saw bites are easily missed if you are just watching the rod tip. For rolling leger, of course, the finger and thumb method is essential. You will be surprised at how sensitive this method is, and how quickly you will learn to understand what is happening on the bottom.

11

Bream

Abramis brama and *Blicca bjoernka*

There are two species of freshwater bream in Britain: the common, or bronze, bream (*Abramis brama*) and the silver bream (*Blicca bjoernka*). Both are members of the carp family.

Only the bronze bream is fished for deliberately, with a record of 12 lb 14 oz. The record for silver bream is still open, with a qualifying weight of only 1 lb 8 oz (though, to be fair, the old record stood at $4\frac{1}{2}$ lb). Most silver bream weigh less than a pound.

The bronze bream is widely distributed throughout England and Ireland, and is also found in southern Scotland and parts of Wales. The silver bream has a more limited distribution, being found mainly in Norfolk and the Fens, and having a scattered local distribution elsewhere.

Young bronze bream are often confused with silver bream. They can be distinguished by complicated scale and fin-ray counts, but identification is difficult without killing the fish and examining the pharyngeal teeth. The bronze bream has one row of five teeth on each side, whereas the silver bream has two rows on each side, with two teeth in one and five in the other. It is best to assume that a silvery-looking small bream is a silver bream and leave it at that.

Both fish are flat, compressed from side to side to give a very slim front section, but a very deep side section.

The bronze bream is a slow, shy—and some say stupid—grazing fish which moves about in large shoals. Fish around the 3 lb mark are found in shoals of up to 200; larger fish, naturally, move around in smaller numbers.

The bream has a reputation for being a poor fighter and, indeed, will often give up easily and just roll on its side to be reeled in. But a big bream which turns its massive flank broadside on to the angler, especially if there is any current to help it, can take a great deal of turning.

It is covered in a great deal of slime, which comes away readily to festoon the landing net, keepnet and the angler himself. Care should be taken, however, to disturb the slime on the fish as little as possible; the bream, like other fish, is vulnerable to fungus diseases which find their way in through breaks in the slime.

Because of their size and shape, and because they can be taken in large numbers once a shoal is located, bream suffer more than most fish from being packed into keepnets.

Throughout the season the angling papers carry horrifying pictures of huge catches jammed into nets, with the proud captors smiling in the background. When these fish are finally put back into the water, almost all will have suffered breaks in the slime, and a fair number will be swimming as best they can with frayed or broken fins. If you must keep bream for the count—and you're only human, after all—use knotless netting and try to afford two, or even three, nets.

Baits

Groundbaits
Bream shoals are large and the fish are greedy, so plenty of groundbait is needed. Pre-baiting for two or three days in advance will increase the chances of a big catch.

Breadcrumbs, bran, sausage rusk and mashed bread can all be used to make a stiff groundbait into which is mixed a sample of the hookbait. You can also add household scraps such as mashed potato, boiled potato peelings, bits of torn-up bread crust and any minced or mashed cooked vegetable leftovers. Add sand or earth if necessary to help the bait sink. The balls of bait should reach the bottom in one piece and break up there.

Hookbaits

Worms, maggots, casters, bread—cube, paste, crust or flake—sausage, cheesepaste and freshwater mussel (tie the mussel on to the hook with wool) will all take bream. If you can find any bloodworms, mix them in with the paste.

Carry several baits with you. Bream are fickle in their choice of food and will often ignore a bait that they pounced on the day before. Use generous portions. Red worms, brandlings and maggots can be used in bunches. Lobs can be halved or used whole.

Large worms can be mounted on a two-hook tackle, with the bottom hook just behind the tail and the upper hook about two-thirds the way up the body, leaving the head free to move about. You may feel that the second hook adds unnecessarily to the ironmongery and doubles the chances of the fish rejecting the bait.

If the fish are in a choosy mood, try a cocktail bait of paste and maggot, flake and maggot, maggot and worm, or any other permutation you think might tempt them.

Tackle

Forget the legend of the bream's poor fighting qualities. A big bream, broadside on in deep water, can give a fair account of himself. And remember that a lot of fishing will be done at a distance with leger weights and large bait.

Use a hollow glass 12-ft rod with a test curve of $1\frac{1}{2}$ lb and a good through action. Line of 4 lb b.s. on a fixed-spool reel will take care of big bream in open water, but for weedy or snaggy swims scale up the line strength to 6 lb b.s.

The most widely used methods for bream are legering or

swimfeeder fishing, so take a selection of your favourite leads and feeders. Bite detectors can include swingtips, quivertips, butt indicators, dough bobbins and—for night fishing—buzzers.

Many anglers, however, still prefer to use a float. The most effective are a peacock quill or sarkandas reed with a balsa body or, for long-distance work, the bottom-weighted zoomer. Sliding floats are indispensable for deep water.

Hook sizes range from no. 4 for the larger baits—crust, paste, large lobs, bunches of worms—down to no. 12 for maggots and small worms.

Hearty feeders though they are, bream are very shy fish. So, though the tackle should be strong, it should also be as fine as possible, bearing in mind the kind of bait, the method of fishing, the distance to be cast and the likely size of the fish in the shoal.

Fishing for bream

Bream like waters with plenty of elbow room; large deep lakes, pits, reservoirs, slow muddy reaches of rivers and basins of canals.

They will eat almost anything they find on the bottom: weed, bloodworms, snails, larvae, molluscs, freshwater shrimps, daphnia and even microscopic organisms. The sucking and blowing involved in the feeding muddies the water and sends up thousands of bubbles—a real giveaway to the angler, who can then lob his groundbait in front of the advancing shoal.

The shoals have a regular 'beat', either along the banks or through the muddy deeps. At the end of the beat they will feed for a while in one spot before turning and heading back the way they came. This turning point, once it can be established, is an excellent place to fish.

Once a moving shoal has passed, it is not a bit of use sitting there and hoping that some of the fish will turn back for another go at your bait. The best thing is to anticipate the movement as the bites get less frequent, head off the shoal and get your groundbait and hookbait on the bottom before the leaders arrive at the new position.

Certain places in lakes, rivers and canals are regular turning places and have local reputations as bream holes. Five minutes' chat with a bailiff or a local angler may save you a lot of time in locating the fish.

Early in the season, the fish will be cleaning themselves after spawning. They do this in shallow water, rolling and splashing on the surface. They can be fished for in these shallows, but their condition may be disappointing. They do not really recover from spawning until the end of July, by which time they have moved back to the deeper water. As a general rule, once spawning and cleaning are finished, it is the deeper water which should be fished.

Bream will roll on the surface in shoals on warm evenings when the water temperature is up. Opinion is divided about whether or not this is a prelude to feeding, but feeding happens often enough after rolling to make it well worthwhile fishing that spot.

If there is any wind about, find a likely looking bay on the leeward side of the water—fish with the wind in your face, that is. The wind will be carrying debris and food across the surface which will build up and sink. The bream will be down at the bottom, picking it up.

They will be feeding too, around sources of food such as weedbeds and around any underwater obstructions which cause food to collect.

Still-water bream are fish of summer and autumn and will hibernate during the winter, although they will emerge during bright warm spells and feed in the middle of the day. River bream can be caught throughout the winter, except in conditions of extreme cold or heavy water.

Before you start to fish, throw in balls of groundbait over a good-sized area. If the shoals are near the bank, throw out the bait in a fan-shaped pattern, converging towards your pitch. For distance fishing you may need a catapult or throwing stick.

The large shoals will contain small to medium-sized fish. If you contact any large fish, go easier on the groundbait. The larger the fish, the smaller the shoal, and too much groundbait will fill them up at the expense of the hookbait.

Float fishing
Although the bigger bream tend to be caught on leger, float fishing is still favoured by many anglers, partly because of the interesting action of a typical bream bite. (It also has an advantage when fishing on the far side of a patch of weed, or beyond a ledge, where the leger would be obstructed. The line from bottom weight to float, because of its steeper angle, is also less likely to be fouled by a bream than a leger line. These two advantages, however, can be had also on float leger.)

For shallow, still water at close range, a small porcupine quill, a short length of peacock quill, or a reed float can be used. Laying on is the most worthwhile method. Place the shot about 18 in from the hook and set the float higher than the depth of the water. Tighten the line from the rod so that the float is laying over at half cock.

When the bream lifts the bait, the float will usually dip out of sight. Strike straight away.

After the strike you should not have too much to worry about, providing you keep the fish away from the weed. On being hooked, the fish's first instinct is to dive for the bottom. Its second is to run for cover. So first, hold it off the bottom. Second, turn its head away from the snags.

For deeper water you can use a peacock or sarkandas reed with a balsa body. For really deep water, or for fishing through surface weed, you can use a slider. For distance fishing, try an antenna float with a shot on both sides of the bottom ring, having just one shot on the bottom and the bulk of the shot about halfway along the line. Or you can use a weighted zoomer float, which will cut down on the amount of lead needed on the line. Both floats are attached at the bottom only.

In deep water, or when fishing at a distance, you will not be able to tighten the line, so the float will stand straight instead of leaning at half cock.

In windy conditions, use an antenna float attached at the bottom only. You can sink the couple of feet of line nearest the float by rubbing it with detergent. This, however, eventually weakens the line, so after six trips, discard it.

In running water, the shot on the bottom will have to be heavier and the float correspondingly bigger. How many and what size shot you use, and how big a float, you will have to work out according to the strength and depth of the water.

Legering and swimfeeder

Use the smallest leger weight—drilled bullet, Arlesey bomb or swan shot link—which will take the bait out and hold it on the bottom. Set the lead about 18 in from the hook.

For fishing in bottom weed, use a leger on a link of length appropriate to the depth of weed. Use a bait of crust or flake, or a balanced bait of paste and crust. The best way of putting flake on the hook is to squeeze the centre of the flake and push the hook through the squeezed bit, not to put the bread on the hook first and then to squeeze it all round.

Bites on link leger are generally quite decisive because the fish usually does not feel any resistance—nor does the bite register—until it has taken the bait and is moving off. On link leger, therefore, there is no doubt about when to strike—straight away.

For a muddy bottom, use either the link or a slow-sinking cork-and-lead leger weight.

For fishing on the far side of weed or underwater obstructions, try float leger. The float will hold the line clear of the snag. The float should be the lightest possible in the circumstances. A long piece of quill or cane is ideal.

Swimfeeder fishing is a deadly way of taking bream. Use a small feeder rather than a large one, and re-pack it at every cast. One trick to help spread the feeder bait around in still water is to pack the centre of the feeder with dry groundbait before blocking the ends with damp bait. As the feeder sinks, the dry bait takes in water and expands. When it gets to the bottom the expansion ends in a gentle 'explosion' of the bait. In running water, of course, this is not necessary; the current itself will wash out the bait.

Freelining and soluble leger weights
Freelining is a satisfying way of taking bream, but it means that the bait must be fairly large to give the necessary casting weight and to stop it being fragmented by smaller fish on its slow way down. A soluble leger weight—a cube of sugar or a piece of block salt—can be tied on the line to give extra casting weight and to help the bait sink faster. After a very short time on the bottom, the soluble weight has dissolved altogether, leaving the terminal rig as a genuine free line.

Because many bream waters are large and exposed, a swingtip can be badly affected by the wind, registering many false 'bites'. The target board is one answer to this, acting as a windshield as well as an aid to bite indication. But in really windy conditions, the best solution is a quivertip, which is less affected by wind, gives fewer false alarms and more accurate indications of the difference between a bite and a snag.

12

Common Carp

Cyprinus carpio

The different varieties of carp can be very confusing. In Britain there are two main species: the common carp (*Cyprinus carpio*) and the crucian carp (*Carassius carassius*).

The crucian carp (dealt with in the next chapter) is the smaller, with a rod-caught record weight of only 4 lb 15 oz 8 drm. Apart from its size, it can be distinguished from the common carp by the absence of barbels, its rounded and less deeply forked tail fin, its convex dorsal fin and its chunkier build.

Two other members of the carp family—the Prussian carp, which is a variant of the crucian, and the goldfish—are rare outside cultivated waters.

The confusion really sets in with the different varieties of common carp. There are two main divisions: the true 'wild' carp and the 'king' carps.

Carp were introduced into Britain from the Continent some time around AD 1300 as a food fish for stocking the lakes and ponds of monasteries and manor houses and the moats of castles. Selective breeding altered the streamlined shape of the wild carp into the solid, hump-backed shape of the king carp.

Various circumstances—the last being the coming of the steam train which enabled fresh sea fish to be carried long distances—resulted in the neglect of carp-breeding, and the fish reverted to their natural shape. Their descendants are today's wild carp.

The king carp in our waters are descended from later imports of specially bred fish, many of them brought from the Continent since the First World War. (Of recent years especially, much stocking of club waters has been done with king carp.) They grow much faster and bigger than wild carp—as much as 3 lb a year—and have a deeper and wider body.

There are three kinds of king carp: the *fully scaled*, the *mirror* and the *leather*. Fully scaled carp are covered with scales of normal size. Mirror and leather carps are partially scaled fish. The mirror carp carries irregularly shaped large scales, which can cover the whole of the body or be arranged in lines or clusters, leaving the rest of the body naked. The leather carp has only a few small, degenerate scales, generally around the base of the fins; the rest of the body is covered with smooth, slimy skin.

The physical characteristics of the common carp, whatever the variety and apart from the scales, are the same. It has a large mouth with thick, leathery lips and carries four barbels, two small ones at the front of the top lip, and two larger ones at each corner of the mouth. The body is broad, and oval in cross section. The back is humped, with the hump exaggerated in the king varieties. The dorsal fin is long, sail-like and concave. The caudal fin is noticeably forked. The colour gives a general impression of bronze, with a back of olive green, bronze or brown. The sides are paler green or bronze, the belly is pale green or yellow, cream or buff.

Carp waters range in size from the tiniest ponds to the largest lakes and reservoirs. The one thing they have in common is an abundance of natural foods: weed, larvae, worms, snails and microscopic organisms.

The carp likes warm, and preferably slow or still, water. This may explain why most carp waters are in central and southern England, with very few north of Yorkshire. The fish has only localised distribution in Wales, Cornwall and Ireland.

The best carp waters are sheltered, either by trees or by surrounding high ground. This shelter keeps off the wind and helps retain the heat built up in the water during the day.

A few rivers, including the Thames, Soar and Nene, hold a reasonable head of carp. More could be stocked, but stocking is mainly done on lakes, ponds and pits.

At one time carp were regarded as almost too clever to be caught on rod and line, and a great mystique surrounded the fish. But research into tackle, baits and techniques by experts like Richard Walker and members of the Carp Catchers' Club showed that it was possible to catch carp not only in numbers, but at sizes hitherto undreamed of.

The record carp of 44 lb was caught by Richard Walker in Redmire Pool in 1952. The fish was taken to London Zoo, where it lived until 1970.

The Carp Catchers gave names to the different types of feeding carp to describe their habits:

Bubblers: Carp grubbing about the bottom for food raise clouds of mud and great patches of bubbles. Bubblers tend to ignore any bait dropped down to them, possibly because their heads are buried in the mud in the search for bloodworms.

Cloopers: Surface-feeding carp make a noise halfway between a smacking kiss and a slurp. Try for cloopers with a floating crust.

Smoke screeners: A smoke screener raises a trailing cloud of mud, but few bubbles, which probably means that his head is not buried. Drop the bait ahead of the cloud so that the fish comes across it naturally.

Margin patrollers: On deep, featureless waters—and at night on most waters—carp will feed in the margins, taking much of the food from the surface. A bait just resting on the surface (see *Margin Fishing*, pp. 133–4) will take these.

Tenters: These are tricky fish to go for, because tenters are those feeding in the weeds, or among the lilies and lifting lily pads clear of the water on their backs. Can be had by dropping the bait over the edge of the lily pads. The problem then is to get the fish out.

The carp is a summer fish, feeding in temperatures between 58° and 70° F. The best months are June to September. The best times are late evening and early morning.

The old idea that carp can only be caught at night dies hard. Carp *are* caught through the night, but so are they caught at dusk, during the first hour or two after dark, at dawn and even during the day. So there is no need to go through the discomfort of a whole night's fishing to catch them. One consolation of night fishing for carp is that the water is usually less crowded than during the day.

Carp tend to lie dormant during the winter in deep, frost-free areas, but they will come out of hibernation and feed during warm spells, especially on sunlit days. They will often come out of hibernation altogether by the end of January and give the end-of-season angler some pleasant surprises.

The fish feeds in weedy shallows, on the margins of lakes and islands, in and around beds of weed, reed and patches of lilies. On deep, featureless lakes it prefers the shallows by the banks. In lakes with variations in depth, it will feed in the shallower water on humps and bars. It is fond of water under overhanging trees and around underwater features such as sunken trees or boats. It will feed at points of difference on an otherwise featureless bottom, such as a weedbed in an expanse of empty water, a bar of sand or gravel in the middle of wastes of mud.

During the day carp move into the shelter of the lily pads. Although they are less active there, they can be tempted with baits dropped over a pad and allowed to dangle near the surface, or gently teased off to fall naturally through the water.

A carp will often give its presence away by the mess it makes, clouding the water and sending up masses of bubbles as it roots around. The eeriest give-away of all is the parting of the surface weeds as the fish moves through the bed. Whatever its size, it never fails to look really big. Although it is mainly a bottom-feeder, it will feed at the surface—particularly at night—making great slurping sounds as it takes food from the top of the water or from the underside of the lily pads.

Mapping a carp water is really worthwhile, especially during the close season, when there is time to do a thorough job and the weed is no problem. The close season, too, can be the time for watching the fish, with the aid of polarised spectacles and a pair of binoculars. All the fish spotted can be recorded on the map, with details of place, times, size, feeding habits and any other information which may come in useful. It will not be long before you see a pattern of activity and behaviour which will be very useful when the time comes to fish.

Baits

Groundbaits

Pre-baiting is necessary, perhaps more than for any other fish, to accustom carp to finding food in a particular spot, and accepting it as part of their diet.

Carp are contrary creatures. They will refuse to accept a strange bait which suddenly appears in their feeding grounds. But, when they have got used to seeing it around, they will try some. If they like it, they will tuck in heartily and have no hesitation about taking a piece with a hook inside. Eventually, however, they will realise that this particular bait means trouble and leave it alone.

This eventual rejection of a bait happens on heavily fished waters where anglers naturally tend to use the baits which have been successful in the past. The only thing then is to start again with another kind of bait.

Make a good basic groundbait of soaked bread and bran and mix it with some generous samples of the hookbait.

Make plenty of it; a hungry carp is like an underwater vacuum cleaner.

If possible, bait up the spot for three or four days in advance. If the day's fishing is to start in the evening, throw in the bait during the afternoon so that any disturbance is over long before the carp move in to feed.

An old dodge, which still works, is to leave a pole sticking out over the water for several days at the point where your rod will be when you start to fish. Remember to take the pole away when you start, or the carp will notice two objects where there was only one before. The snag about this trick is that it gives your swim away to other anglers who might be there before you.

Hookbaits

Hookbaits for carp can be large. A decent-sized fish has no trouble in sucking in a piece of paste as big as a tennis ball, or a potato a couple of inches in diameter.

Potato and bread are the classic carp baits. The bread can be in the form of paste, flake, cube or crust. Paste should be stiff enough to stand the strain of casting and to stay in one piece in the water.

Many anglers like to mix sugar or honey in with the paste, and certainly the carp seems to have a sweet tooth. The number of other additives is almost as great as the number of anglers. Everyone has his own special favourite: cheese, fish oil, custard powder, cocoa, syrup or treacle, dried blood, mashed-up pilchards, minced worms, dripping, corn oil, butter, minced liver, meat extract, chopped bacon, mashed bananas, sausage or luncheon meat. The choice is dictated as much by the angler as by the fish, but the carp seem to enjoy them all.

Potatoes can be boiled until soft, or merely parboiled. The fairly hard potato produced by parboiling, while appreciated by the carp, is less attractive to fish such as tench or bream which may be sharing the swim. Hard potatoes should be only lightly hooked so that the hook can come free easily on the strike. Light hooking with biggish potatoes precludes long casting, so for distance work use only a piece of potato.

Soft potatoes are threaded on to the hook length with a baiting needle, and the hook pushed into the potato until it cannot be seen. The advantage of a soft potato is that the

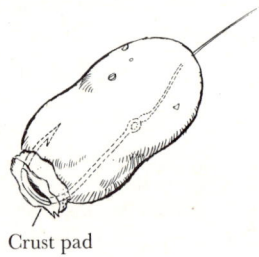

Crust pad

FIG. 38

hook comes out easily on the strike. The disadvantage is that the same softness may allow the potato to fly off in a long cast. This can be overcome by putting a pad of dry crust into the bend of the hook.

Worms are very attractive to carp. Unfortunately they are attractive to every other fish, so their use is best restricted to the times when you know that the carp are there. Either lay them over the edge of a lily pad or drop them in front of a smoke screener.

Natural baits such as caterpillars, caddis grubs, freshwater mussels, water snails, slugs, wasp grubs and maggots can be used, like worms, once the carp are feeding.

Other proven carp-catchers are wheat, peas, green beans, sweetcorn, luncheon meat and sausage.

Tackle

There are many purpose-built glass-fibre carp rods on the market. Possibly the best for all-round carp fishing is the 10-ft, two-sectioned MK IV with a test curve of $1\frac{1}{2}$ lb, designed by Richard Walker. For heavier work with big fish and/or weedy conditions there is the stepped-up MK IV with a test curve of $2\frac{1}{2}$ lb.

A rod such as the MK IV will take a line of between 7 and 10 lb b.s. Line strength should be chosen according to the possible size of the fish and the amount of snags or weed about.

Except for fishing with the smaller baits, hooks should be large. The most useful sizes are nos. 4 and 2, though for the big baits you could go as large as a no. 1/0. For the smaller baits, such as maggot, wasp grubs and wheat, go down to a no. 6 or 8. If you want to try fishing really light, try an Avon rod with a 4-lb line, and use maggot, caddis or wasp grub on a no. 12 hook. To penetrate the carp's leathery mouth, the hooks must be really sharp. Give each one a thorough rub with a sharpening stone before use. The reel should be a good fixed spool, with a slipping clutch.

The landing net must be big. You may feel it is tempting fate to set up a net with 42-in arms, but you will need all of that if you hook a carp of any size. Have a good length of handle—6 ft is not overdoing it—so that you can net a fish on the other side of a reed bed. The netting should be knotless and of fairly small gauge, so that the carp comes to no harm.

Carp should never be put into a keepnet. Their bulk and weight make them too prone to damage. Instead of a net, use an open-weave sack. Make sure it is clean, and certainly avoid one which has held any kind of chemical. Thread some thick string in and out around the mouth of the sack to make a drawstring. Soak the sack thoroughly and submerge it in a deep, shady place.

Ordinary disgorgers are of little help in getting big hooks

out of the carp's tough lips. Use surgical forceps or long, needle-nosed pliers. Rather than pull out a hook against the barb, cut the line above the shank and work out the hook point-first.

The rod rest should be of a type which allows the line to run freely. Use a back rest also to allow the rod to point at the water, so that there is no resistance to a running line from the rod rings. Best of all, if you can afford it, is an all-purpose rod rest with two forks which can be adapted to almost any rod position.

Bite indicators can range from the simple cylinder of aluminium foil around a drawn-down length of line between the butt rings, to one of the sophisticated audible bite indicators which buzz whenever any line is taken out. Because of the time which can elapse before a carp bites, the audible indicator is a good investment. Watching a piece of foil for hours can hypnotise you and eventually send you off to sleep—and that would be the time that the foil lifted. . . .

Fishing for carp

Above all things—caution. Tackle up well away from the bank, use all the stalking techniques to get down to the water, and make sure you have plenty of cover. Once you are in position, having crouched or crawled all the way, remember not to spoil it all by standing up.

You will have an idea of where the carp are likely to be— from your notes; from looking around for likely weedy shallows, underwater humps and bars; by spotting mud clouds or bubbles; by seeing or hearing carp rolling on the surface or clooping down floating food; or simply by spotting them through polarised spectacles.

Groundbait with several small balls of bait, rather than one massive one whose impact would send the fish running for cover.

Get your hookbait into the water, get the rod in the rest with the bale arm of the reel open, have your landing net ready . . . and settle down to wait. Carp bites seldom come quickly. It is more often a matter of hours than of minutes.

A 'typical' carp bite is one where the bait is mouthed and fiddled with for a while before it is swallowed and taken away in a strong, steady run. The strike should be held until this run has developed and is noticeably accelerating. Like all things typical, this does not apply in every case.

A fish which has eaten unattached samples of bait may take the hookbait down in one go and start its run without a moment's hesitation. Surface feeding fish will suck in a bait and turn down immediately, spitting out the bait at the first hint of any check. For a surface feeder the strike should be lightning fast.

The strike must be strong. A big hook has to be driven into lips as tough as old boots. If the bait is any distance out, there is also the slack to be taken up and the stretch of the line to be compensated for.

Strike horizontally and well back, even walking backwards two or three paces as you do so. You've hooked him, and your troubles are just beginning . . .

Hooking a large carp has been described as hooking a speeding lorry, hooking a runaway elephant—hooking, in fact, almost anything big and unstoppable. But your first job is to stop him, or at least to turn him before he can dive into a tangle of lily stems or take a turn around a sunken log. Use sidestrain to turn him and rely on the slipping clutch to give line when necessary.

As soon as his head is turned, strike again. Firmly, but not fiercely. The first strike may not have been enough to drive the hook home beyond the barb. To gain line, pump the fish and wind in as you drop the rod tip without slackening the line. Do not attempt to wind against the pull, and certainly do not wind as you pump.

Be prepared for a long fight. Give line whenever it seems

necessary, always keeping the line taut. You are dealing with a very powerful creature which must be tired before it gets to the net. A short, hard fight, skull-dragging the fish to the bank, could result in your trying to net a fresh and angry fish, whose last lunge could pull out the hook or break the line.

Float fishing
Float fishing, although not favoured by many carp anglers, is very useful for getting the line out past a ledge into deeper water, or beyond an obstacle, without fouling the line.

The float should be sensitive and not affected by wind, and that means an antenna, fastened at the bottom only. If the bait is fished by laying on, with about 18 in of the line flat on the bottom, there is less risk of the carp bumping into the line and taking fright. A shot can be placed to rest on the bottom and stop the float wandering about.

Freelining
Freelining is an excellent method for carp, particularly when fishing close to the bank or in shallow water. There is neither weight nor float to arouse the fishes' suspicions.

Any bait heavy enough to cast can be freelined. A floating crust is very effective, particularly if you can cast it dry so that it lands lightly on the water. If you need extra weight for the cast, dip the crust in the water first.

Potatoes, soft or parboiled, can be used. For fishing over soft bottom weed, try a slice of raw potato. This goes down slowly with a fluttering motion and comes to rest on the top of the weed. A balanced combination of crust and paste will also sink slowly and lie on top of the weed without disappearing.

Baits like crust, flake and worm—or a bunch of worms—can be cast to land on lily pads. The line can drop across the pad, leaving the bait to hang over the edge just a few inches below the surface. Or the bait can land in the middle of the pad, to be eased gently off into the water so that it sinks naturally and without disturbance.

When the carp are sucking snails from the underside of the pads, a good technique is to land the bait smack on the edge of the pad so that the carp will see it and suck if off. With a large lobworm, try to get it half on the pad and half off, so that part of it is waving attractively at the surface.

When fishing over lily pads, remember to strike as soon as the fish takes the bait and to get the fish out of the lilies before it can dive through the stems.

With bunches of worm, you will have no weight problem. Use red worms or brandlings, and thread them to cover the whole of the hook.

Legering

For distance fishing you will often need the help of leger weights to get the bait out. Use a link leger to get over the problem of bottom weed, or try a slow-sinking cork-and-lead-wire leger weight.

A crust bait can be used without a stop on the line, so that it floats on the surface anchored in position by the leger weight below. Or a stop can be put on the line so that the crust floats in midwater.

For fishing on soft bottom weed, try the raw potato or balanced paste and crust baits.

Margin fishing

This needs extra caution, because you are fishing literally over the top of the fish. Choose a margin where carp are known, or are likely, to patrol. One fringed by reeds, behind which you can take cover, is best.

The best results are had after dark when the carp patrol the bank to see what goodies the day's anglers have left floating about.

Set up two rests one in front of the other, or an all-purpose, two-armed rest. Unless there is any wind about, there need be no weights on the line.

Bait up with crust, traditionally matchbox-sized. Poke the rod out so that the tip sticks out over the water of the margin, and lower the crust gently . . . very gently . . . on to the surface. With the bale arm on, lay the rod carefully on the rests. There should be just enough line between the rod tip and the crust to allow the crust to swing about gently in the current, but not enough to leave any loose coils of line on the water.

Use a dough bobbin between the reel and the first ring as an indicator, and be ready to strike as soon as it rises-- although you will probably see or hear the fish take the bait. As the fish sucks in the crust, it will turn down quickly. If it feels any pull from the rod tip it will let go immediately.

Margin fishing need not be all surface work. You can lower sinking baits—worm, paste, potato—on to the bottom.

For margin fishing where there is no cover on the bank, sit further back from the water. Place a third rod rest at the water's edge and lay the line over this to prevent it getting fouled on the bank.

13

Crucian Carp

Carassius carassius

It is a pity that the crucian carp has swum for so long in the shadow of its giant cousin. It is a shy and delicate biter, a hard fighter, and on light tackle a joy to handle.

A crucian of 2 lb is worth remembering. A crucian of 3 lb is a fish a light-tackle man is hardly likely to forget.

Its distribution is more limited than that of the common carp, but not so limited as was once thought. The capture of many a good-sized crucian has gone unrecorded either because it was caught by a carp angler who regarded it as a nuisance or because it was caught by an angler unfamiliar with the fish, who mistook it for a small common carp.

More than a few anglers today are fishing deliberately for the crucian, and discovering it in more and more waters. With this kind of interest, it may not be long before the record moves into the 5 lb bracket.

The crucian, more so than its larger relative, is a shoal fish. The shoals grow smaller as the fish grows larger, and the biggest crucians are probably solitaries.

It likes still or slow water with plenty of weed. A classic swim—and ideal for the use of light tackle—is a stretch of clean bottom alongside or in between weedbeds.

Like the common carp, the crucian is mainly a summer fish and feeds best in the shallows when the water is warm. When the water cools down, it moves to deeper lies. Early morning and late evening is the best time to fish, but the crucian also feeds through the night.

Baits

Groundbaits

If possible, groundbait for two or three days in advance with a light mixture of breadcrumbs, bran, pulped bread or rusk. Samples of hookbait can be added, but do not at this stage add any maggots or worms to avoid attracting eels. Once the fish are feeding, small balls of cloudbait and samples of hookbait will hold their attention.

In heavily weeded water, a stretch can be cleared with a drag made from two garden rake heads tied back to back and flung out on a length of nylon cord. Drag the swim in a fan shape, with the cleared area narrowing towards the bank.

The carpfisher's dodge of leaving a pole sticking out from the bank can be used during the groundbaiting period.

Hookbaits

Maggots, worms, bread (as crust, cube, paste and flake), cheese paste, hemp, stewed wheat, caddis grubs—the crucian will take them all. Maggots, as always, are an excellent standard bait, and can be used in cocktail with bread flake, brandlings or small red worms.

The mouth of the crucian is not nearly so large as that of the common carp, so the baits need not be so big. Although some anglers use walnut-sized lumps of paste to discourage roach and rudd, there is no evidence that the crucian itself prefers large baits.

Tackle

On a clear swim, roach tackle is strong enough: a 12-ft roach rod, a fixed-spool or light centre-pin reel, and a line of $2\frac{1}{2}$ lb b.s. On a weedy swim it is best to scale up to a MK IV Avon rod and a 4 lb b.s. line.

Hooks can range from no. 16 for maggots, hemp and

wheat, to nos. 10 and 12 for small worms and paste, and no. 8 for crust, cube, flake or larger worms.

The float should be the smallest quill or reed which will do the job. Leger rigs can be used in different combinations.

Fishing for crucians

Whatever method you use, get down to the water cautiously and quietly after tackling up away from the bank. Crucians are extremely wary fish and, furthermore, *shoal* fish. The shoal will move off at the signal from its most alert or timid member. It will not return without the agreement of the majority, therefore probably taking longer to get over the fright than a solitary fish.

Float fishing
Laying on is an effective method, with the bait about 18 in from the shot. Or the bait can be fished with a self-cocking float set about 6 in deeper than the depth of the swim. Ideally, there should be no weight on the line but if the bait has a tendency to float, or there are fish nearer the surface after the bait, place a shot above the hook length to help the bait down.

When fishing over weed, adjust the depth so that the bait just touches the surface of the weedbed. Or for a more natural presentation set the float deeper so that the bait and several inches of line lie on the weed. For this the best bait is one like flake, or balanced paste and crust, which will not sink or wriggle into the weed.

Legering
Use only the tiniest weight on a sliding link, or make up a link with a couple of swan shots.

For legering over weed, use a slow-sinking cork-and-lead leger weight on a sliding link. The weighted cork should rest on top of the weed, but even if it sinks into it, the link will allow the bait to stay on the top. Again, a good bait on top of weed is a balanced paste-and-crust.

You can detect the leger bites with a dough bobbin or a quivertip. The crucian carp bite can be a typical carp performance; the bait is fiddled with, nibbled at, nosed about and put down. Just when you think the fish has lost interest, it will come back, swallow the bait and move off. This is the time to strike. When the fish—or rather, the shoal—is really confident about a bait, the bites will reflect this, so be prepared for un-carplike bites, at which the float goes under and away with no more warning than a brief tremble.

Float leger can be used if you are fishing at any distance. Use the lightest possible antenna float.

Freelining
Crucians will occasionally leave the bottom to feed on snails under lily pads, giving themselves away by the sucking noises and the movement of the leaves.

Try for them with floating crust, or use the carp fishing dodge of casting a worm over the edge of the lily pads to dangle in the water a few inches below the surface.

14

Catfish

Silurus glanis

'Ugly' is the one word which best describes the catfish. It is certainly the ugliest European freshwater fish, and among the ugliest anywhere.

The catfish family is a big one, but the catfish found in Britain is the Danubian catfish, or *wels*. Several importations were made in the 1870s and 1880s, and they particularly flourished in a lake at Woburn Abbey. Many of their descendants have been transferred from there, and they can now be found in waters in Bedfordshire, Buckinghamshire and Hertfordshire, including Tring Reservoirs and the Grand Union Canal.

The catfish is a scavenger whose sole preoccupation is eating. This gives it a rapid growth rate and also, in the opinion of some anglers and fishery managers, makes it a menace to other fish. Catfish are good parents: they lay their eggs in a nest and guard them until they hatch. This means a lower mortality rate among the catfish fry, and consequently a prolific breeding rate.

The record catfish is one of 43 lb 8 oz, caught in 1970 at one of the Tring Reservoirs, but they can live for sixty years and grow to a weight of 300 lb. One of 73 lb was netted at one of the Woburn Park lakes. So the next record catfish may really be something.

The fish is unmistakable, with its huge mouth and long 'whiskers'. Ugly though it is, it makes good eating, and was in fact first introduced in attempts at fish farming. Its skin is leathery and the scales are not visible. The back is black or grey-brown. The sides are a mottled brown.

Baits

Use deadbaits, offal, lengths of chicken gut, threaded right up the shank to form a bunch on the hook. Baits don't have to be fresh.

Groundbait with chopped fish, dried blood or offal.

Tackle

Pike tackle, with line of at least 10 lb b.s. No. 2 hooks or large trebles for deadbait snap tackle.

Fishing for catfish

The catfish likes still or slow water, with plenty of mud on the bottom, and will feed in quite shallow water around margins and in channels between the weeds.

Groundbait with chopped fish or offal. The groundbait can be put in a pierced and weighted tin, and thrown into the swim on a piece of cord. This allows the smell of the groundbait to drift out and attract the fish without feeding them.

The hookbait can be legered, freelined, or laid on under a float.

There is no hesitation about a catfish bite. The float goes straight under as the cat sucks in the bait. Strike hard and well back.

The catfish, with its weak tail, does not look as if it is built for fighting, but for a little while at least it will make you think you have hooked a record breaker.

Don't be frightened by the look of the catfish at close quarters. (Some anglers are so repulsed that their first reaction is to beat the fish to death.) Those feelers cannot hurt you. The teeth can, though, so take care when you extract the hook.

15

Chub

Leuciscus cephalus

'The chevin is a stately fish and his head is a dainty morsel. There is no fish so strongly enarmoured with scales on the body. And because he is a strong biter, he hath the more baits.' So the chub was described by the author of *The Treatyse of Fysshynge with an Angle*, published in 1496 as part of a larger book, but possibly written as a pamphlet as early as 1450. Chevin is one of the chub's alternative names. Others are chavender, alderman, loggerhead and skelly.

The chub is a most stately fish, with a long and thickset body.

The reference to the head as a dainty morsel is puzzling: the chub has never been highly regarded as a food fish. Indeed, he has been described as tasting like cotton wool stuffed with needles. (Although Izaak Walton gave a recipe by which 'you will find him a much better dish of meat than you, or most folk, even than anglers themselves, do imagine'.) Certainly the writer cannot have been referring to the size or beauty of the head, which is large, broad, big-mouthed and thick-lipped—a real loggerhead.

He is, however, 'strongly enarmoured with scales', large brassy ones which give him the appearance of being encased in a very flexible and finely jointed suit of mail.

'A strong biter ... and hath the more baits ...'. He is greedy. Nothing much, animal or vegetable, seems to come amiss. This makes the range of baits for chub a very wide one. And he does bite boldly, with a strong and definite bang—but only when he is satisfied that there are no hooks attached. What's more, he bites all the year round.

The chub is a bundle of contradictions. As a young fish he moves around in large shoals and has a liking for fast water. As he grows older he is likely to occupy a hole by the bank, often under tree roots, perhaps in the company of one or two other chub but often as a solitary.

Bold as he is when he is sure of himself, he balances this with a caution bordering on timidity. ('The fearfullest of fishes,' Walton called him.) The merest hint of anything wrong with the bait, and he will either spit it out or ignore it altogether. The merest hint of a possibly hostile presence— a footfall, a shadow, the flash of a rod—and he will melt slowly from sight, disappearing before your eyes with an uncanny effect which has been likened to a television fade-out or the disappearance of the Cheshire Cat. A whole shoal, just like a single fish, can fade away in a matter of seconds.

Chub are widespread in England and southern Scotland, not quite so common in Wales, and have a localised distribution in Ireland.

By now you probably have an idea of what he looks like: long, thickset body; heavy shoulders; big, blunt head with a large mouth; grey-green, grey-brown or grey-blue back, shading to a brassy colour on the flanks and into a silvery belly. Dorsal and anal fins are convex, which is the quickest

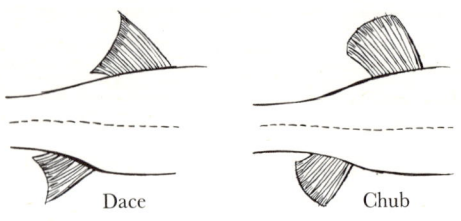

FIG. 39 Fin shapes of dace and chub.

way of telling a young chub from a dace, whose dorsal and anal fins are concave.

You can look for chub in moving water where there is plenty of cover and plenty of food. He can also be found in some lakes, mainly around the mouths of feeder streams, in canals where there is a fair movement of water, and even in some pits and ponds, but these last two are very much the exception.

He does not need a lot of water; very fine chub are taken regularly and often from rivers so small that they almost qualify as streams, although obviously the bigger shoals are in the bigger rivers.

Look for chub also in bankside runs under overhanging trees, in holes by tree roots and behind rocks, in runs *under* the bank where the side has been eroded away to leave a ledge at the surface, at the junction of feeder streams with the main flow, at the tails of weir pools and mill runs—anywhere, in fact, with the combination of cover and food.

In summer, chub will spend a lot of time near the surface. In winter they will seek out the deeper water. In late April and early May, they move into shallow, weedy runs to spawn. It takes them until July or August to get back into proper condition, getting into their peak condition by the autumn.

The chub's natural foods are insects, worms, water snails, caddis grubs, crayfish, frogs, fish and weed. Like other members of the carp family, chub crush their food with the pharyngeal, or throat, teeth. These are particularly powerful in the chub—as you can find out, if you have a mind to.

Baits

Groundbaits

The best groundbait for chub is samples of the hookbait, dropped in only a few at a time, but regularly and frequently. It is worth doing this for as much as twenty minutes or so before you try with a hooked bait, so that the chub has had time to sample your offerings and decide that he has nothing to fear from them.

You can, if you wish, mix the hook samples with an ordinary groundbait preparation on the principle that this will attract other fish into the area and arouse the chub's jealous, bullying instinct and make him less cautious about taking food. This *can* be successful, but it can also result in your catching the intruders and not the chub.

For the faster or deeper swims, mix the hookbait samples with clay to get them to the bottom quickly.

Hookbaits

It is not difficult to think of a bait for chub. It is much more difficult to think of something he does not like. You can try with any of these:

Bread: As crust, flake, cube or paste.

Cheese: Especially smelly cheese such as Danish Blue, either as straight chunks, mixed to a paste with milk, or added to a bread paste.

Slugs: Large black and orange ones or small grey ones. Some anglers slit the undersides of the big slugs so that the innards hang out in the hope of making them more natural and attractive. Apart from its being messy, and not too pleasant for the slug, it is doubtful whether many slugs find their way naturally into the water with their insides hanging out.

Maggots: In bunches, threaded along the hook from barb to shank, or in cocktail with casters of worms.

Worms: Small reds, brandlings, lobs or blueheads, singly or in bunches. Do not worry if a bunch of lobs looks a little on the large side—the chub was not given that great big mouth for nothing.

Insects: Almost any you find by the water's edge, especially any from overhanging trees: their relatives will have been groundbaiting the spot for weeks. Look for large spiders, caterpillars—especially the big, hairy ones—grasshoppers, beetles (a cockchafer if you can find one), moths, wasps, bees, dragonflies or daddy longlegs.

Baits from the water: Silkweed, caddis grubs, swan mussels, water snails (shelled or partly crushed). And crayfish, killed with a quick squeeze of the shell and hooked in the second segment of the tail.

Soft fruits: Cherries (ripe and stoned), gooseberries, elderberries, raspberries, ripe hips and haws.

Beans, peas and sweetcorn: Either cooked until tender or straight from the tin.

Baits from the pantry: Luncheon meat, boiled or raw pieces of sausage, cubes of banana, lengths of macaroni, strips of bacon or bacon fat, chunks of catmeat.

Deadbaits: A minnow, gudgeon or elver, lip-hooked or threaded with a baiting needle on to a treble hook.

Tackle

The rod you will use for chub will depend on the water and the method. But two things remain constant: the size of the hook and the strength of the line.

A chub has a big mouth, so never think in terms of a hook smaller than a no. 8. A medium-sized chub will take a no. 6 without a qualm. If there are big chub about, a no. 4 or even a no. 2 can be used.

The fish is not noted for his fighting ability once his first dash has been checked, but that dash is powerful. To check it, and to cut through any weed or snags, you need line no weaker than 4 lb b.s., and up to 6 lb if there are hopes of big fish.

You will find a choice of two rods useful. A 13-ft float-leger rod will enable you to fish over obstacles and get to otherwise awkward spots. A 10-ft MK IV Avon rod will help with weedy swims or big fish.

Fishing for chub

Whichever method you use, remember the chub's shyness. Keep quiet and stay out of sight.

Float fishing

Chub expect a certain amount of their food to fall directly from above. What they do not expect is for this food to be followed by a clump of weights and a float. So only fish directly above a chub hole by dapping (see pp. 149–50).

Much of the remaining food they expect to be brought down by the current, sinking slowly down as the speed of the water drops in an eddy or behind an obstruction. Try to simulate this natural delivery. Position yourself upstream of the lie, cast in, and let the current carry the bait down to the lie. Set the bait deeper than the swim and check the float every now and again so that the bait is swinging out in front of it.

On float tackle you can use all the baits mentioned, not forgetting the lip-hooked deadbaits.

As well as a normal float, you can try using a small bubble float or a wooden controller to send down weightless baits.

Do not be in too much of a hurry to strike. The chub is facing you. And it has a habit of taking the bait between its lips and sinking down without turning away. This will pull the float under, but it does not mean that the fish has the bait in its mouth. A strike too early will simply pull the bait from its lips. Count one-two-three . . . and strike on three—sideways.

Long trotting

This is an excellent float fishing method for chub, because you are fishing a long way from your quarry. Again, before you cast, throw in small balls of groundbait. Here you might have to throw it well downstream to cover the more distant runs and lies, so mixing the hookbait samples with clay will help.

Use your Avon rod, with a free-running centre-pin reel. With the check off the centre pin, the pull of the current should be enough to take the line out. Finger pressure on the drum can check the line whenever necessary.

A fixed-spool reel can be used by taking off the bale arm and letting the line run out through the fingers, or you can leave the bale arm down, take the check off, and turn the handle backwards.

Use a line of 5 lb b.s., and dress it down to the float with floatant. The float should be a cork-bodied one, with a top big enough and bright enough for you to see right to the end of the swim, or a specially shaped streamlined trotting float.

By checking the float as it travels downstream, you can turn it into the likely spots on either side of the main run. Mend the line automatically every now and then to make sure that the bait is travelling in front of the float. (Surface water travels faster than the lower layers, so an unattended bait generally finishes up behind the float.)

You need not worry about giving the chub enough time to swallow the bait. By the time you have given the over-the-shoulder strike necessary at long distances, and by the time all the stretch in the line has been absorbed, the fish should have the bait well inside its mouth.

Once you have hooked the fish, get him away from whatever hole or eddy he was in, and into the main current. Play him back towards you as quickly as you can without putting undue strain on the rod. Keep the line tight and use sidestrain to keep him away from the snags along the bank.

Freelining

Freelining is a very successful method with chub. Using neither float nor weights, the bait can be drifted downstream to the fish or cast upstream ahead of him, to reach him either on the surface or underwater in the most natural manner possible.

Surface-fished baits, which are especially good in the

summer, include floating crust, big caterpillars or beetles, grasshoppers and moths. For surface fishing, of course, the line should be greased right down to the hook.

Sunken freelined baits are just about everything else. Paste, worms, bunches of maggots, crayfish, wasp grubs, sausage, luncheon meat, cherries ... everything, in fact, which you would use when float fishing or legering.

Downstream freelining—where you cast in and let the current take the bait down to the fish—is easiest. As the strike is being made away from the fish, give it time to swallow the bait before you strike.

Bites on surface baits are easy to spot. The bait disappears in a swirl of water, with a noise like badly drunk soup, or simply disappears.

For bites below the surface, watch the line where it enters the water. It can dimple down under the surface, move to one side, stop, or make any one of a number of movements which could be a current or a snag, but which could be a chub. There is almost always, however, a subtle difference in the movement of the line which you will recognise once you have caught one or two fish this way.

Again, do not be in too much of a hurry on the strike. Let the line run under a little before you act.

Upstream freelining puts the bait in front of the fish and to one side. This has the extra advantage that the fish is facing *away* from you as the bait drifts down towards it. It also means that on the strike the hook is pulled back into the fish's mouth, so that if you do strike too early there is a chance of the hook going home.

Take up the slack as the bait drifts back towards you. Keep an eye on the bait, if it is on the surface, and an eye on the line if the bait is sunken. Again, a bite on a sunken bait will be indicated by some erratic movement of the line at the point where it enters the water. Before striking on an upstream freeline, give a couple of quick turns of the reel to take in any slack.

Dapping

Chub are very fond of swims and holes under overhanging vegetation, in tangles of roots and behind obstacles which leave only one approach open—straight down.

The technique for this is dapping: simply poking the rod out over the water and lowering the bait on to the surface. *Simply* is not really the word. It is often simple enough to get the bait down, but far from simple to get the fish up. Mind you, dapping need not be restricted to overgrown lies. You can use it on a clear bank, providing you keep well back and out of sight.

First, you need a strong rod. Match its length to the individual problem spot. A really treed-up spot might give you no room for manoeuvre with a long rod. But where there is room, or where you are poking the rod out over a bed of reeds, a long rod will enable you to keep your distance from the fish and lift the line more easily over obstructions.

The first problem, then, is getting the bait down to the fish. The second and bigger one is getting the fish to the bank without snarling up either rod or line, or allowing the fish to dive into a snag.

Make sure first that you have room, either upwards or sideways, to play the fish. If you spot any likely dapping spots on your way along the bank, you can make room by trimming or bending the weeds or twigs, and calling back later when the fish will have got over the disturbance.

Use a 5-lb or 6-lb b.s. line. Once the fish is hooked there will be no chance of fancy playing.

For bait, choose a hairy caterpillar, beetle, grasshopper, daddy longlegs, or a piece of floating crust.

If it is breezy or the bait is very light, one or two large shot pinched about 6 in above the hook will provide the weight to take the line straight down to the water.

Poke the rod out over the lie, and let out the line gently until the bait rests on the surface. The wriggling of insect baits will advertise their presence quite effectively. If nothing happens to the floating crust after a little while, jiggle the line gently up and down so that the crust makes a series of concentric ripples on the surface.

When the fish takes, give it enough time to mouth the bait properly as it sinks—but only just enough. Strike firmly and play the chub directly to the nearest bit of open space.

Anglers are often told that they can dap through a small hole in a tangle of branches. They are *not* told what to do when the fish bites—and there is not much they can do, except to try and haul the thing up at great risk to rod, line and the fish itself. So attempt dapping only when there is room to get the fish safely to the bank.

Spinning
Spinning for chub is not practised nearly to the extent it could be, perhaps because so many anglers, subconsciously, still do not look upon the chub as a predator.

A chub will take small spinners and plugs quite greedily, especially if they are worked past a shoal where the competition for food overcomes some of the chub's normal caution. Spinners, bar spoons, wobbling spoons, diving and surface plugs—all in small sizes—can be cast downstream of the shoal. The lure is worked past the shoal to one side, at a fast and even pace.

You can search the clear runs between the weeds, and pools at the end of fast runs, by letting the lure hit bottom and then working it back just inches above the river bed.

For treed-up sections of bank where there is not much room for manoeuvre, you may need to use a shorter spinning rod, say 6 or 7 ft long. Smaller holes can be searched with a popper, which will make the most fuss at the slowest speed across the limited surface area.

16

Dace

Leuciscus leuciscus

The dace is a little, lively, silver fish of the clear, fast runs. Also known locally at one time as the dart, dare or graining, its name is said to have come from the old English word *darse*, meaning to dart.

The record is only 1 lb 4 oz 4 drm, and a pound dace is a whopper. But many an angler who has sneered at the size of the fish has been converted after catching a few on light tackle.

It has a back of dark blue, olive or brown-green, sides of silver; greenish or pink-tinged fins; small head and mouth; slim, neat body and forked tail fin. It is not a fish which impresses with bulk or gaudiness, but a shining, dapper little fighter. Often confused with a small chub, it can be told apart by the fact that its dorsal and anal fins are concave, while those of the chub are convex.

The dace is found over most of England and Wales, but not in Scotland or Ireland. Seldom found in still water, it likes the streamy runs of rivers. It does not need a lot of water, and is often found in tiny rivers and side streams.

Baits

For groundbait use bread mixed with bran, rusk or meal, and samples of the hookbait.

Maggots, small red worms or pieces of lob, wasp grubs, caddis grubs, water snails, bread paste, small cubes of bread or pieces of crust, hemp, woodlice and any small insects likely to find their way naturally into the water—caterpillars, grasshoppers, daddy longlegs, spiders—will all take dace.

Tackle

Use light, tip-action rod with a 2-lb b.s. line, small floats and hooks between nos. 18 and 12.

Fishing for dace

Dace-fishing is often a roving pursuit. The angler locates the shoals in the runs, catches them for as long as he can, and then moves on when the surviving fish realise that something is wrong and refuse to bite.

In summer, explore the runs between weedbeds and over gravelly shallows. In winter, try the deeper runs into which the dace will have moved. In both summer and winter, explore eddies, bays and tails of weir pools.

Dace do not seem to mind sudden changes of temperature and like plenty of light for their feeding. They feed during the day, anywhere between bottom and surface, and stop when the light starts to fade.

If you cannot see the fish, start with float tackle just off the bottom and trot it downstream. Adjust the depth until you find the shoal. In really fast water you may have to use a bigger float to take the weight needed to keep the bait down in the current.

Dace bite very quickly, and just as quickly eject a suspicious mouthful, so the strike has to be made as soon as the float dips.

As well as straightforward trotting—and on clear water you may have to use long trotting—you can try stret pegging. In the deeper runs of winter you can use a static leger or a rolling leger. The rolling leger is useful at any time, and is especially useful for fishing under the opposite bank.

For surface-feeding summer dace, you can freeline baits on floating line, or present them with a streamlined bubble float or wooden controller float. Dapping will take them under overhanging trees and bushes.

Groundbaiting should be little and often. One trick of the old Thames dace fishermen was to fish from a moored punt and groundbait by raking the river bed, letting the current carry the disturbed debris and insects downstream.

If you get the chance to visit a likely swim the night before, you can try a groundbaiting dodge with a large tin filled with maggots. Holes are pierced in the bottom of the tin, just big enough to allow the maggots to escape one by one. The tin is hung over the swim late at night, so that through the night and the early morning a steady stream of maggots has been dropping into the water. Some keen dace men use a biscuit tin which, filled with maggots, makes the whole thing a bit expensive.

A cheaper, but more long-term and rather revolting method, is to hang a dead chicken or pieces of meat or offal from the branches of an overhanging tree. The meat is soon crawling with maggots which drop off naturally over a period into the water.

Fly fishing for dace can be very productive and exciting in the summer when the fish are at the surface to feed on hatching flies (see pp. 100–3). Traditionally, the flies for dace should be bright ones, but they often prefer dark ones. The real answer is to match your fly as nearly as possible to those upon which the dace are feeding.

Dace are often predatory in their habits, taking minnow and fry. It is well worth spinning with a small, flashy barspoon, especially when the minnow are seen to be jumping at the surface to escape the dace beneath.

17

Eel

Anguilla anguilla

The freshwater eel does not fare too well at the hands of many anglers, who treat it as vermin, a slimy nuisance which takes bait meant for other fish and whose strength and agility make it awkward to deal with on the bank. It is treated not at all well, either, by fishery managers who not unnaturally dislike its taste for the spawn of other fish.

An increasing number of anglers, however, are fishing deliberately for this powerful and mysterious creature, either for the pot or for the lusty sport it provides.

The eel has a fascinating life story, starting with its hatching in the Sargasso Sea in the western Atlantic. The larvae—tiny, transparent, leaf-shaped creatures called *leptocephali*—drift on the Atlantic currents towards Europe. Other leptocephali drift towards the American coast to populate American rivers.

Scientists are still arguing about whether the American and British eels are separate species. One theory is that the European eels never survive the long and dangerous journey back to the spawning grounds, and that it is the American eels which provide the massive crop of spawn every year in the Sargasso.

In March and April, about three years after hatching, the young eels arrive at the estuaries of western European rivers. They have now changed into *elvers*, still only 3 in long, but by now cylindrical and almost miniature copies of their parents.

Millions and millions of elvers make the run up river together, but it is a wonder that any at all survive. Waiting for them are not only the predatory birds and fish, but man as well—scooping up the tiny creatures by the thousand to be made into elver pie.

As they work up river, many of them turn off into tributaries. The males, for some reason, stay in the rivers, but many females move on to colonise still water. (The records of the National Anguilla Club, and those of Liverpool University, indicate that only female eels occupy still water.)

Canals, most or all connected at some point with a river, take their full share—not that the eels need the connections. Their ability to survive in the smallest and dirtiest trickles of water, plus their ability to wriggle overland through wet grass at night, enables them to colonise the tiniest and remotest of ponds.

After a summer acclimatising to freshwater life, the bootlace eel spends the winter hibernating in the mud. The following spring finds it ready for ten or eleven years of hearty eating and growth. Nothing much comes amiss: crustacea, molluscs, insects, larvae, spawn, fry, frogs and carrion.

One September or October, at the end of a decade in freshwater, the eel turns again to the sea. If it does reach the Sargasso, it apparently dies after spawning, for none has been known to make the return trip back to the river. If the alternative theory is correct, it fails to reach the Sargasso at all, leaving the perpetuation of the species to its American cousin.

Eels are generally regarded as fish of the summer and autumn. Although a spell of mild weather will bring them out of hibernation, they tend to bury themselves in the mud for the winter. In the main, you can discount November to February for eel fishing. Ironically, just as the eels begin to stir in March, the three-month close season clamps down on coarse-fish waters.

If you want to be sure of eels, especially the bigger ones,

the best times are the two hours before daylight and the two hours after dusk, preferably on a moonless or overcast night. More eels *are* caught during the day, but this is because most anglers are active during daylight—and generally fishing for something else.

Baits

Groundbaits

The first essential in eel fishing is really attractive groundbait. Eels hunt by smell, so for attractive, read smelly. Chopped-up fish or offal, liver or chicken guts, meat, chopped worms, dried blood—any or all of these should bring the eels sniffing around. Some anglers swear that breaking an egg into the water is a sure attraction. I have no evidence that it is any more effective than any of the nauseous ingredients already listed, but if there is a cracked egg in the pantry you can mix it in. Or you can use it by itself, mixed with bran into a stiff ball. You can incorporate the groundbait in a ball of clay or stiff soil to make it easier to throw and slower to disperse.

A method of attracting eels without feeding them uses a lidded tin, punctured all over with a large nail. Fill the tin with chopped meat, fish or offal and a couple of stones for extra weight. Fix the lid on firmly, tie the tin to a length of cord and throw it in the swim, tying the cord to the bank to keep it in place. In moving water, fish a little downstream of the tin. In still water, fish as close to it as you can. The smell from the mess inside will drift through the water and bring the eels homing in. Alternatives to the tin are a piece of fine netting, open-weave fabric or a sock, filled with groundbait, weighted and thrown in in the same way. The disadvantage, however, is that the eels can soon rip a hole in the fabric, gorge themselves on the contents, and ignore the hookbait.

Hookbaits

Few eels can resist a lobworm. Unfortunately few other fish can resist one either, and it is not much fun pulling in perch or roach on eel tackle. Still, lobs are an excellent bait if you don't mind hooking other fish and small eels.

You could try a piece of liver, meat, a string of chicken entrails, a strip of kipper. Or a deadbait, part or whole of a dead fish such as roach, bleak, dace, gudgeon or sprat or part of a herring or mackerel. Whichever bait you use, make sure that the hook is well covered. For the dead fish, use a baiting needle. Pass the needle through the mouth, through the body and out near the tail. This leaves the hook sticking out of the side of the deadbait's mouth. Pinch a half-moon lead or a split shot on the line where it comes out of the bait near the tail, to stop the bait from sliding up the line.

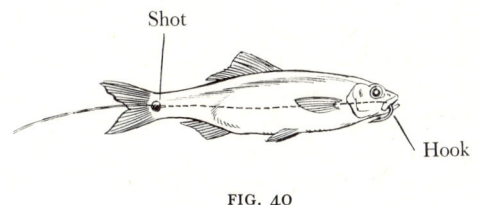

FIG. 40

Use the baiting needle, too, for the liver or meat. With chicken entrails you can either use the baiting needle, or pass the hook point through several times to make sure there is a good bunch of entrails all the way up the shank, and no loose lengths waving about.

Tackle

Use strong, simple tackle. There is no time or room for fancy rodwork, especially with the larger eels. A hooked eel should be pumped straight to the top before it can take a couple of turns of line around a snag, or before its tail can take a grip of anything.

A 10-ft pike rod, a 10-lb b.s. line on either a fixed-spool reel—well filled for quick recovery—or a multiplier, and no. 6 hooks are the basic equipment. The hooks should be attached to 12-in wire traces which have a snap link swivel at the other end. This snap link can be attached to a split ring—or another swivel—at the end of the reel line.

The swivels not only stop the twisting of the eel from kinking the line, but the use of a snap link makes it a simple matter to detach the trace and drop a big or awkward eel into a sack. (More of that later.)

Depending on which method you prefer, take a selection of large floats, leger weights or paternoster rigs.

Fishing for eels

Float fishing

Lay on with the swivel and hook length on the bottom. In slow or still water the swivel itself may be heavy enough to hold the bait in position, but it may be necessary to add a half-moon lead or one or two split shot just above it.

The eel is a fiddly biter, mouthing at the bait and trying to tear bits off it, picking it up and moving off for a little way before finally taking it and running. So be patient. Ignore the first twitches and bobs, the first short runs. When the eel finally takes the bait, it will run hard and fast. The run is the time to strike.

Legering

You can leger with an Arlesey bomb, with or without a link, but in any case attached to the line with a snap link swivel. The trace, again, should be fixed to the reel line with a snap link.

You can watch the rod tip for bites, or use a dough bobbin, but after the first indication hold the line between the fingers.

This will give you a better idea of what the eel is up to. Remember to let the line slide out through the fingers as the eel makes its first short runs.

Freelining
In absolutely still water you can freeline, using the same techniques as with legering for detecting the bites.

Dealing with eels
The first essential is to get the eel out of the water. If you are on an open bank, you can walk or run backwards to help get the fish away from snags.

For eels up to medium size, many anglers prefer not to use a landing net, but to lift the eel straight from the water. With a strong rod, a small eel can be simply swung clear. With larger eels you can take hold of the line and lift the fish straight from the water, smoothly and without jerking.

A large, carp-size landing net—with a small mesh—will help to take care of bigger eels. A small landing net, or one with an open mesh, is worse than useless.

With the eel out of the water, your troubles have only just begun. If you do not act quickly you will have your line in an impossible knot and your clothes covered with an unbelievable amount of slime.

FIG. 41   Holding an eel

Small to medium-sized eels can be held quite firmly with the middle finger on the back of the neck (for want of a better word) just behind the head, and the two fingers on either side under the throat.

Another trick is to lay the eel on its back in a groove in the ground. This helps to quieten it and gives it less room in which to thrash about.

Big eels often need more drastic treatment. Some anglers have a sack or plastic bag propped open on a tripod of branches. The snap link swivel on the trace can be unclipped and the eel—trace and all—dropped into the sack to be dealt with later.

Wrapping an eel in newspaper makes it easier to hold. Rolling it in sand or dust clogs its nervous system and quietens it. But an eel never stays quiet for long.

Night fishing

Night fishing brings the bigger eels, and here leger is the only practicable method.

There are several ways of detecting bites:

1 Hold the line between finger and thumb.
2 Use a piece of aluminium foil on the line if there is enough light to reflect.
3 Use an electric bite alarm.

Step up the line strength to 20 lb b.s., and use traces of 18 lb b.s. Use a really strong pike rod or a sea rod. Give the eel the usual time to take the bait and run, but after the strike be even more ruthless in getting it to the bank.

Never go night fishing for eels on your own. An eel is trouble enough in daylight. By night, especially if it is over the 3-lb mark, it can be almost impossible to deal with alone.

Your companion's first function is to hold the torch, then to hold open the sack while you drop in the eel—simple enough tasks, but absolutely vital if you are going to retain the eel.

Remember that the eel is a fish, however snake-like and sinister it may look. Treat it as far as you can with the same care given to more 'conventional' fish. Take out the hooks as painlessly as possible, and put back any unwanted eels unless there is a club or authority rule forbidding their return.

Killing an eel is not easy. Their hold on life is very strong and even a 'dead' eel will wriggle sometimes for hours after death. You can chop off an eel's head. This kills it, but does not stop it wriggling, and makes it difficult to skin for the pot. The tidiest way of killing an eel, after dropping it in dust or sand to quieten it, is to hit it sharply just above the *tail*, and then to cut through the spinal cord behind the head with a sharp knife.

The best way to skin an eel is to cut through the neck, but to leave a third of the skin unbroken. Hold the head with a cloth, the body with another, and draw the head backwards towards the tail. The skin will peel off like a glove.

18

Grayling

Thymallus thymallus

The grayling, perhaps the most beautiful fish in British waters, is a member of the *Salmonidae*, the salmon family, and has the characteristic adipose fin, the small, fleshy dorsal fin just in front of the tail.

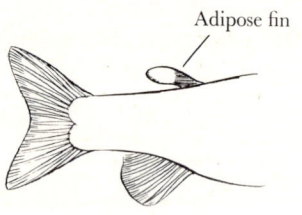

FIG. 42   Grayling.

Strictly speaking, it should be a game fish, but because it spawns at the same time as coarse fish it is generally treated as one—even to the extent of being scorned by died-in-the-wool trout fishermen.

Because of its alleged liking for trout spawn, it is ruthlessly netted and electrocuted out of trout rivers every season. (This argument is losing ground now that more and more trout waters are being stocked from hatcheries.) Such is its capacity for survival, however, that it usually turns up again before long.

The grayling's basic colour is silver, but it is shot through with tones of purple, indigo, green and yellow, which give it the delicate shimmering quality of watered silk. The fins often carry a purplish tinge.

Apart from its colour, its most recognisable characteristic is the sail-like dorsal fin, which continues the purple tones of the body and is speckled with dark marks which often range to look like horizontal stripes.

Old names for the fish were umber, oumer, silver lady, and lady of the stream, all of which testify to the beauty of its form and colouring. The fish is even supposed to *smell* nice, with a faint scent of thyme (hence its Latin name). This I have never been able to confirm, perhaps because of a poor sense of smell, but many anglers swear that the grayling does smell like a flower and not a fish.

The grayling is fairly well distributed in the fast rivers of northern England—particularly in Yorkshire—in southern Scotland and in parts of Wales. It can also be found in some waters in Hampshire and Dorset. It does not appear in Ireland.

Because it spawns with the coarse fish, the grayling is tired and flabby up to mid-July, and up to this time the trout-man's scorn may be justified. But from then on her strength and condition improve rapidly. By September, as the trout season is drawing to its close, she is plump and fighting fit, and many enlightened trout anglers pursue her on the fly until Christmas as an extension of the season.

Baits

Grayling will take maggot, wasp grub, grasshopper, small red worms, and the tiniest spinners. They will also take dry and wet flies and imitation shrimps.

Tackle

Use a 12-ft trotting rod with a line of 3 lb b.s., either a

fixed-spool or free-running centre-pin reel, and hooks nos. 16–20. For fly fishing, use a 9-ft trout rod, fly line and centre-pin reel.

Fishing for grayling

The grayling likes the uncommon combination of a fast flow and a muddy bottom, preferably in midstream. The water must be absolutely clean; at the first hint of pollution, the fish disappears.

They feed anywhere between bottom and surface. It is best to search the water from top to bottom, and then to stick at the depth the grayling dictates—it is no use trying to tempt her to feed at a depth she does not approve of.

A grayling nips, rather than bites—hence the small hooks. When she nips, she turns sharply down, so the strike should be immediate and need be no more than a turn of the wrist, tightening the line and letting the fish literally hook itself.

Many anglers blame the grayling's soft mouth when they lose a fish, but the fault is the angler's not the fish's: the grayling does not have a soft mouth. Izaak Walton seems to have started the misconception which has lingered on ever since. The grayling's mouth is *small*, not soft. By contrast a perch has a soft mouth, but a gape like a Gladstone bag.

A grayling hooked downstream takes full advantage of the current, spreading the sail of her dorsal fin and turning broadside on to the force of the water. When this happens, try to turn her head towards you and use sidestrain to keep it there whenever necessary. Move her into slack water and try to get below her for the netting. The grayling has a habit of kicking at the last moment; when this happens you stand a better chance with the net downstream of her.

A delicate way of taking the fish is by trotting down a maggot, wasp grub or red worm on a fine line (3 lb or even 2 lb b.s. if the current is not too fierce). Use a grayling float—a slender quill with a pear-shaped cork 'body' near the top.

With the last shot on the line about 9 in from the hook, the bait is free to swing about just off the bottom. Keep the bait ahead of the float by occasional checks on the line. The grayling takes the bait just like a river roach. Strike, gently, as soon as the float bobs, quivers, sidesteps, tilts or checks.

You can try fly tackle as well as trotting tackle to search the different depths for grayling feeding. Try on the surface with a small, flashy dry fly, or below with wet flies or leaded shrimps.

The grayling has keen eyesight, so even dry flies are generally cast *downstream* and across. This has the advantage of presenting the fly before the line, but it needs extra care to avoid drag.

Often the fish will make messy and inaccurate rises which would seem to indicate that her eyesight was not as good as it was supposed to be. Misses like these, however, are caused because she has shot up right from the bottom to take the fly, contending with a fast current on the way. Missing a fly does not worry the grayling, so do not let it worry you. Send the fly back so that she can have another go.

For wet fly fishing, fish downstream and work the flies downwards from the surface until you make contact. If the fish are lying really deep, or the flow is really fast, add some lead to help the fly down. Do not cast right on top of the fish. Let the fly land several feet upstream of her and float down, so that she has more time to sight the lure and can come up at a less acute angle.

When looking for grayling, either on fly or trotting tackle, keep in mind the combination of a fast flow and muddy bottom. If there are no locals about to volunteer information, it is worth wading around and poking about with a landing net handle to find the right conditions—always taking special care not to step out of your depth or wade into too strong a current.

19

Gudgeon

Gobio gobio

The gudgeon is small and not very pretty. Consequently many anglers do not take him seriously. For his size, however, he is probably the hardest-fighting fish in the water and a great delight to catch on ultra-light tackle, especially on hot summer days when nothing else is stirring.

In Victorian times gudgeon fishing parties were great social and family occasions, often followed by a meal, because the little fish make delicious eating.

The gudgeon is common in England and Wales, though rare in Scotland, the Lake District and Cornwall. It has a reasonable, though localised, distribution in Ireland. (There is at least one stretch of water in Ireland on which the gudgeon is advertised, along with its larger cousins, as one of the angling attractions.)

It looks like a miniature barbel, but can easily be distinguished by its two barbels (the barbel has four), the speckling of its body, its grey or greeny-brown colour, and its more sharply forked tail.

The record gudgeon weighs in at just 4 oz, but they have been known to reach a weight of 8 oz. Anybody who does find himself with a half-pound gudgeon on light tackle is in for a real thrill.

Baits

Groundbaits
Simply raking the bottom will bring the gudgeon shoals

along to investigate the disturbance. Occasional hookbait samples—maggots, chopped worms, minced raw meat—will keep them there.

Hookbaits
The small red worm is the classic bait. They will also happily take maggots, wasp grubs or bits of raw meat and, perhaps less happily but quite readily, paste.

Tackle

Tackle can be as light as you like. Use the slenderest rod in your holdall; line of 1 lb b.s., fixed-spool or centre-pin reel; hooks nos. 12–16. The gudgeon has a big mouth for its size and never seems to object to a no. 12. The float should be your tiniest quill.

Fishing for gudgeon

Gudgeon have a long spawning period, starting as early as April and carrying on until as late as July. The female deposits her 3500 eggs in batches of only a hundred or so at a time, so each fish may take up to a month to complete the spawning. Later summer and early autumn are therefore the best times to fish for them.

They like a river with a gravel or sand bottom and a reasonable flow, and are often found fairly deep although they also congregate in shoals in shallows by the bank. Though a river is their ideal habitat, they also live happily in the slower waters of a canal, and can even be found in a lake or pond, often lying around the mouth of a drain or feeder stream to pick up the food carried down by it.

They are not fussy feeders. Their natural food includes worms, shrimps, aquatic insects, larvae, spawn, insects, molluscs and even fry. They feed by stirring up the gravel, using their barbels to locate the food.

Fish as light as you can. In still water, lay on with the shot set about 6 in from the hook. In moving water, set the bait a few inches over the depth so that it trips the bottom. You can leger for them with the smallest possible weight, although it's not so much.

In moving water, note where the cloud disturbed by the raking has drifted to. The fish will most probably be feeding at that spot, rather than the site of the original raking.

There is no hesitation or delicacy about a gudgeon bite. The float dives suddenly straight under. Strike immediately. On leger, you will get a quick 'bang' of the rod tip.

On the light tackle you will be surprised at the power of the fight, even after catching a dozen or so. The numbers, incidentally, are another delight of gudgeon fishing. When they are really on the feed it is possible to hook out the whole shoal, one after the other. Fifty or sixty fish in an hour or so's fishing is a very satisfying result—even if the size of the fish is an anti-climax after the fight they put up.

20

Perch

Perca fluviatilis

'The perche is a daynteous fysshe and passynge holsom and a free biting', wrote the author of *The Treatyse of Fysshynge with an Angle*. Dainteous he is—handsome, dashing, colourful with his green back, green-gold flanks, black zebra stripes and bristling dorsal fin. Wholesome he is—a perch makes a delicious meal. Grilled with butter, he has a unique nutty flavour which many people prefer to trout. And free-biting—young perch, ever hungry, ever on the lookout for food, snatch at almost anything which looks like a meal. Possibly the first fish of most young anglers is a perch—or was, until disease cut their numbers drastically in the early 1970s, a setback from which they are slowly recovering.

The perch could be confused with only two other fish—the ruffe and the zander—and then only at a passing glance. The ruffe grows no bigger than 4 oz, has its two dorsal fins joined together, and is a drab olive or brown colour, speckled with dark spots. It looks what it is—an ugly poor relation. The zander is longer and thinner and, though striped, is paler, with eight to twelve stripes as against the perch's usual six. It also has a set of pike-like teeth in the front of its mouth. The perch's teeth are tiny; it relies on its powerful pharyngeal, or throat, teeth to chew up its prey.

At second glance the perch really is unmistakable. As well as the splendid colouring of his flanks, his pectoral, ventral and anal fins are a rich, glowing red.

His first dorsal fin, grey-green but sometimes tinged with

red, has a distinctive black spot at the rear end and is made up of between fourteen and sixteen stout and very sharp spines. The second dorsal fin carries one or two spines at the leading edge. More spines are present on the ventral and anal fins, and even the gill covers end in a very sharp point.

When the fish is in any kind of trouble, up come the dorsal fins and out stick the spines on the others. Even the spines on the gill covers are used as the fish puffs and blows.

All in all, he is not a very comfortable fish to handle—even his scales are like knobbly sandpaper—and most anglers find this out the hard way, with a palm full of dorsal spines. The safest way to pick up a perch is to slide the hand backwards from the head, so smoothing these spines down.

Apart from his colouring, the perch's most distinctive feature is his shape: big head, humped back, small tail. His shape can be likened to that of a fighting bull, and he has many of the same characteristics of movement, apart from the same peppery temper. All the power is in those shoulders. The tail itself is relatively weak. A perch turns with a flick of the tail, using the bulk of the humped back as a pivot, just as a bull will give a kick of its back legs, but spin around on the front ones.

This explains the jagging, thrumming fight of a hooked perch. He is weaving from the shoulders in an attempt to throw the hook. It also explains why his lunges, though exciting to the angler, are not really powerful—certainly nothing like the fierce jagging of a pike or the steady pull of a tench.

For all that, the perch should be played carefully. His mouth, though large, is very soft, and the hook can easily come away, especially if it is lodged only in the membrane above the upper lip. He also never knows when he is beaten and will often give a final lunge as he is being drawn over the net. The lesson here is not to slacken the line at all until he is actually in the net.

Perch are found all over the British Isles, in all kinds of

waters: rivers, streams, lakes, ponds, canals and pits. They prefer the quieter water, and in rivers will tend to stay away from the main force of the current in eddies, holes, in and around reed beds, behind rocks and in laybys.

The perch is mainly a predator. Because of his swashbuckling appearance and dashing fight, he has none of the sinister associations of the pike. But predator he is, eating fish—often smaller perch—molluscs, worms, insects and crustacea.

Until he gets really big he is a shoal fish. Small perch hunt in really large packs, like wolves, often patrolling regular beats. Like wolves they will drive their prey before them, bunching them together before rushing in for the kill. A sign of a hungry perch shoal is often the scattering of fry on the surface, leaping clear of the water to escape the pack underneath.

As the perch grow bigger, the shoals grow smaller, probably not because the bigger fish really want to be alone, but because the mortality rate among small perch is very high: their curiosity and sense of adventure make them easy prey for pike, eels and predatory birds. All the fish in a shoal are the same size. Perch of more than 2 lb shoal in groups of four or six, and the biggest perch of all are probably loners.

Baits

Groundbaits
Raking the bottom helps gather the perch around by disturbing worms, larvae and insects, and by attracting swarms of fry. (These can be attracted also by the odd ball of cloudbait.) Apart from that, the only form of groundbaiting needed is samples of the hookbait, say, maggots or bits of worm.

Hookbaits
The perch is a meat-eater, so this cuts out bread, cheese and

cereal baits. Perch *are* caught on them, but not regularly or often enough to make their use worthwhile.

Worms are a deadly bait, especially large lobs. You can try the head or tail of a lob for smaller perch, or to make your bait go further, but the perch does not hesitate to tackle the biggest lob or bluehead. Red worms and brandlings also do very well, either singly or in bunches.

Deadbaits will be taken, either wobbled on spinning tackle, lip-hooked and worked sink-and-draw, or simply cast out and left on the bottom. The fish should be fairly small: minnows, young gudgeon and roach generally do well. Small dead crayfish, hooked through the second tail segment and worked sink-and-draw are always worth a try.

Artificial baits, plugs, spinners and spoons, make for exciting perch fishing. The best spoons and spinners seem to be the small flashy ones, and the best plugs the smaller ones with a fussy action. The perch has a habit of biting at the tail of its prey in an attempt to cripple it. To encourage this, tie some red wool or silk in the form of a tassel at the end of the lure.

Maggots, the good old standby, will take perch, especially when they are being a bit fussy about their food. They can be used singly or in bunches, and are more attractive when they are lively on the hook, or when the tackle is kept on the move.

Tackle

Tackle for perch need not be too specialised, so long as it matches the method used. A line of 3 lb b.s. is certainly strong enough for small to medium-sized perch. For bigger perch, for long casting, or for fishing a water containing possible snags, the line strength can be increased to 5 or 6 lb b.s.

Remembering the perch's big mouth, hooks ought not to be too small. Certainly no smaller than no. 12 for maggots, no. 8 for large lobs, no. 6 for deadbaits and an appropriate size of deadbait flight for spinning or wobbling.

For float fishing in slow or still water you can use an 11-ft hollow glass rod, a fixed-spool reel, and a line of 3 lb b.s. The float can be either cork bodied or a quill of a size appropriate to the bait.

For distance casting or for legering, use a MK IV Avon rod.

Fishing for perch

In summer, perch move around in midwater, often following their quarry into the shallows. In winter, again following their quarry, they move down into the deep holes, though a spell of fine weather will bring them up on patrol again.

Their diet is made up of small fish, larvae, insects, worms, snails. Like all predators, they want the most return for the least effort. So, when not patrolling, they spend their time in and around places such as weedbeds, old pilings, underwater brickwork, stonework, woodwork, treed sections of the bank with a maze of underwater roots, sunken barges and lock gates. In these places, where there is weed and cover, there is plenty of small animal life. There are also backgrounds which suit the perches' natural camouflage, and plenty of hideaways from which they can dash to seize passing fish.

Perch panic easily, and it is essential to get a hooked fish away from the shoal quickly, to prevent him frightening the others. But do not try to skull-drag him to the bank. This will probably result in the hook tearing loose, and then the shoal certainly will panic. Play him firmly, but try to gauge what is happening below the surface, and turn him with sidestrain rather than straight, unyielding pressure.

Float fishing

Depending on the conditions and the position of the shoal, you could fish midwater, just off the bottom, or lay on.

A perch sucks in and blows out its food several times before swallowing it and the resulting bob-o-bob of a float, when the bait is fished off the bottom, is unmistakable. Hold the strike until the float slides under or sideways. Strike firmly, with just a turn of the wrist, but not fiercely.

A strike too soon, while the float is still bobbing, can mean a miss or a fish very lightly hooked. Too fierce a strike can tear the fish's soft mouth. Either way you would have an angry and frightened fish panicking the rest of the shoal.

Too late a strike can mean that the fish is hooked in the gut, injuring it and making the removal of the hook a difficult and messy business. (With small and greedy perch, often even a quick strike is too late.) To take the hook from the gut, you can cut off the barb with a pair of wire-cutters and withdraw the hook without damage. Or cut the line above the shank and withdraw the hook point first.

If neither is possible, and the fish is obviously hurt, kill it straight away. (The fish need not be wasted. Its red gill fringes and short lengths of its gut make effective bait for its comrades. A big enough fish can be taken home, cleaned, opened out like a kipper, and grilled with butter.)

If there are no bites after a while, adjust the depth of the bait and try again. If nothing has happened by the time you have searched the swim from end to end, and from top to bottom, move on. When the perch shoals are roaming, you must be prepared to roam too. The consolation is that when you do find a perch, you find a whole shoal, and you should go on catching the fish until the survivors lose interest or are frightened by a fish breaking free.

With a laid-on bait, the sucks and blows may not register as bobs on the float, and the first indication you have of a bite may be when the float moves under or away. Strike then.

In still water, do not leave the bait just hanging there in one spot. After a few minutes, lift the rod and move the float back towards you a little. This will lift and move the bait in a short sink-and-draw motion and may well attract the attention of a passing fish.

Spinning

Small, flashy, fussy and working slowly: these are the qualities the perch likes best in an artificial lure. Mackerel spinners, small bar spoons, Colorados, wagtails and small plugs such as the Plucky all work well. The Devon minnow is not so good because it cannot generally be worked slowly enough.

These small plugs work best on a nylon trace with, of course, a swivel at each end. There is often no need for an anti-kink device. If there are pike about, you may have to use a wire trace instead of the nylon, accepting the slight muffling of the lure's action that results from this.

The perch has not got the speed of a pike, but can manoeuvre better and will follow the lure, nipping at its 'tail' in an attempt to cripple it.

These nips will be felt as plucks on the line. Ignore the plucks and keep winding in. The take will be signalled by a definite 'braking' of the lure. Strike.

One school of thought advocates a jerky, uneven recovery, varying the speed and movement of the lure. Another advocates a steady reeling in with no variation in the pace. Though I prefer the uneven recovery, perch on different waters have their own preferences. On strange water alternate the techniques until you get a bite on one or the other, and then stick to that for as long as the fish are taking.

The even-speed technique does not mean just a straightforward recovery. Even though the pace remains the same, you can vary the action of the lure by moving the rod to turn it from side to side, and then giving it a gentle sink-and-draw movement.

The uneven recovery is meant to imitate a sick or injured fish, to get the perch interested in the prospect of an easy meal. Exaggerate the sideways and sink-and-draw movements, and occasionally stop reeling altogether so that the lure sinks like a crippled fish.

Even with the uneven recovery, keep the lure working

fairly slowly. Although the perch can manoeuvre better than the pike he is not renowned for his patience, and may soon lose interest in a lure which can move faster than he can.

Perch will often pick dead fish from the bottom, so try now and again letting your lure sink right down to the bottom and leave it there for ten seconds or so. Keep your eye on the line at the surface. If it moves, strike. If there has been no sign at the surface as you pick up the lure again, give a gentle strike just in case.

Dead fish can be used as spinning baits, either hooked through both lips or mounted on scaled-down wobbler tackle. Lip-hooked fish often benefit from having some form of weight—swan shot, lead wire or half-moon lead—fixed on the line about 4 in from the hook. This weight helps in casting and gives the bait a better sink-and-draw action.

Large lobs can be spun, mounted on two-hook Pennell tackle, with the upper hook just in front of the saddle and the lower hook below it, leaving a fair length of tail to wave about naturally.

A weightless worm is the most attractive. It is cast out and allowed to drift to the end of the swim, sinking slowly as it goes. It is then retrieved by sink-and-draw. The distance of the cast or the speed of the water may dictate the addition of weights in front of the worm.

Leger and sliding paternoster
Legering can be used throughout the year, providing you are willing to put up with marauding eels during the summer. It is especially useful, however, for distance fishing, for seeking out deep-lying winter perch and for exploring holes in flood conditions.

Baits are worms or deadbait—minnows, small roach, gudgeon, crayfish or sprat. Remember to pierce and deflate swim bladders of fresh fishbaits.

On a 'straight' leger in still or slow water leave a trace of 3 or 4 ft between weight and hook, so that the perch can suck, blow and fiddle about without feeling any resistance. Alternatively, use a link leger about 2 ft from the hook.

To reduce the chances of the fish dropping the bait, arrange the rests so that the rod 'points' at the water, and use only the lightest of bite indicators.

The best weight for a distance cast is the Arlesey bomb, designed by Richard Walker to catch deep-lying perch in Arlesey Lake, Bedfordshire.

The bite indicator may give several twitches before the perch takes the bait and moves off, or the first indication may be the run itself. Do not be in a hurry to strike. Wait until the run starts and then count to five.

For not-so-deep fishing, or for fishing not so far out, a float leger can be used. Or the float can be attached above a sliding paternoster which can be adjusted to hold the bait at any distance above the bottom.

Freelining
If the perch are feeding close in, a deadbait or worm can be freelined. It can be cast out, allowed to sink slowly and left for a while on the bottom. It is then reeled back in, either 'inched' back towards the bank or lifted in slow and short hops of sink-and-draw.

21

Pike

Esox lucius

With the pike we move into a controversial area of angling. No fish, with the exception of the eel, has been so badly treated over the centuries. Even today, after years of campaigning by enlightened individuals and angling groups, pike are hauled out of the water and clubbed or stamped to death without a second thought. Some angling clubs even give official sanction for this by insisting that no pike be returned to the water.

Although there may be a need on some waters for *selective* culling of pike, the fact remains that the fish is a very important factor in maintaining the ecological balance of the water. Many a club has cleaned out every single pike from their water—and then found it full of small and sickly fish, stunted because there were too many of them for the natural food supply, and wide open to disease because they were overcrowded and because sick fish survived long enough to pass on the sickness.

Greedy as he is when he is on the feed, the pike could never be accused of killing for the sake of killing. He is far too lazy to chase and kill more than he needs. This laziness also makes him a natural regulator of underwater disease: he goes for a sick or crippled fish simply because it is slower and easier to catch than a nippy, healthy one. He actually does the selective culling of all the crippled, sick, weak and aging fish which a bailiff would like to do.

Possibly the main reason why the pike is still so badly

treated is fear. The fight of a pike underwater is powerful and savage; a fierce, jagging fight which keeps the rod jerking madly right up to the time he comes to the net. His fight *above* the surface is spectacular: a series of thrashing leaps, with the great head shaking in an attempt to throw the hook. A pike at close quarters is an awesome sight. The lean, cruel jaws are packed with teeth: crocodile-like teeth on the lower jaw, and hundreds of small, needle-like teeth on the upper . . . all pointing inwards. Few fish which get between those jaws stand much chance of ever getting out. An incautious finger can take quite a mauling, too.

So the whole of the pike's actions and armoury are pretty fearsome, but perhaps the main cause of the fear in anglers is the eyes. They are set high on the head, looking upwards and forwards, giving the fish the binocular vision, the focus, that it needs for a lunge at its prey. The setting of the eyes makes the pike the only fish which can look—or appear to look—the angler straight in the face. It is a cold and seemingly malevolent stare which invests the pike with a look of more intelligence and more evil intent than it possesses.

But however big it is, however full of fight, however evil-looking, the pike is still only a fish. Once on the bank he is completely at the angler's mercy. The hooks can be taken out without damage to either the angler or the fish. The country's best specialist pike anglers make a point of treating the fish with care and returning it to the water—to grow bigger and to be caught again.

The pike is found everywhere in the British Isles, and in every kind of water—rivers, streams, canals, lakes, ponds, pits and reservoirs.

It is a loner, a solitary fish even as a 6-in pikelet. Though a number of pike may be caught from one 'hot spot' when they are on the feed, they have moved there individually after a shoal of other fish, rather than gone along together.

Its dark green back speckled with lighter green and its

lighter green flanks marked with short horizontal bars of creamy yellow make it almost invisible against most underwater backgrounds. It lies absolutely still except for the quivering of its fins, until a food fish approaches. Then, with a flick of its tail—aided by the dorsal and anal fins which are set far back towards the tail—it lunges from cover and seizes the fish across the body. (One estimate of the speed of this lunge puts it as fast as 12 ft a second.) After seizing the fish, it sinks back and then turns the fish head first into its mouth to swallow it.

Pike spawn between February and May—generally in March and April—moving into shallow water or into side streams to do so. A 15-lb female can lay about 150 000 eggs, and a 30-lb fish has been estimated to contain half a million. The eggs are attached to weed stalks, but by the time waterfowl, eels and other fish have been at them, only a fraction hatch out.

The great mortality among the eggs, and among the small pike (which are constantly part of the diet of larger pike) keep the numbers down. This, plus the havoc played by anglers in the past, has led some clubs and river authorities to extend the close season to 1 October and to fix size limits on pike which may be taken away, generally from 18 to 24 in.

Another reason given for the extended close season is that pike take a long time to recover from spawning, but it is hardly likely that it needs six or seven months. It seems strange, too, that pike fishing can be illegal in September, when the fish is fighting fit, yet legal in February and the first fortnight in March when they may be spawning.

Baits

Groundbaits
Very little groundbaiting is done for pike, but chopped mackerel, herring or sprats will attract them to a spot in

which deadbaits are to be fished. It is important not to overdo the groundbaiting, otherwise the pike will gorge themselves on the free offerings and probably ignore the hookbait. All the three fish mentioned are oily—the mackerel in particular—and a little of this oil spreads a long way.

Hookbaits
Livebaits: at the risk of repeating myself, and boring you, I can only ask that you do not use livebaits. And that you politely but firmly refuse requests from anglers for roach or gudgeon in your net to be used as livebait.

Deadbaits are very effective and often account for the bigger pike.

Whole sprats can be used. Herring and mackerel can be used whole or halved. The advantage of halving, apart from giving you two baits for the price of one, is that the oil is released much more quickly and in much greater quantity. (To help release the oil from a whole fish bait, puncture the sides with a baiting needle.)

Dead freshwater fish—roach, dace, rudd, chub, trout—can be used whole. Although not as effective as the oilier sea fish, their harder skins make it more difficult for eels to break up the bait before the pike can get to it. With a fresh deadbait, puncture the swim bladder (about the middle of the fish) with a baiting needle and squeeze the air out, otherwise it will float to the surface. Hard-skinned deadbaits can be mounted on wobbler or spinning tackle and worked through the water like a spoon.

Deadbaits do not have to be fresh. Sizable pike have been caught on baits which the hungriest cat would have run away from. But *you* may have some views on it, even if the pike don't.

Artificial baits
Buy those you think the pike will like, not those *you* like. If you have any spare cash, by all means buy some pretty

ones to play with, but start off with a few tried and tested plugs, spinners and spoons.

Bar spoons, Colorado spoons, wobbling spoons and wagtails are all proven pike-takers. The first three can carry coloured thread or wool lures as an extra inducement, but not if they interfere with the action.

Plugs can be one-piece or jointed. The best kind is one with an adjustable diving vane at the nose, which can be set to change the plug from a surface worker to a deep diver.

You will, of course, buy more plugs—floating plugs and sinking plugs—to suit particular waters and conditions, but one with an adjustable vane makes a good all-round lure.

As a general rule of thumb, use a light coloured lure in deep or coloured water, or when the sky is overcast or the light is failing. Use a darker lure in clear water or on a bright day.

The size of the lure may often be dictated by conditions. Fishing a small bay, or a narrow patch in the weeds, may mean the use of a small lure. The pike, however, is more likely to stir itself for a larger lure, especially if the pike itself is a respectable size.

Neither spoons nor lures should be too flashy. The plugs which do best seem to be those with the darker coloured backs, and the spoons those which carry a different colour on opposite sides—generally a permutation of green, red, gold, white or yellow.

Worms

If for any reason you find yourself without dead or artificial baits when there are pike about, try working a large lob or a bunch of worms with a sink-and-draw action.

Tackle

There are several custom-built pike rods on the market in hollow glass, generally 10 ft or more in length and with a test curve of $2\frac{1}{2}$–$3\frac{1}{2}$ lb. Don't be tempted to buy the short—6–7 ft—so-called pike rods, especially those made from solid glass.

A MK IV hollow-glass carp rod with a test curve of $1\frac{1}{2}$ lb and a length of at least 10 ft is suitable for spinning and for deadbaiting with medium-sized baits at short range.

For big deadbaits, long-range casting or spinning with really large spoons, you can use a stepped-up MK IV carp rod with a test curve of $2\frac{1}{2}$ lb.

Use a fixed-spool reel. For long-range work a sea reel is best. For lure fishing you can use a multiplier.

A line of 10 lb b.s. will take care of most pike under normal conditions. For work among snags, casting large baits, or for chasing a possible monster, step up to 15 lb or even 20 lb b.s.

Carry a selection of hooks, singles and trebles, with the sizes ranging from nos. 8 to 4. This will allow you to match the hook to the size of the bait and to make up your own rigs for deadbait legering and spinning. Because of the lack of holding places in a pike's bony mouth, many anglers will use only trebles, but single hooks can be used quite successfully with small deadbaits.

Whatever else, the hooks must be sharp. This applies to pike fishing more than any other. So make absolutely sure that the point is sharpened right down to the barb. Take special care when buying artificial lures that the hooks are of good quality. The main fault with artificials is that the trebles tend to be thick in the wire, and have had insufficient attention paid to the finish of the points.

Snap tackle, often called Jardine snap tackle after its inventor, carries two treble hooks a short distance apart on a wire trace. One point of each of the trebles is stuck into the deadbait, leaving the remaining two points on each treble for hooking the fish.

An improvement on the basic Jardine snap is the Ryder hook. This is a treble with an eye at the end and a ring at the

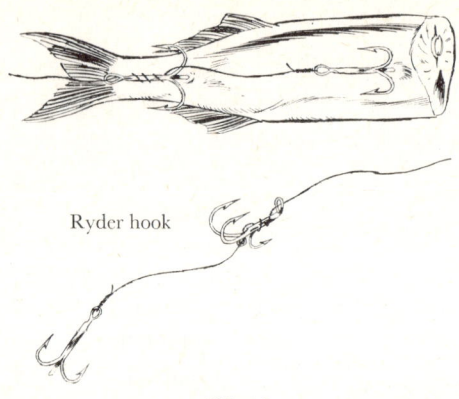

Half herring or mackerel on snap tackle

Ryder hook

FIG. 43

bend of the hook. The Ryder is used as the upper hook on the rig, with the trace passed through the eye and through the ring at the bend of the hook. This enables the hook to be moved up and down on the trace to suit the size of the bait.

All pike fishing should be done with a 2-ft wire trace between hook and reel line. Traces can be bought ready-made, but both braided and single-strand wire can be

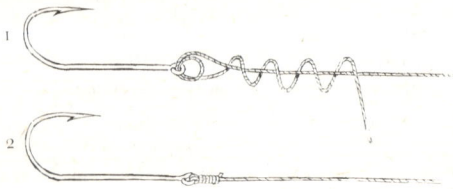

FIG. 44 Fixing a braided wire trace to an eyed hook. 1 Pass the wire through the eye *twice*, leaving about an inch at the free end. Twist the free end tightly around the wire above the hook. 2 Push the turns down tightly towards the eye. Seal with a smear of adhesive.

bought in lengths, as can nylon-coated wire. Which wire you use is up to you. Braided wire tends to fray; single-strand wire tends to kink.

The diagram shows how to fix a trace to an eyed hook. Use a smear of adhesive to stop the wire from unwinding. Nylon-coated wire can be sealed with the touch of a lighted match before being smeared with adhesive. At the other end of the trace, tie on a swivel or split ring in the same way.

For spinning, the trace should be fitted with a swivel at each end (barrel swivel between reel line and trace, link swivel between trace and lure). An anti-kink device should be used. This can be either a half-moon lead clipped to the reel line immediately behind the second swivel, or a celluloid anti-kink vane which incorporates its own swivels.

When choosing floats, the first one to forget is the old-fashioned pike bung; it was designed for livebaiting anyway, and even for that it has dropped out of favour because it offers too much resistance to a taking pike.

Long, slim sea floats are fine for piking. You can make your own with a length of dowel and a couple of corks. A swivel can be added to the bottom ring, or two side rings fitted, to turn it into a sliding float. A sliding float can be made also by substituting the case of a ballpoint pen for the centre dowel. The line goes through the centre of the case, and can be stopped with a drilled bead underneath an elastic band tied on to the line as a stop knot. The simplest of all sliding floats is a small ball-shaped pilot float threaded on to the line and, again, stopped by a bead and a stop knot.

For landing a pike, use a large, small-meshed carp net. Many pike anglers still carry a gaff in case they hook a big fish, but it is surprising how few of them use it properly in the heat of the moment. (The correct way is to slide it under the jaw and lift it so that the point penetrates the thin skin behind the point of the jawbone. Not only is this difficult with a big, thrashing pike, but there is a fair chance of dislocating the jaw.)

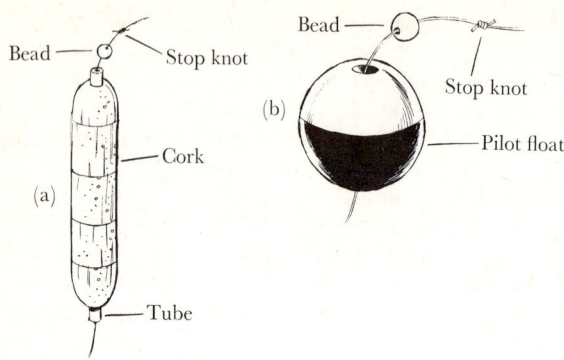

FIG. 45 (a) A sliding float made with a ballpoint case and corks. (b) A simple sliding float.

For disgorging pike, wear a pair of stout leather gloves. Use a pike gag to keep the fish's mouth open, but not the old type with the forked ends. Either buy a gag with flat ends, or file down the point of an old-type gag and cover the ends with adhesive tape. (You do not need those prongs, honestly.) Use the clip on the gag to hold the fish's mouth open to full stretch and no more. Just to slip in the gag and allow it to spring open, unchecked, is asking again for a dislocated jaw.

Carry a long pike disgorger and a pair of long-handled surgical forceps or a pair of special disgorging pliers. You may find yourself working a foot down inside the pike to take out the hooks, so you will need every inch of those long pliers.

Now and again a set of hooks will be stuck irretrievably in the wall of the pike's stomach. Often the kindest thing to do is to cut the trace as near to the hook as you can get, and leave the hook where it is. For this, use a pair of wirecutters whose handles you have lengthened by jamming or soldering them into lengths of metal piping. If you can reach the hook itself, cut through the shank below the eye. You may be able to draw out the hook, barb first. If the barb has not come back through the stomach wall, just cut through the shank or the trace and then leave well alone.

Fishing for pike

The pike will be found where the food is—that is, where the other fish are. The most popular idea of the pike's hunting technique is the ambush, taking up station in or near beds of reed or weed, by underwater obstructions—rocks, masonry, woodwork, or anything else which offers cover or background camouflage. This is generally true of small to medium waters with plenty of different physical features. But on waters such as reservoirs and pits, which are lacking in variety of form and contour, the pike will roam in search of the shoals.

On rivers, the pike is more predictable. Because it dislikes fast water it will take station in bays, eddies, lay-bys, pools at the end of weir runs, and behind any feature—weedbeds, rocks, sunken trees—which slows down the current and offers concealment.

In summer and autumn the pike will hunt or lurk in the shallows. In winter it will move to the deeper water where the other fish have retreated. When a warm spell brings the shoal fish out of the deeps, the pike will follow them—often to indulge in an orgy of feeding which is a gift to the angler. At night, too, the pike will follow the shoal fish, to hunt in the shallows and along the margins.

As well as fish, its diet includes water voles, frogs, ducklings, cygnets and the chicks of coot and moorhen. It will also stoop to scavenging dead fish and small drowned birds or mammals.

Float fishing
A deadbait can be fished off the bottom, horizontally, under a float. Snap tackle is used, with one hook of the first treble behind the gill cover, halfway down the depth of the body,

and one hook of the second treble set just in front of the dorsal fin.

The double advantage of this method is that, firstly, the bait can be set at whatever depth the pike are feeding and, secondly, it looks lifelike, especially if there is any current or wind on the water to move the float. Remember to puncture and squeeze the swim bladder of a freshly killed fish.

Laying on is a sensitive method in still water, and a useful one for fishing on the far side of a weedbed, the float keeping the line clear of the edge of the weed.

The float for laying on need only be big enough to carry the weight of the line or the swivel, providing it can be seen clearly. In deep water a sliding float should be used.

Freelining

A deadbait can be freelined, with the bites registered by dough bobbins, swingtips or buzzers.

Buoyant baits can be used for fishing over weed. With newly killed freshwater fish, the buoyancy is obtained

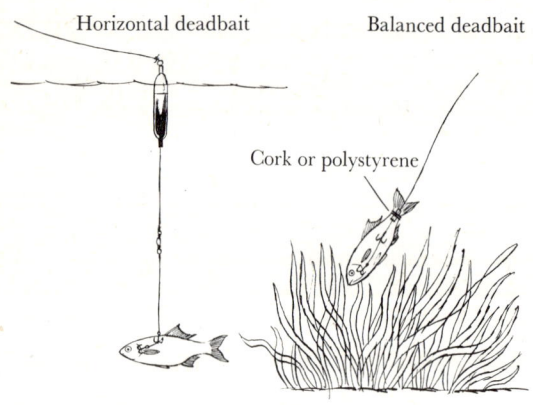

FIG. 46

simply by not puncturing the swim bladder. Where the swim bladder has deflated, or when using saltwater fish, buoyancy can be had by binding a piece of cork or polystyrene to the bait with copper wire or nylon, or by pushing pieces of either material down the throat of the bait fish.

The depth of the bait can be altered by adjusting the amount of buoyant material. The angle of the bait in the water can be altered by moving the position of the material. A bait with the buoyancy placed near its tail will lie on the weed head downwards, as if it were feeding. One with the buoyancy strip at the centre of its body—or pushed far enough into its innards—will lie horizontally. One with the material just inside its mouth, or tied behind its gills, will float head up.

Heavy deadbaits for big pike can put a great strain on the rod if they are cast out in the normal way, so many anglers cast them either by hand or with the help of a forked stick. A deadbait casting stick can be made from a forked branch cut from a hedge. Lay the bait across the fork to throw it.

To cast by hand, take off the bale arm of the reel and hold the trace about a foot above the bait. Throw under-arm and start the swing slowly to avoid dislodging the hooks—and do be careful of those hooks as you throw.

Leger
With larger baits, or for close-range fishing, there is no need to use leger weights; the bait can simply be freelined. But with the smaller baits, say, sprat or gudgeon, or for fishing at a distance or in running water, a leger weight is a great help.

Deadbaits can be mounted on snap tackle or, in the case of smaller fish, with a large single hook pushed through the eye sockets.

If nothing has happened for a while after a distance cast, and you know the bottom is free of weed or snags, try retrieving the bait no more than a foot or so at a time, and letting it lie again for a little while. As well as covering more ground, the occasional movement of the bait may attract the attention of cruising pike.

With all the methods so far described, you can increase your chances of finding pike by using two rods and 'leap-frogging' along the bank. If nothing has happened for a time, pick up the first rod and cast in again on the other side of the second rod. A little later, take the second rod and cast on the other side of the first, and so on. With any luck, eventually you will find the fish.

Spinners, spoons and plugs

Piking with spinners, spoons and plugs is very popular in autumn and winter, when the weed has died back. This enables the lures to be worked with less risk of a snag, and the activity keeps the angler warm in the colder weather.

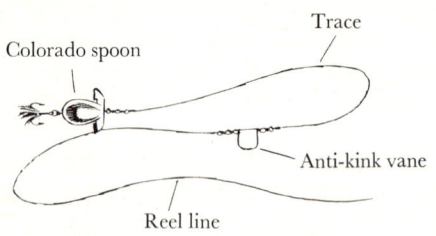

FIG. 47 A spinning rig.

'Deep and slow' is the old pike-spinners' motto. Slow, certainly. Pike are idle and love nothing more than to have the meal come to them. Even more than with a perch, you have to be careful not to outmanoeuvre or outpace the fish. Deep, yes—providing you remember this means fishing near the bottom, rather than fishing in any specific depth of water.

As a general rule you will have better luck nearer the bottom but, like all general rules, it is made to be broken. If the pike are feeding at the surface, try for them there with a floating plug. If they are feeding in midwater, try with a diver.

If there are no obvious signs of pike, you will have to search all the likely places: weeded bays, holes, eddies and around piling, bridge buttresses and underwater obstructions. In lakes, because of the lack of current, pike will be more widely spread than in a river, and a boat is a great help in seeking them out.

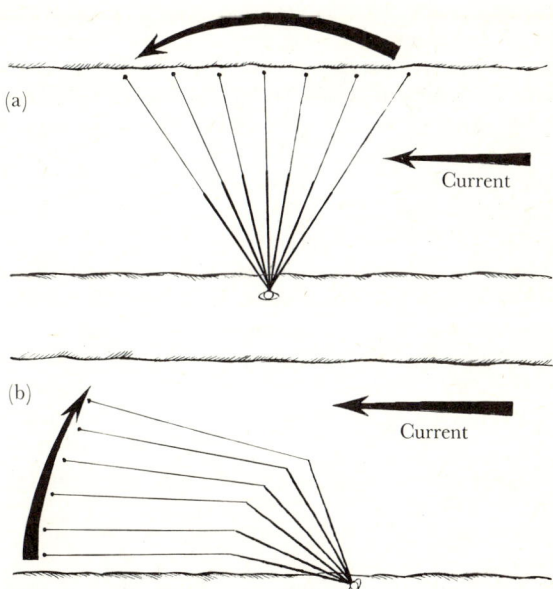

FIG. 48 (a) Spinning on a narrow river. Cast across to the far bank, starting upstream. Make each successive cast further downstream. (b) Fishing your own bank. Fish downstream, start close to the bank, and make each successive cast further out.

On a narrow river, search out as many pike lies as you can reach, starting from the opposite bank with the first cast upstream and working downstream with each successive cast (see Fig. 48 (a)). When you have covered as far downstream as you can reach, move further downstream and start again.

When fishing your own bank, cast downstream and make each successive cast further out (see Fig. 48 (b)). When you have covered that area, again move further downstream and begin again.

When fishing weedbeds and the fringes of bays from a boat, try to anchor the boat out of the sun and to do it quietly. Lower the weights at each end of the boat as slowly and gently as you can, and keep movement in the boat down to a minimum. However big a fish you hook, don't panic, don't hurry and, above all—don't stand up.

To deep and slow could be added 'uneven'. Pike are intrigued by a broken, uncertain action, possibly because the lure looks like a sick or injured fish. The motion of the bait on a basic sink-and-draw can be varied by reeling in different lengths of line at irregular intervals, twitching the rod tip and moving it sideways now and again.

A spoon can be allowed to flutter to the bottom under its own weight, the rod tip being raised and lowered slightly as it falls, producing an effect like a sinking fish making vain attempts to get back to the surface. When the spoon reaches the bottom it can be retrieved with the broken sink-and-draw action.

Whatever lure you use, remember that the main idea is to make it look like a fish in trouble.

On an artificial, don't wait for the pike to run with the bait after the take. The fish will of course drop the metal or plastic as soon as it realises the deception. Strike immediately, hard and sideways, at any sudden stopping of the lure.

Deadbait spinning

Deadbaits can be spun in the same manner as a spinner and using the same terminal tackle, not forgetting the anti-kink vane.

Small deadbaits can be spun on a single hook, pushed either through both lips or both eye sockets. Larger deadbaits will need either the addition of a treble hook halfway down the fish, or the substitution of snap tackle.

A very effective form of snap tackle is the wobbling tackle which gives a more enticing movement to the fish. (There are several forms of spinning flights, now going out of fashion, which make the bait revolve like a metal spinner, but there seems little point in making a real fish spin round and round like an artificial.)

Freshwater fish are best for spinning and wobbling because of the firmer skin and flesh. Don't forget to puncture the swim bladder.

Deep and slow—and uneven—is again the rule. Let the bait sink, reel it in slowly with an uneven sink-and-draw movement, let it drop right on to the bottom, lift it, drop it, reel in a little more . . . and so on, in a series of slow, irregular movements, varied with the occasional twitch from the rod tip.

When a pike takes a spun deadbait you have a little more time for the strike than on an artificial. But don't hang about waiting for the pike to turn the fish. Let him take, and let him run, but as he runs—strike sideways.

Striking and playing a pike

A pike goes through a peculiar ritual when it takes a fish deadbait. It seizes the bait across the body and 'runs' with it for some way. Then it stops, turns the bait head first into its mouth and moves off again. (This does not apply, of course, to artificial lures.)

Many anglers insist on waiting for the pike's second run before striking, but others strike earlier. When to strike really depends on the size of the bait, the size of the pike, how quickly the pike swallows the bait after turning it, and whether the pike has become suspicious of the bait. The only thing you can be sure of at the time is the size of the bait. Too soon a strike, especially with a big bait or a small pike, may pull the hooks clear. Too late a strike, and the pike may have dropped the bait or be hooked far down in its gut.

With a small bait, then, or if you suspect the pike is a big one, let the first run go to a slow count of five, and then strike. With a big bait, let the pike run and stop. Another slow count of five from the end of the run, and then strike.

The bony roof of the pike's mouth gives no hold for a hook, so the strike should always be made *sideways*, firmly and far back, in the opposite direction to which the pike is moving.

Use sidestrain to turn the pike away from the snags it will almost certainly head for. Don't let the jag-jagging of his great head panic you into giving him any slack. Give him *line* by all means, if necessary, but keep up the tension between the rod and the fish.

Many pike are lost when the fight moves to the surface and the fish shoots out of the water with wild, head-shaking leaps. At this stage, there is a risk of the hook being pulled out by a jerk of the fish's head, or of the reel line being broken, either by a jerk or by the pike falling back on top of it. As the fish falls back into the water after a leap, follow it by dropping the rod tip to water level, but still try not to let the line go slack.

Roach

Rutilus rutilus

As the most common angler's fish in the British Isles, the shy and gentle roach was taken for granted until disease and parasites cut its numbers drastically in the second half of the 1960s. Though stocks are now more or less back to normal, the roach's temporary disappearance has given anglers a new respect for it.

It is a pretty fish in a delicate, unassuming way. Its colours vary according to the water. Its back can be grey-green, blue or olive. Its sides are silver, its belly white. Dorsal and tail fins are reddish brown with black edges. The other fins are red and grey. The eye is red, and just above each eye is an orange patch. Anal and dorsal fins are concave.

It is mainly a bottom feeder and the bottom jaw recedes, giving the fish a chinless, timid look.

The roach is widespread over England, southern Scotland, eastern Wales, rare in northern Scotland, the West Country and western Wales. Since its introduction into Ireland at the turn of the century it has been spreading steadily, and in many places has ousted the native rudd. (The situation in Ireland is confusing, because there the rudd has always been called the roach.) It is also common throughout western Europe.

Roach are sometimes confused with rudd, but the differences are quite marked. The rudd's bottom lip protrudes, giving it a bulldog look in complete contrast with the 'frightened' look of the roach. The roach's dorsal fin is set

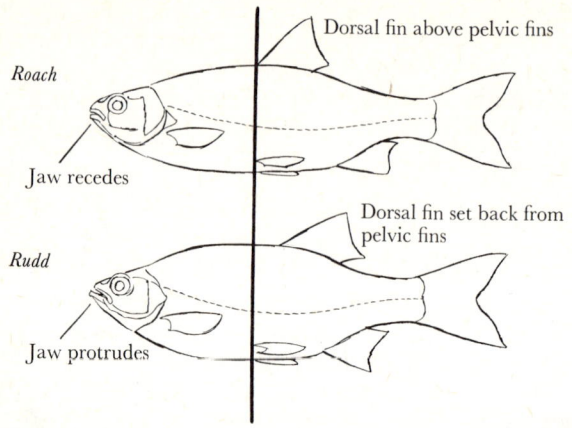

FIG. 49   Roach and rudd.

almost above the pelvic fins, while those of the rudd are set back nearer the tail. The rudd is deeper in the body, more heavily built and much more strongly coloured.

Roach–rudd hybrids are often difficult to identify without expert dissection, so except in the case of a specimen fish, it is best not to go beyond a look at the mouth, the dorsal fin and the general shape of the body. A fish with a receding chin, but with a dorsal fin set back towards the tail—or vice versa—is likely to be a hybrid.

More easily identified is the roach–bream hybrid. The bream's dorsal fin, like the rudd's, is set back much nearer the tail. But the most definite difference is in the number of rays in the anal fin. The roach has only nine to twelve rays; the bream has between twenty-three and twenty-nine. A fish carrying between fifteen and nineteen rays is therefore a hybrid.

Roach are shoal fish and are found in almost every water from dirty canals and pits in industrial areas to clean rivers like the Hampshire Avon. The ability of the roach to survive in polluted water—even though it stunts them—led to the popularity of angling in northern and midland industrial areas and to the start of match fishing.

It is difficult to say what is a typical roach haunt, because the fish is everywhere that food is likely to be. It has a preference for a clean bottom—gravel, rock, sand—rather than a muddy one, likes to be near weed, and in a river tends to stay in the gentler currents. But beyond these preferences—and even then there will be exceptions—it seems quite happy almost anywhere.

The size of the fish varies according to the food supply. Even here there are contradictions: the average size of fish from seemingly identical waters can vary greatly—possibly because of the greater number of predators in one water or another. A water holding big pike, for instance, will almost certainly hold big roach as a consequence of the pike thinning out the smaller fish.

Roach spawn between the middle of April and the end of June, and move into weedy and reedy shallows to do so. They spawn as shoals, often in company with shoals of rudd and bream—hence the hybrids. After spawning they move out of the reeds to clean themselves. In rivers they will move for the summer into the weir pools, tails of mill pools and into streamy runs between the weed—often still in fairly shallow water. In pits and lakes they will patrol the shallows near the weed, moving into deeper holes in the evening as the shallows cool down.

In autumn they seek out the deeper holes, away from the current and colder water. While the leaves are falling, souring the water, and the current is bringing down silt which irritates the fishes' gills, they tend to go off their feed and sulk at the bottom of the holes.

When the river has settled down and the frost has killed off the weed growth, the fish will be feeding again, and feeding heartily. With the weed gone, food will be short, and they will be more than ready to consider your offerings.

A winter or spring flood which moves over the bank and into surrounding fields, will bring the fish themselves into the fields after the worms, slugs and insects being uncovered by the floodwater (see pp. 232–3).

Baits

Groundbait

A bread and bran groundbait, mixed with samples of the hookbait and any of your own favourite flavourings will do nicely. In still water, cloudbait will keep the attention of the fish without feeding them.

Use all groundbait sparingly: roach are nowhere near as big or greedy as bream and can soon overfeed.

Hookbaits

As a general rule, baits for roach should be small. The fish has a small mouth and is a dainty eater. It is also extremely tackle shy, so the small baits should be matched with small hooks and fine lines. Perhaps the one exception to the small bait is the use of a lob when there are likely to be big roach about.

Roach feed on larvae, molluscs and insects in the weeds, and on the weed itself. They also eat insects, grubs, worms and small fruit which find their way into the water from the banks or trees alongside. So there is a wide range of:

Natural baits, such as caddis grubs, wasp grubs, caterpillars, woodlice, dock grubs, small grey slugs—and whatever else you find crawling about the bank are worth a try. Elderberries, in season or preserved, are very successful. Swan mussels can be used, cut into small pieces. Silkweed can be deadly. Bloodworms can be used with a paste bait, or threaded singly or in bunches on a no. 20 hook, and can also be added to groundbait.

Maggots are the most widely used roach bait. Take care to hook the maggot correctly so that it stays alive longer.

Change a maggot as soon as it stops moving. Watch out for 'blown' maggots—roach can suck the inside clean out of a maggot, leaving only the skin on the hook, without disturbing the float by so much as a tremble. Single maggots are more likely to deceive bait-shy roach than an unnatural looking bunch.

Although the roach seems happiest with natural maggots, it will sometimes prefer coloured ones on a heavily fished water. Sometimes when the fish are being really finicky, a pinkie fished on a tiny hook—no. 18 or 20—will tempt it when the larger maggot would not.

The old-time match fishers used to keep maggots under their tongues in cold weather to keep them lively for the hook. A less revolting way of keeping them active is to keep a selection in a small container in your trouser pocket. An empty tobacco tin, well-scoured, is ideal.

Small worms—red worms or brandlings—are excellent bait. So is the tail of a lob, especially under conditions when worms are being washed down naturally from the bank. Whole lobs can be used, hooked about a third of the way down the body to keep them moving naturally, when decent-sized fish are expected.

Bread can be used as crust, flake, paste, small cubes or punched pellets. The paste should be only just stiff enough to stay on the hook and certainly not so stiff as to impede the strike or arouse the roach's suspicions. Think *small*, both for the bait and hook size. Bloodworms can be worked into the paste, as also can cheese, sugar, honey, fish oils, or any other favourite additive.

Casters must be hooked with care, otherwise you may squash them or tear the shell. When selecting casters at the bank, put them in a shallow container of water. Any which have turned into floaters since you left home will, of course, float, and the true casters sink to the bottom. Keep the casters in water until you need to use them to stop them turning into floaters.

Hempseed can be a deadly roach bait where it is allowed. Use with a hook of size no. 16–12 pushed into the split of a cooked grain. Groundbait with hemp as a loose feed, but do not overdo it. Always use freshly prepared hemp; it goes sour quickly and then the fish will not look at it.

Wheat and *tares* are baits whose success varies with the water. Always worth a try if the locals do well with them.

Cheese can be used in small pieces, or mixed with bread to make a paste. Cheese will often tempt roach which have become tired of being offered nothing but maggots or bread.

Tackle

For all-round roach work, a hollow-glass rod with a tip action, between 12 and 14 ft long is about right. Roach are quick biters, so a quick response is essential.

For small roach in numbers you could try the roach pole, which uses neither rings nor reel, but just a length of line tied to the tip. It was the deadly weapon of the old Thames roachmen, but fell out of favour in Britain between the wars. It has since made a revival, helped by anglers on holiday trying it out on the Continent, where its popularity has never waned. A roach pole can be as long as 30 ft.

For river work, or legering, an Avon rod gives the necessary strength and a tip-and-middle action.

Line should be as light as the rod and conditions allow. For slow or still water, $2\frac{1}{2}$ lb b.s. is quite strong enough ($1\frac{1}{2}$ lb b.s. can be used in absolutely still and snagless water). The line can be stepped up to $3\frac{1}{2}$ lb b.s. for snagging or weedy conditions, or for trotting down a briskly flowing river.

You can use a centre-pin reel for trotting if you wish, but most anglers prefer a fixed-spool reel for all roach work.

Keep thinking small when choosing floats: small quill, balsa, reed, cane, cork. Have some antenna floats for windy conditions and a trotting float for river work. For distance casting you will need some larger cork or balsa-bodied floats to support the weight, or a bubble float which will provide its own weight. Small floats in still water should be fastened by the bottom only and made almost self-cocking so that as little weight as possible is on the line.

Hooks can be as small as no. 20 for bloodworms and casters, up to no. 10 for crust.

Leger weights should be very much on the small side.

Fishing for roach

Roach feed throughout the season, being put off mainly by sudden changes—either a drop in temperature or flooding. It is the *change* that puts them off, rather than the conditions: after a few days they get used to things and start to feed again.

Strong light during the day puts them off their feed. As the light fails towards evening, they come back on the feed again. Evening is a good time to try for them under the bank: like carp they come foraging along the margins towards the end of the day. They can also be fished for at night.

In winter, although the fish spend most of the time in the deeper holes, they will often emerge to search the shallows, especially during a mild spell.

Float fishing

Although roach feed in midwater, and at times on the surface, they most often feed close to the bottom. A slow-sinking bait, used with a self-cocking float, can be set to arrive eventually on the bottom. Because of its slow, natural action, it will be taken by roach at whatever depth they are feeding. If you discover that they are taking in midwater, you can adjust the depth of your bait accordingly.

The bait can be fished right on the bottom by laying on, with the shot about 18 in from the hook. Or the laying on can be modified into the lift method by placing the shot only about 3 in from the hook, so that the float rises and lays flat on a bite.

Strikes for still-water roach should be fast—but not hard—as soon as the float moves under the water or, in the case of the lift method, as soon as the float rises.

In moving water, you can use normal trotting-the-stream techniques with the bait just off the bottom. Check the float now and again to make sure that the bait travels in front of it. This also gives the bait an upward lift, a movement very attractive to the fish.

The float can be set higher than the depth of the water for *tripping the bottom*. By controlling the line, the bait will trip along the bottom looking like a piece of natural food. The extra length of the line will allow it to be dropped into any deeper holes along the way. Holding back the float will lift the bait so that it can travel over known obstacles.

In rivers you can try both stret pegging and long trotting. Neither is simply a case of letting the float travel downstream: it should be checked and turned to explore every interesting feature along the way. In stret pegging, where the weight is in contact with the bottom, the float will have to be lifted every so often so that the weight will rise and settle again further downstream. With both techniques the line from float to rod should be treated with floatant.

Strikes on moving water have to be especially fast. On heavily fished waters where the roach have become extra cautious, a strike should be made as soon as the float behaves oddly: whether it dips, stops, moves sideways or simply trembles. When fishing the swim, strike at the end of every run, just in case.

Hempseed fishing needs very sharp striking indeed, for the fish take the grains without hesitation. Use a very small quill, attached bottom end only, so that just the smallest bit of tip shows at the surface. Strike as soon as the float dips. Ordinary split shot can cause false bites, when the fish mistake it for the seed. To avoid this, weight the line with mouse-dropping weights, or a piece of coiled lead wire held in place by a dust shot above and below the coil. Be sparing with the hemp you use as groundbait, throwing in a little frequently rather than a lot all at once.

Once the fish are really feeding, you can try slipping an $\frac{1}{8}$-in piece of black valve tubing on the hook in place of the hemp. The fish will take this quite freely. It has the advantages of staying on the hook, making hookings more certain, and does not need replacing after every strike. When the fish stop feeding on hemp, it does not necessarily mean that they have gone away. They may have simply changed their feeding level. So keep casting with the bait moved to different levels until you find the shoal again.

Float legering
This method is a bit on the clumsy side for ordinary roach fishing, but in deep water it can be a help in spotting bites. A sliding float with the line running through the bottom ring only is the most sensitive one to use.

Legering
Keep the leger weights as small as possible. In still water, the simplest of shot-legers can be used: just a single shop clipped on to the line, 18 in from the hook, to hold it on the bottom. In moving water, always leger downstream.

Bites can be detected in still water by having the line just slack enough to form a curve between the rod tip and the surface of the water. When this curve straightens out, strike. Alternatively, a swingtip or quivertip can be used. The swingtip and quivertip can be used on faster water, or the line can be held between finger and thumb. Faster water is ideal for the rolling leger technique, with all the bites detected by finger and thumb.

Rolling leger can be worked by casting across under the far bank, keeping a tight line and letting the pull of the current move the bait back to the near bank in an arc. Or the weight can be allowed to roll straight downstream as the line is paid out.

Surface fishing

On warm summer evenings roach feed like rudd at the surface. They can be taken with a bait only a few inches under a self-cocking or a bubble float, or by freelining.

Because of the lightness of tackle and bait, freelining for roach is a good bit trickier than freelining for carp or chub. The fish may be close enough in to be reached with a match rod or a roach pole. If not, try a rod with a more flexible action and work it backwards and forwards a few times to build up enough flex in the rod to flick the bait out. Dry fly fishing is also successful with surface-feeding roach (see pp. 100–3).

If the fish are feeding bang on the surface, the line should be treated with a floatant to within a few inches of the hook. If they are a foot or so under the surface, leave more of the line ungreased so that the bait sinks slowly and naturally. The straightening of the floating line, or a dimpling at the point of entry, will indicate a bite. The strike should be immediate.

Roach pole fishing

The roach pole looks clumsy, unwieldy and—because of the absence of rings and reel—primitive. But it works, and is especially effective in deep water close to the bank.

The old poles were made from cane, but modern ones are generally of hollow glass. There are metal poles on the market, but these are too heavy for a long session; even a glass pole can leave you with aching arms and back by the end of the day.

The line is attached directly to the tip of the pole, more often than not via a rubber shock absorber. If the pole ends only in a ring, with no shock absorber, a stout elastic band will suffice.

The pole is fished with the least possible length of line between float and rod tip. The length of the pole is determined by the distance of the fish from the bank. Do not try

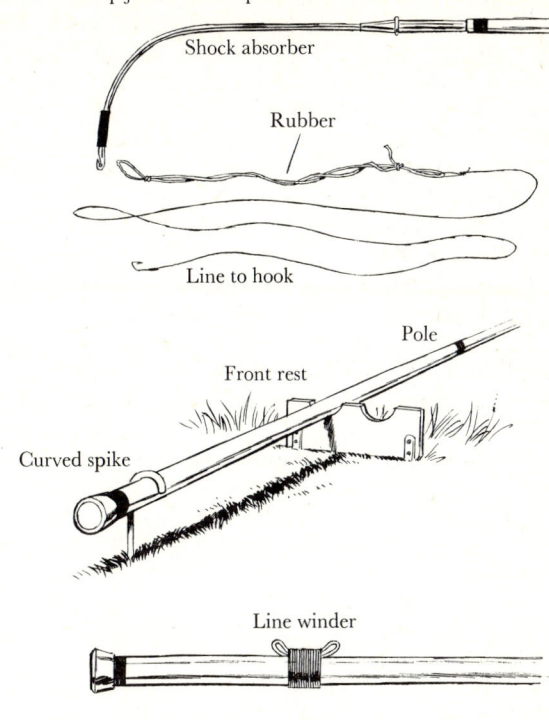

FIG. 50   Roach pole features.

to flick the line out to the fish: add another joint or two until you reach them.

When the length of line from pole tip to hook is appreciably less than the length of the pole, then one or two joints have to be unshipped to land the fish. This might seem tedious and likely to lead to loss of control, but with a bit of practice you will be able to do it automatically.

Telescopic roach poles, in which the joints slide back

into each other, look more efficient and up-to-date than the conventional poles, but they do have their drawbacks. They can telescope when the pole is lifted up, leaving the angler trying to control a fish on a very short pole. Another snag is that the joints cannot be unshipped, so that you cannot set the pole at the length you want merely by removing a section or two, and you cannot use the shortening of the pole to help you land a fish.

A short pole can be held and used like an ordinary rod, but the longer poles are obviously much heavier and need a different striking technique. To fish with a long pole, sit down on a basket or stool. Take the weight of the pole on your knee. Have the left hand in front of you, under the pole, and the right hand back towards the butt. Use both hands for a strike, lifting with the left and pushing down with the right.

The strain can be eased by using a rod rest, but ordinary rod rests are not much good. You can make a front rest from a piece of board or plywood, cutting three or four semi-circular depressions on the top edge. On the bottom edge, fix two or three spikes which can be pushed into the bank to hold the board firmly upright.

For the back rest, use a long spike with a curved top like an umbrella handle, or one with a screw end known as a whirligig. The spike or whirligig is pushed or screwed into the ground and the butt of the pole pushed under the curved top. The butt further along rests in one of the depressions in the board. This arrangement holds the pole securely, while allowing it to be lifted instantly for a strike. The depressions along the length of the board allow the pole to be fished in different positions.

The pole can be fished with float tackle, a free line, or a leger. Groundbait can be put exactly where you want it by using a bait dropper on the line between casts.

To save untying and shortening the line every time you want to change depth, you can whip on a winder made either from two end rings or pieces of wire. The rings should be flattened down to give a shallow angle.

Spare line is stored on the winder. The remainder is wound around the pole from the winder to the tip, and passed through the ring at the end of the pole.

23

Rudd

Scardinius erythrophthalmus

At first sight the rudd looks like the more glamorous sister of the roach. Where the roach's beauty is delicate and understated, that of the rudd is full-blown and colourful, enhanced by an altogether bolder look about the head and body.

> 'A kind of roach all tinged with gold,
> Strong, bold, and thick, most lovely to behold'

was how one anonymous writer of old put it. Indeed, the arguments can go on for ever between the champions of the grayling and the rudd about which is Britain's most beautiful freshwater fish.

The rudd is bulkier than the roach, both in width and depth; weight for length, it is the heaviest British freshwater fish. Its dorsal fin is set further back than that of the roach, and its lower jaw sticks out beyond the upper, to give it a pugnacious expression in direct contrast to the timid look of the roach.

The most striking difference is the colour. From olive green on the back, the colour turns into shimmering golden-bronze on the sides, shading into gold and yellow down to the silvery white belly. The fins are scarlet and the eye is bright red. There is a variety called the golden rudd, which has lemon-coloured fins.

The rudd is common in Ireland (where it is called the roach) but in England it is more localised, being confined mainly to the southern and central parts of the country, and rare in Wales. There is a water in the Lake District which holds some fine rudd, but this is an isolated freak.

Although it is bigger than its cousin the roach, the rudd seems to suffer from competition with it. The roach has taken over in many Irish waters since its introduction.

Rudd–roach and rudd–bream hybrids are quite common. A rudd–roach hybrid can be suspected if the under jaw recedes, or the dorsal fin is set immediately above the pelvic fins, on what appears otherwise to be a rudd.

A rudd–bream hybrid can be identified most readily by the number of rays in the anal fin. A rudd has ten to thirteen, a bream twenty-three to twenty-nine, so a fish with, say, eighteen rays would be a hybrid. As an extra check, the scales along the lateral line can be counted. A rudd has thirty-nine to forty-four scales, a bream forty-nine to fifty-seven. So a fish with, say, forty-six scales is likely to be a rudd–bream.

The rudd is a fish of still or slow water—lakes, pits, canals, reservoirs and the slower reaches of the slower rivers. The Norfolk Broads are classic rudd waters. The Great Ouse and the Nene are two rivers which hold the fish in numbers.

It dislikes acid and thrives in alkaline water, sometimes too well for its own good because of its tendency towards population explosions, which crowd the water with stunted fish. On waters with a good head of pike, the numbers are thinned out and the sizes of the individual fish go up.

The rudd's diet is mixed: weed, caddis grubs, snails, worms, freshwater shrimps, flies and insects and larvae. It will also eat smaller fish, including its own fry.

It feeds in shoals, at or just under the surface, near weed or reed and in sheltered spots out of the wind. Bigger rudd, however, will sometimes feed on the bottom in shallow water. Unlike those of most fish, the shoals are made up of mixed sizes, with the bigger fish lying rear of centre or below the main shoal.

The rudd spawns in shallow, sheltered weedbeds fairly late, from late April into June. It recovers very quickly, however, and is usually in condition by the time the coarse season opens.

It is a fish of the warm weather, going off its feed when the temperature drops below 45 °F. A fresh wind, which cools and ruffles the surface water, can put it off its food. A warm, calm day is best, with light cloud just taking the fierceness out of the sunlight.

In autumn the shoals start to move to deeper water, where they stay for the winter. In winter they feed only occasionally, generally about midday during mild spells.

Baits

Groundbaits

With the rudd feeding mainly between surface and midwater, and seldom below a depth of 4 ft, groundbaiting is hardly the word.

Small balls of cloudbait, dampened just sufficiently to hold it together, can be flicked in at intervals.

Bran, meal, powdered biscuit or maggots can be placed on a floating crust, and the crust set adrift in a slow, circling current. The fine stuff on top of the crust will be washed off, little by little, into the water. The snag here is that, if the current is anything but circular, the crust will go floating off out of the swim, taking the fish with it.

The classic and very effective rudd groundbait—and the complete opposite of the word—is the floating crust, anchored by a piece of thread to a stone.

The swim must be plumbed first, to get the exact depth. The thread should be about a foot longer than the depth to allow the bread to float naturally. The bread should be thick —some anglers use half a loaf—and either stale or toasted to avoid its breaking up too quickly. Tie a twig or matchstick to one end of the thread and push the free end through the crust. Pull the thread through so that the twig is tight against the crust. Tie a stone on to the other end.

Your bait is now ready to be lowered into the swim from a boat. You can use two or three crusts in different parts of a large bay, or bait up several smaller bays. If you have no boat, tie a loop above the twig or matchstick. With the help

FIG. 51

of this loop, poke the bait out over the water on the end of a match rod or roach pole. Lower it gently on to the water and withdraw the rod. If the bait is being lowered gently on to the water, it can be topped with loose dry bait. This will not work, of course, when the bait has to be thrown into the swim if you have no boat and the fish are feeding beyond the reach of the rod.

Do not, incidentally, use nylon thread. It will not rot and will lie about underwater as a snare for unwary water birds, voles or shrews. Use either cotton or paper-based string.

Hookbait samples can be thrown in, sparingly. Maggots can be mixed with casters. The two sinking at different rates stand a better chance of interesting the fish at any given depth.

Bread can be soaked and mashed into a consistency only just this side of sloppy. Bits thrown in every now and again will sink slowly, opening out into attractive ragged-edged pieces as they do so. Or pieces of dry flake can be thrown in, squeezed first to make them easier to throw.

Use a catapult or throwing stick to get your groundbait to distant spots.

Hookbaits

Rudd will take practically any roach bait. Bread—crust, cube, flake, paste—cheese and cheese paste, maggots, casters, hempseed, wheat, tares, small grey slugs, worms—lob, red worm, brandling—bloodworms, freshwater shrimps, bits of swan mussel (bigger than for roach), caterpillars, wasp grubs, spiders, caddis grubs, moths, dragonflies, bluebottles are all welcome. Practically any insect you find along the bank or in the water is worth a try. Artificial flies can be used, fished on ordinary tackle with a bubble float to give casting weight, as can small and shiny spinners.

Tackle

In rivers and canals, or in lakes where the fish are feeding near to the bank, a roach rod or match rod is fine. Where they are feeding at a distance, an Avon rod will give the extra action for the longer casts.

Use a light line—3 lb b.s. is as much as you should ever need—on a fixed-spool reel.

For short casting in still water, use the tiniest self-cocking floats. For longer range work, use the smallest antenna if the surface is being ruffled by wind. Small bubble floats are useful, but can be difficult to see at any distance.

Hooks will vary with the size of the bait, ranging from no. 20 for bloodworms, no. 16 for casters and maggots, no. 12

for a bunch of maggots or a worm, up to as large as 8 for a piece of flake, crust, or a large lob. A rudd's mouth has more gape than that of a roach, so the fish will take bigger baits (and hooks) without any fuss.

Fishing for rudd

A warm day, sheltered and shallow water, and weed are the four main ingredients for success. If the wind is blowing, choose a bay on the leeward side of a lake into which the wind is carrying surface debris.

Look for patches of surface weed, or patches of water lilies. Try under overhanging trees, where the rudd may have congregated to feed on the insect life falling into the water. Look for clouds of hatching or mating flies. Check the margins of reed beds, especially if the outer reeds are moving with a motion suggesting that something below the surface is nuzzling at the stems.

If no rudd are giving themselves away by the rings on the surface of the water, try looking below the surface in likely places with the help of polarised spectacles.

On a river, investigate the slack water, the slow eddies, the bays, the cattle drinks.

Although rudd are not bait-shy, they are angler-shy. So unless you can keep your distance—'fine and far off' was the old dictum—keep low, use all the cover you can find, move slowly and quietly.

On a large, featureless water you may need a boat. Row or drift gently until you locate a shoal. Or try to find underwater humps, banks and bars, and groundbait there. Investigate all the bays in the reed beds.

Keep your boat in the shade, if there is any; if there is none position it so that you do not cast shadows across the shoal, either from yourself or from your rod.

Rudd are not as tough as they look. Keepnet casualties are high, as is the incidence of fungus disease after the slime has been broken by rough handling. So treat them gently and don't confine them for longer than you have to.

Float fishing

For close work, keep the float as small as you can. A tiny quill or plastic float, either self-cocking or made so by a couple of shot clipped on the line either side of the ring, should be attached by the bottom end only. Use no weight on the line below the float, so that the bait sinks slowly and naturally.

If the fish pecks at the bait on the drop, the first sign of a bite will be the float going straight under and zigzagging away. Strike. If the bait has gone down the full distance before being taken, the first sign will be an almost perch-like bobbing of the float. Wait until it goes under before striking.

A wooden controller float attached at both ends, or a small bubble float, can be used to give casting weight to a surface-fished bait. Grease the line from the hook to several feet beyond the float. Do not wait for the float to move before striking: keep your eyes on the floating line beyond the float and strike when it starts to disappear below the surface.

The drag of a bubble float on a take can be eliminated by letting it slide free on the line, held in check by a nylon stop knot 18 or 24 in from the hook.

It sometimes helps to cast the bait beyond the fish, to avoid disturbing them, and to draw it back gently into the feeding area.

Freelining

The heavier baits, such as crust, paste, flake, cheese or large worms, can be freelined. The line can be greased right down to the hook for surface fishing, or the last 18 in or so can be left ungreased to present a slowly sinking bait to a pre-determined depth.

With a free line you can use the trick of casting the bait on to the lily pads. Either drop the line across a pad, so that the bait dangles over the edge a few inches into the water, or get it just to the edge of the pad so that the fish can nose it off; alternatively, tweak it back gently right off the pad so that it sinks down slowly and naturally to the waiting fish.

Legering
Though legering is not over-popular with rudd fishermen, it can be useful in some circumstances. It gives the necessary weight for long casting, and can be used with a link to present a suspended crust, either at the surface or in midwater.

Spinning
Rudd can be taken on small, bright spinners—really small ones, with a piece of red wool as an additional attraction. Try them in shallow water, in clear patches between the weeds. Work them slowly and unevenly. It sometimes pays to let them drop to the bottom and lie there for a little while, starting them in motion again with a few short, uneven twitches.

24

Tench

Tinca tinca

The tench is such an individualist, such a secret creature, that even nowadays it is difficult not to credit it with all sorts of special—if not magical—qualities.

It is a fish of the long, drowsy days of summer, a fish of still and mysterious waters. It seems to make its own rules, and then goes right ahead and breaks them. The ultimate contradiction is the power of its fight after its delicate and deceptive fiddling with the float.

Of old it was credited with all kinds of healing powers. Its 'gallstones' were said to have curative qualities. Such gallstones were almost certainly the otoliths, small 'stones' found in the ear cavities which help the fish keep its balance. Izaak Walton told of 'two little stones' found in every tench's head 'which foreign physicians make great use of'. He went on to write of a reported cure in Rome in which a whole tench was applied to the feet of a sick man. It got short shrift, however, in *The Compleat Angler*. Walton described it as 'a fish I have not often angled for'.

The healing reputation still persists in the legend of the 'doctor fish'. Sick fish—even the pike—were said to rub themselves against the tench's healing slime. In return for this the pike was supposed to grant the tench exemption from its menu. Obviously, nobody has told the pike. Small tench are found quite often in pikes' stomachs and are also used by some pike men as livebait.

In a heavy, chunky kind of way, the tench is a very beautiful fish. Its colour is a deep green-bronze. Its small eyes are an orange-red. There are two small barbels at the corners of the mouth.

The fins are very broad and the tail is thick and muscular. It is this tail which gives the tench its powerful, boring run—a steady and seemingly unstoppable progress to the nearest patch of cover.

The scales are small and the slime abundant and sticky. (To give the doctor-fish legend some credence, it may be that an injured fish knows instinctively that a break in the slime is dangerous—it allows fungus diseases to penetrate the skin—and that it will seek out a slow-moving fish with plenty of slime for a quick repair.)

The tench is distributed widely over the south and midlands, becoming less common north of the Ribble, though some tench are found in southern Scotland. Although not common in Wales beyond the border country, they nevertheless seem to flourish in isolated waters which provide the right conditions. Their numbers are increasing in Ireland, where they are an introduced species.

The right conditions are still or slow-moving water, with plenty of mud, weed and small animal life—worms, insects, larvae, snails. The fish is found in lakes, ponds, pits, canals, and in quiet stretches of some slower rivers. The water need not be too deep: tench seem to prefer shallow water and are quite happy with between 3 and 6 ft.

It feeds on the bottom, in and around the weed. At dusk in summer it will move into the shallows to feed, just as carp do. In colder weather it will move to the deeper part of the water.

Tench congregate in large numbers in the shallows to spawn, splitting into groups of three or four—two or three males and a female—for the actual spawning. Here the tench shows its individuality by spawning later than other coarse fish and shedding the eggs only during warm spells. The female sheds her eggs in batches between

May and July, sometimes carrying on as late as the end of August. After a thunderstorm seems to be a favourite time to do it.

A hearty but selective eater, the tench is assumed to feed generally only in a summer water temperature range of between 58° and 70°F. In the winter it is assumed to sink into the mud and hibernate.

But even these two generalisations are thrown by the appearance of feeding tench in still water in the middle of winter, and the fact that river tench seem not to hibernate at all. For several years there have been reports of occasional quite large tench catches in still water between December and March. River tench, perhaps because they have to keep on the move and consequently replace the energy they use up, are active throughout the winter, feeding in deep holes near the bank.

In still water, however, winter feeding tench are the exception. It is best to assume that you will take them normally only between June and October. But if you ever do see a tell-tale line of tiny bubbles during a mild spell in winter, do not hesitate to tackle up for tench.

The tench's bubbles are unmistakable—and another mystery. A feeding tench releases thousands of very tiny bubbles, which rise to the surface in dead straight lines, just like the bubbles in a bottle of fizzy lemonade. It is still being debated whether these bubbles come from the mud which is being nosed through, or from the tench itself. The bubbles are so tiny, so many, so regular in their size and movement—very different from the big, wobbling bubbles released from the mud by carp and bream—that they are more likely to come from the tench's gills than from the disturbed mud.

No two tench seem to have the same taste in food. You may catch one on maggot, but the next one might look at nothing but a red worm. The fish will also act collectively and refuse to eat at all. Tench waters have a habit of going 'off' for no apparent reason, and just as mysteriously coming 'on' again.

Like the carp and the eel, the tench has a strong hold on life. Once the fish was prized for the table and was carried long distances in wet sacks, arriving alive and well at either market or stewpond. (They can be carried from the water to a garden pond in a loose wrapping of wet moss.) There are reliable accounts, too, of tench surviving hot summers by burying themselves in the mud of dried-up ponds, and reappearing with the autumn rains.

Another strange quality is the great strength of the fish. Is all its power really necessary in still water? It has been suggested that the tench needs its great, muscular tail to move through dense weedbeds—its barrel shape is not so well suited as the bream's for slipping through tall underwater growth—and for digging in the ooze. If that is so, it has a really generous safety margin. With one thrust of that mighty tail, the fish could be into most weedbeds and out the other side. Nor does the tench seem to dig deep for food; it certainly makes far less mess than the piggy grubbings of a carp. Still, whatever the reasons for that tail, no doubt the tench is glad of it—and so is the angler.

Baits

Groundbaits

A basic groundbait of breadcrumbs, bran and sausage rusk, mixed with sand or earth to help it sink quickly without breaking up, will keep the tench busy on the bottom. To the basic mix you can add samples of the hookbait and your own favourite additives. Fish oils—halibut or cod liver oil—or dried blood certainly seem to increase the appeal.

Cloudbait, with additives if you wish, will help lead the fish to the heavier groundbait on the bottom.

Baiting a spot for two or three days previously, or at least the night before, will increase your chances of success. But do not forget to be at the water at first light. Tench fishers get up early and you could arrive to find someone else reaping the rewards of your pre-baiting.

Hookbaits

Although a tench's choice of food is unpredictable, the range of baits it will take is very wide.

Worms—small reds, brandlings, blueheads, lobs—or maggots are perhaps the safest all-round baits. After them comes bread, as crust or flake.

The maggots and smaller worms can be fished singly or in a bunch. The bigger worms are best hooked in two places, so that the fish cannot simply bite off a length.

Wild baits include wasp grubs, earwigs, caddis grubs, slugs, snails and swan mussels. Wheat, peas, sweetcorn, cheese and small parboiled potatoes are also well worth a try.

Tackle

Though the tench is a shy fish, and a fiddly and choosy feeder, it is no use using light tackle. The powerful steady run must be turned before the fish gets into a weed patch.

For both float fishing and legering, the best rod is an Avon: a 10-ft one for legering and a 13-ft one for float fishing.

Even in a clear swim, the line should not be less than 4 lb b.s. and the hook length 3 lb b.s. On a weedy swim, the line strength should be increased to 7 lb or even 8 lb b.s. Camouflaged or smoke-coloured line is a help in overcoming the tench's caution.

Hooks need not be smaller than a no. 10. A no. 8 or even a no. 6 will be more certain of finding a hold in the tench's leathery mouth. (This said, on some hard-fished gravel pits, many tench are taken on light tackle, with no. 18 hooks and $2\frac{1}{2}$-lb b.s. reel line.)

Floats should be as light as possible: quill or reed for

close fishing in the shallows, cork-bodied antenna to take the extra weight for distance fishing.

Leger weights and swimfeeders should be on the small side.

Fishing for tench

You will do best with tench by getting to know a water, either by fishing likely spots over a period or, more quickly, by asking locals or regular angling visitors where the best spots are. You will do even better, once you know the likely places, by preparing them: groundbaiting for two or three days in advance and by dragging a swim the day before.

A typical tench water is fringed with reeds and carpeted underwater with soft weed. To clear a swim, first cut an opening in the reeds so that you will be able to land your fish without obstruction. Make the opening only as wide as you need to play the fish up to the landing net: the reeds left standing will make excellent cover.

You can drag the swim with two garden rake heads bound back to back with cord or wire, and tied to a long length of strong cord. A less expensive drag can be made by wrapping barbed wire around an iron bar, and tying the bar in the middle to a length of cord. Be careful of the wire when you throw the drag out.

Do not drag too big an area. All you need is a cleared path through the weeds, narrowing as it nears the bank. A great, bare gap where earlier there was a cosy weedbed could make the fish suspicious and afraid to venture too far from cover. Put the cleared weed to one side *in the water*. Leaving it on the bank will dry it out and kill all the tiny creatures which live in it, and upon which the tench feed. Sort through the weed for caddis grubs, mussels and snails to use as bait.

This kind of preparation, of course, is not always possible. So on a strange water, or when time is short, bait up a spot at the edge of a bed of soft weed. And keep an eye open for the bubbles.

Tench bubbles are only the size of a pinhead and come up in continuous streams. These bubbles will be the only sign, because tench are not such messy feeders as carp or bream, and do not discolour the water.

Float fishing

Despite the increasing popularity of legering for tench, many anglers still prefer to watch a float, especially as the fish's fiddling makes the movement so fascinating.

In still water the main shot should be just under the float, making it practically self-cocking, with just a dust shot to take the bait down in a natural looking drift. Set the hook about 12 in deeper than the water so that the bait is laying on.

The tench's bite starts with the smallest trembling of the float. This can be caused by the fish gently mouthing the bait, blowing water at it to clear away debris, or by vibrations from the fish's tail as it stands on its head to inspect the bait. Eventually the float will move, perhaps lie flat on the surface, and then slide gently under.

The lift method is a popular and effective one. A small quill is attached at the bottom end only and a single shot set 2 in from the hook at a depth slightly greater than the swim. After the cast, the line is reeled in taut so that just the tip of the float is showing. When the fish takes the bait, the float lifts up in the water and lies flat; then it slides under.

At one time the gospel was to hold the strike until the float went under, but a growing number of anglers are striking as soon as the float lifts. The argument against waiting for the float to go under is that by this time the tench will have felt the drag and may drop the bait. The argument against striking on the lift is that the fish may have only the bait, not the hook, in its mouth. Perhaps the only satisfactory answer is to study every bite, try to work out what the fish is doing, and strike when it feels right.

The results will show whether or not your deductions are correct.

Strike firmly. The tench has a tough, leathery mouth which takes some penetrating.

If the fiddling with the bait goes on for a long time, with no more action from the float than a continued trembling, it sometimes helps to move the bait a few inches. This can make the tench feel that its meal is trying to get away, and make it do something positive—like swallow it. Moving the bait can help, too, when the bubbles are rising all around your float, but nothing is happening to the float itself.

Legering
As there is generally weed or soft mud in a tench swim, the leger weight should be a link of swan shot or an Arlesey bomb attached to a link. The weight can then sink into the weed or mud, leaving the bait on top.

To make sure that maggot or worm baits stay on top of the weed, they can be used in cocktail with a piece of bread-flake or crust.

Legering can be done with a swimfeeder attached about 18 in from the hook. Maggots, of course, will find their own way out. To spread groundbait in the absence of a current, you can pack the middle of the feeder with dry groundbait, sealing the ends with damp groundbait. The water will make the dry groundbait swell on the way down, and it should eventually burst out in a cloud at the bottom. Alternatively, jiggle the rod tip when the feeder hits bottom to loosen the bait.

Groundbait can also be squeezed round the swan shot on a link leger, to fall away when the weights hit bottom.

Bite detection in still water and calm weather can be done by watching the slack line under the rod tip, or with a dough bobbin if there is any wind or current. Strike as soon as the bobbin lifts, because this means that the fish has already taken up the slack line and is moving off.

Float legering

This can be useful when fishing at long range, providing the float is not heavier than it need be for the job. Self-cocking or weighted antenna floats are best. The float will carry most of the weight needed for the cast, allowing the leger weight itself to be as light as possible.

Freelining

Freelining can be deadly when the fish are feeding in the shallows close to the bank. The absence of float and weights means that the bait can be presented with the minimum disturbance and looks absolutely natural.

As in leger fishing, bites can be detected by watching the slack line or by the use of a dough bobbin.

When the day begins to warm up, tench often move from the bottom and, like carp, suck snails from the underside of lily pads. Here the freelining technique can be used to drop the line across a lily pad, leaving the bait dangling in the water a few inches below the surface.

25

Zander

Stizostedion lucioperca

The zander, or pike–perch, is an imported fish whose rapid breeding and growth rate could change the whole angling scene in the British Isles within the next ten or twenty years.

It is neither a pike nor a perch, but a completely separate species. One look at a zander, however, explains why it got the name and why the name stuck. If there ever were a cross between a pike and a perch, this is what it would look like. The zander has a large head and long, almost pike-like body. The two large, spiny, dorsal fins and the striping on the flanks are very reminiscent of perch.

Continental names for the zander include sander, sandel, snockbaar and gos. A related fish in America is known as the sauger, or walleye, and there is a Biritsh record for this, too. (The walleye record was made in 1934; for all practical purposes we can forget this fish and concentrate on the zander.)

The first recorded importation of zander was in 1878, when twenty-four fish were bought from Schleswig and, all but for one casualty, placed in a lake at Woburn Abbey. (The casualty did not die in vain; it was eaten—zander taste very good.)

There were several other imports later and in 1948 some of the Woburn fish were moved to a pit at Leighton Buzzard, Bedfordshire, and in 1951 some to Claydon Lake in Buckinghamshire.

The move which really established the zander, however, was in 1960, when 500 fingerling fish were introduced as an experiment into the Great Ouse Relief Channel. Since then the fish have spread through the drains of the fenland system, and are likely very soon to appear in the Great Ouse itself.

Some anglers welcome the zander for the exciting sport they provide. Others fear that they will deplete the shoals of roach and bream and ruin the existing sport. Many roach and bream caught in the fen drains bear the marks of a zander's teeth.

Baits

Zander will take the small, flashy artificial lure used for perch, and will also go for small spun or wobbled deadbaits. Baits which have proved particularly effective are small legered deadbaits or strips of fish mounted on small (no. 8) trebles.

Tackle

An Avon rod with a 4-lb b.s. line will handle small to medium-sized zander. Where bigger fish are likely to turn up, it is safer to use pike tackle. Wire traces to the bait are needed to survive the zander's teeth.

Fishing for zander

For some reason, zander prefer murky, even dirty, water. They feed best at dusk and dawn. They move in big, wandering shoals and seem fond of margins fringed by reeds.

They are attracted to lures worked with a side-to-side zigzag motion, and will follow a lure right to the bank. When retrieving a lure, keep it in the water until it almost hits the bank. You may get a bite almost at your feet. Another reason for keeping the lure in the water until it gets to the bank is that a lure pulled out close to, or in the middle of, a shoal can frighten the fish and put them down.

Zander appear to prefer small deadbaits or fish strips to larger baits, although their mouths are quite capable of tackling a big bait. Apart from being more attractive to the fish, a small bait means there is no problem about when to strike—as soon as the zander picks it up and runs.

The fight of a zander is unpredictable. Some will put up a fight which would shame a pike. Others seem to give up easily and come tamely to the net.

26

Wading and Boating

Wading

A good pair of waders will extend the range of your fishing quite considerably, taking you that vital 2 or 3 ft nearer to an awkward swim, getting you away from bankside trees or bushes, putting you within accurate casting distance of swims on the far bank, or enabling you to stand in the middle of a shallow river to use trotting tackle more effectively.

Like every other activity on or near water, wading has its dangers, especially in spring and autumn when rivers run fast and deep, or on narrow, high-banked rivers in changeable weather. These dangers can be minimised by learning to wade properly.

The first thing to remember is that wading is not *paddling*. You will be in water far swifter and deeper than you normally experience in gumboots or bare feet. So do not attempt to *wade* in gumboots. They are useless for both grip and depth.

Spend extra money on a pair of good-quality waders rather than take a chance with cheaper ones. The most important part of a wader is the sole. It should either be studded or properly ridged so that it cannot slip forwards, backwards or sideways. It should be equally effective on rock, weed, mud, sand or gravel.

Beware of deep, fast or rough water. A cloudburst a few hours earlier may not have affected the level on your stretch —yet. But it will, so keep an eye open for the first signs of change.

Do not burden yourself with any more gear than you really need. But *do* use a wading staff, scout pole or long-handled landing net, both for support and for probing the next bit of the river bed. The changes in contour can be quite dramatic, especially on a narrow fast river. A probe ahead with a staff may save you from stepping straight into a deep hole or finding yourself on a steeply shelving bank of gravel which will give way beneath your feet.

Take special care on fast *smooth* runs. The very smoothness can mean that the run is deep and powerful. Keep an eye open for weed-covered rocks. Proper soles will be a help on these, but even they are fallible.

Move slowly, using short and deliberate steps, probing ahead with the staff all the time. Make sure that your foot is firmly on the bottom—and that you can feel the grip beneath it—before transferring any weight.

To come out of unfriendly water in a hurry, wade *with* the current. If the only way back is against a strong current, turn *sideways* on to it. Stand still and collect yourself before moving, very slowly, to the bank.

Above all, *don't panic*. If you are really stuck, do not be ashamed of using the old-fashioned, tried and trusted aid to survival—shout for help at the top of your voice.

If your footing gives way and you find yourself suddenly underwater, again—don't panic. You are in trouble, but there are ways out of it. First of all, get rid of everything you are carrying. It may be expensive equipment, but it is all replaceable; *you* are not. As you feel yourself going, suck in air quickly and deeply. Do not flail about or struggle. Let your natural buoyancy bring you up. Kick off your waders. This is difficult, but try. They will be full of water and constitute a surprisingly heavy deadweight.

If you can swim, your troubles should be soon over

If you cannot swim: when your head breaks surface, blow out quickly and breathe in again. Keep your arms down—don't try to raise them unless you are sure of grabbing an overhanging branch or some other firm hold. If you keep your arms down, and do not struggle or panic, you should be able to float until you reach the shallows or are able to grab some firm object—tree, rock, bridgework or piling.

In wading, as in boating, the one sure way of getting out of trouble is—not to get into it in the first place.

Boating

A boat adds to the fun of fishing, as well as giving you access to just about anywhere you choose. It will give you even more fun—and much better results—if you use it properly.

Firstly, and obviously, make sure the boat is waterworthy. Small leaks can suddenly become big ones; a boat which is taking in water is not only uncomfortable but also dangerous. These are obvious points to make, but the obvious is too often overlooked or ignored.

Keep your gear down to a minimum. Rods over 10 ft long are difficult to handle in small boats.

Anchor the boat, whenever possible, in the shade, so that shadows will not scare away the fish. Most small rowing boats have a weight as an anchor. *Lower* this gently over the side from a *sitting* position. If you just throw it over, you can say goodbye to the fish for a while. If you stand up to lower the anchor, you may find yourself in the water with it.

Try not to knock anything against the side of the boat. This is another way of telling the fish to clear off.

Don't be ashamed of wearing a lifejacket. There is nothing cissy about wanting to stay alive. Wear rubber- or rope-soled shoes, never gumboots.

Keep movement in the boat to a minimum. Move slowly and deliberately, keeping low, and if possible with one hand on the gunwale. Never stand up. If you are changing places with a companion, try to do it so that only one of you moves at a time, remembering to keep low and hold the gunwale.

If there are several of you in a boat, don't all crowd to the same side to watch a fish being pulled in.

If you are fishing on commercial waterways, always keep to the right and stay close to the bank. Never cut across the bows of an approaching craft.

Unless you are close to the bank, and a good swimmer, stay with a capsized boat. It will support you until help arrives and can be seen from a distance.

Large open waters such as reservoirs take a great deal of wind and can work up some very choppy surfaces. If this happens when you are out in the middle, head back for the bank with the boat facing directly into the wind. Never turn broadside on.

The Royal Society for the Prevention of Accidents publishes an excellent Water Safety Code, available from RoSpa at Royal Oak Centre, Brighton Road, Purley, Surrey CR2 2UR.

27

Fishing Floodwater

The sight of a river high over its banks, flooding the surrounding fields, is a depressing one, and one you are likely to be faced with several times after the heavy rains of autumn and late winter. (February did not get the nickname of 'Filldyke' for nothing.)

Floods can destroy weeks of observation and patiently acquired knowledge of the river's contours. Chub holes are filled in with a tangle of vegetation and muck, or gouged out into great, scoured arenas. Gentle shallow runs are stripped of their oozy beds overnight. Overhanging or protruding bits of bank suddenly are not there any more.

The fish themselves, for a little while anyway, are in no mood for food. The heavy suspension of silt irritates their gills and their main concern is to get out of the way of it.

Before the river rises to bank height, you can try for the fish in the holes out of the main current. Lay-bys, cattle drinks, deep holes and eddies, sheltered spots behind rocks or piling, eddies at the mouths of side streams—anywhere, in fact, which is protected from the main rush of water. Unless the spot is really protected, float fishing must give way to leger. If the bottom is covered with a layer of soft or tangled debris, then link leger or running paternoster may be the answer.

When the river rises above its banks and spreads into the fields, the situation looks really hopeless. But here you have, if anything, an even better chance of finding the fish. Roach, dace, chub, will be *in* the fields, following the flood line for the rich pickings of worms, slugs, snails and insects. Perch and pike will have followed the foragers to see what they can pick up.

Baits for this shallow water should match whatever the fish are likely to find: slugs, worms, beetles, woodlice, or any other insect in evidence. If the water is still enough, you can try freelining or fishing with a small float. Or you can use a link leger, keeping it on the move and exploring as much of the area as you can.

Spinning in the shallows is not much use: there will be too many snags in the grass and vegetation underneath. But you could take a chance on finding a pike with a floating plug or a legered deadbait. Perch will be quite happy to come across a worm.

Before attempting to fish a flooded field, it is vital to find out exactly where the bank is, and what ditches and hollows are concealed by the water. Do not do any wading without probing every step of the way in front of you with a stick or landing net handle. Move slowly and do not transfer the weight to the leading foot before you are sure it is on a firm base. However well you think you know that particular bank, do not assume that you are moving on firm ground. Apart from the fact that a great spread of water can mask all the familiar landmarks and confuse your sense of place and direction, whole chunks of bank may have been completely washed away.

If the results of fishing the floodwater are not very encouraging, you can console yourself with the thought of what will happen when the water starts to go down. When the suspended silt settles on the bottom, the fish come back good and strong. The river bed is now one gigantic table of food, with holes lined inches deep with animal and vegetable deposits. Get your bait down there at this time, and the bites should not be long in coming.

28

Care of Your Catch

As we said earlier, a certain amount of cruelty is involved in angling. Maggots and worms certainly do not like being hooked. Nor do fish.

But a fish which is cleanly hooked, properly played, properly netted and unhooked, does not suffer a great deal. Fish which have been returned immediately to the water have often reappeared with the very next bite.

Although fish undoubtedly feel pain, their receptivity to it is nowhere near that of warm-blooded mammals. A fish's mouth is not a delicate, sensitive structure like ours. A well-set hook will pierce little more than either skin or gristle. In fact, fish suffer far more from unskilful handling and from being crowded into keepnets, than from the actual penetration of the hook.

What can we do to make their experience, if not pleasurable, at least not so painful?

Start with the strike. This should be enough only to set the hook, certainly not enough to dislocate a jaw or to heave a small fish clean out of the water. Wherever possible, just a quick turn of the wrist.

Timing of the strike is important. If a fish is allowed too long to run with the bait, the hook may go home into the lining of the throat or the stomach. Perch especially, after a few sucks and blows, have an unfortunate habit of taking the hook right down. So wherever possible, try to imagine what the fish is doing under the surface and strike as soon as you feel confident that he has taken the bait.

Playing a fish is a pleasurable experience. But do not drag it out unnecessarily. Once the fish is under control, turn it to the bank and net it. Do not let it charge up and down the swim until it is absolutely exhausted.

Good netting technique is important. Remember always to have the net in the water and to draw the fish over the net. Don't bring it in and then attempt to jab the net under it. Not only may this frighten it into a desperate leap which could break the line, but it can also scrape off a patch of protective slime and a dozen or so scales.

Gaffing is out. The only coarse fish for which it can be justified is the pike, and then only for big pike, and *then* only if the gaffing can invariably be done properly through the skin behind the point of the pike's lower jaw. Few anglers, faced with a big thrashing pike, can muster the necessary skill or coolness.

Handle the fish properly. The protective slime is the fish's defence against waterborne fungus diseases. Once the slime is broken, the fish is in danger of a fatal infection. So always handle it with a *wet* hand. Many anglers advocate using a wet cloth. But however smooth the cloth, the weave will always take some kind of hold on the slime. With a smooth, wet hand, the danger of slime removal is far less.

Take out the hook as gently as you can; do not just twist, jerk or rip it out, however impatient you are for the next fish. As well as the conventional disgorgers, always carry a pair of needle-nosed pliers or artery forceps.

If the hook really is deep down, perhaps through the intestine, and its removal is obviously going to injure the fish beyond recovery, then you must kill it. But kill it properly.

A small fish can be killed by quickly snapping its head back. Larger fish should be killed with a blow behind the head from a priest or similar object heavy enough to do the job in one. The old mild steel rod rests were generally heavy enough to deal with, say, a medium-sized perch, but today's light alloys are not. So carry a priest as part of your tackle even though, hopefully, you will not have to use it more than three or four times a season.

If you can bear to, return a fish to the water straight away without a spell in the keepnet. If you want to photograph the fish, try to do it quickly and out of the direct glare of the sun. If you are photographing a group of fish on the ground, soak the ground first.

If you are weighing a fish on a spring balance, do not stick the hook under the point of the jaw, and certainly *not* under the gill cover. Put the fish in a plastic bag and weigh it bag and all. Plastic bags weigh next to nothing, but if you are anxious to be exact to the nearest dram, weigh the bag by itself later and subtract it from the total. Use a plastic bag even if you are weighing on scales. It keeps handling down to a minimum and prevents the fish flopping out of the pan and injuring itself.

Use as big a keepnet as you can afford, however ridiculous it may look with only a couple of forlorn tiddlers swimming about in it. Knotless micromesh is far less likely to damage the fish than the conventional knotted large mesh.

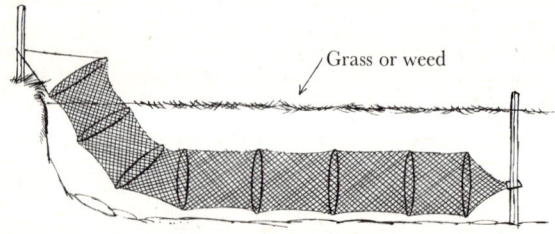

FIG. 52 Staked out keepnet.

Put the keepnet in the water before you start fishing, in a shady place with, if possible, a gentle current. Stake it out at each end so that it is held fully open. If there is no shade on the water, use your fishing umbrella to provide some, or spread some floating weed or grass on the water. Big fish like carp, pike and barbel are best kept in large open-weave sacks rather than nets.

Don't overcrowd the net. As soon as you can afford it treat yourself and the fish to a second one. Don't mix perch or pike with other fish. Apart from the fact that you might find yourself a few fish short at the end of the day, the perch's dorsal fin can do some real damage in a confined space. And if you have caught some crayfish for bait, don't keep them in the net with the fish. Either the fish will eat the crayfish, or the crayfish will gang up on a small or injured fish and finish it off.

When first placed in the net—*placed*, not thrown—fish will often turn belly up and float around upside down for a minute or so, but it seldom takes them long to recover. If they persist in this, however, take them out and return them to the water, first 'walking' them to get some oxygen into their gills. To 'walk' a fish, hold it gently but firmly, head upstream, and push it at a steady pace against the current. The flow of water over the gills brought about by this is usually enough to liven up a fish well inside a couple of minutes.

Look into the net regularly, without lifting it if possible, to check on the condition of the occupants. Take out any which seem to be distressed, 'walk' and release them.

In any event, empty the net halfway through the day's fishing. Remember that not only are the fish in cramped, unnatural conditions—possibly losing slime and scales and going short of oxygen—but they are also unable to feed.

To release the fish, lower the open end of the net into the water, gently lift the other end, and let the fish find their own way out. It is amazing how many anglers look after fish quite well until the time comes to return them. Then they will lift them out one by one to gloat over them, and send them sailing through the air to belly-flop back into the water.

All this might seem a lot of trouble to take over a few fish. But those fish, treated properly, will stay alive and healthy, and be there to catch another time. Apart from the purely practical considerations, they will have given you a lot of enjoyment: the least you can do is to see that they don't come to any lasting harm by it.

29

Care of Your Tackle

Modern fishing tackle—glass-fibre rods, artificial fibre lines, nylon keepnets, plastic floats, plastic reels—does not need the same scrupulous care as did cane rods, silk lines, gut casts and string nets. It may not need the *same* care—but it still *needs some*.

Too often it gets none, and the result in time is, at best, a tackle box filled with broken odds and ends and smelling like a drain; at worst it is a jammed reel, frayed line, broken rod—and lost fish.

The close season is the time for a thorough overhaul of all your tackle, and a discarding of anything which is beyond repair, but the best maintenance of all is that carried out after every trip.

Bait containers
Care of bait containers starts at the end of every day's fishing with the discarding of surplus bait.

Don't just tip all the surplus bait into the water. You could distract the fish from another angler's swim, or foul the water.

If other anglers don't want your surplus groundbait, take it home. You can leave it out for the birds or tip it on to the compost heap. Don't attempt to keep wet groundbait for the next trip; it turns sour very quickly.

If your maggots are not fresh enough to last until next time, kill them by pouring boiling water over them. Put them in a bucket to do this—boiling water can turn a plastic bait container into a very funny shape.

Don't throw either maggots or casters on to the garden. Those that escape the birds will visit you later as bluebottles. Tip worms back on to the flowerbed, or into the wormery. They will be easy enough to dig up next time, and far healthier than if they are left crammed together in a tin for a week.

Wash the containers in warm, soapy water, and rinse clean under the tap. Discard any plastic containers which are cracked, or any metal ones showing signs of rust.

Landing nets and keepnets
Nets made of artificial fibres do not rot but they certainly hold enough water, even after a thorough shaking, to dampen everything else in the basket and to rust metal rings or frames. They also hold enough mud, slime, fish scales and bits of weed to set up a powerful smell and support a healthy growth of mould.

So wash out the nets under a running coldwater tap—without any soap or detergent—and hang them on the washing line to dry.

Lines
Artificial fibre lines will take a lot of punishment, but they are not indestructible. After every trip, cut off the last foot of line. This will have been weakened by knotting and taken a lot of abrasion from sand, grit, and even fishes' teeth. If you spot any weakening or chafing further up the line, cut off more.

Wind the line on to an old-fashioned line dryer. Run it through a damp cloth as you wind (no soap or detergent) to get rid of any grit, mud, slime or weed. Leave it overnight to dry out thoroughly.

This ensures that no bits of grit are left to work their way into the coils and fray the line, or drop down into the reel mechanism; that the reel is not left wrapped in a damp bundle which could cause rust; and that the line has a chance to recover from the coiling caused by being wrapped around the spool.

Hooks

Discard hooks of size no. 16 and smaller after every trip. Sharpen larger hooks with a piece of emery paper or small sharpening stone before you start fishing. However sharp a new hook may look, or feel, there are few which do not benefit from this extra attention.

After using a tied hook, examine the cast for any chafing, or for compression from a split shot. Discard any hooks with weaknesses in the cast, any which have been bent, or any showing signs of rust.

Give sound hooks a sharpening before you put them away, and make sure that both they and the packets are completely dry.

Plugs, spoons and spinners

Wash them to get rid of slime, grit or weed. Sharpen the hooks. Dry thoroughly before putting away. Protect the hook points with bits of cork.

Floats

Wash under running cold water all the floats you have used, and dry them thoroughly. Discard any which have been bent or broken unless you really mean to repair them. (Most anglers' tackle boxes are cluttered with dozens of broken or damaged floats which they mean to repair one day.)

Replace any split or damaged rings. Rubber and soft plastic rings are often cut into by the line.

Rod rests

You will doubtless have swished them around in the water to get rid of most of the clinging mud. There is bound to be some still left, so wash and dry them, rubbing down any rusted parts with emery paper, and straighten out any bends.

Reels

Reels are best kept in individual drawstring felt or cloth bags to keep out dust and grit.

Back home, after taking off the line, wipe down metal reels with a lightly oiled rag. Give a drop of oil to the works inside. If there is any evidence of grit in the works of a metal reel, take it to pieces and clean and oil each piece. A dunking in methylated spirits will ensure complete cleanliness. Oil at the points shown in the manufacturer's leaflet.

With plastic reels, or reels containing plastic parts, follow the manufacturer's cleaning instructions to the letter—plastics can be affected by cleaning spirits which are completely harmless to metal.

Whether or not you have the leaflet showing the parts and order of assembly, *do* remember to lay out the pieces in the order in which you remove them. Otherwise, you may assemble the reel and be left wondering what to do with the couple of bits left over.

Rods

Most rods nowadays are of glass, and not subject to 'setting' (bending in one direction, particularly the top joint) as cane rods are. Nor are they liable to split, or to be covered in varnish which eventually cracks. Nevertheless, they should still be given very much the same care as a cane rod.

Wipe off slime and grit, paying particular attention to the rings, whippings and ferrules. Sticking metal ferrules should be parted by gripping the ferrules themselves, not the rod sections. A pair of rubber gloves will help give a better grip. When the ferrules are parted, the male ferrule should be given a rub with a piece of candlewax.

Spigot joints give very little trouble, but they too should be cleared of every trace of grit to avoid jamming.

Rings should be inspected for damage which could fray the line. Roughness or rust on metal rings can be eliminated with emery paper, but any which are badly pitted or scratched should be replaced, as should broken agate rings. Agate rings can be protected in transit by pushing a small piece of cork through the centre. Check the alignment of the rings and straighten any which have been bent out of position.

Cane rods should be given an extra check to make sure that the varnish is sound. Small chips or scratches can be repaired with a dab of nail varnish. Make sure the joint is absolutely dry before you do this, otherwise you seal water in.

If the varnish is really damaged, all of it should be removed from the affected joint with varnish remover. Then the joint should be rubbed down with a piece of fine emery paper, and given a new coat of *matt* varnish. If the rest of the rod has a gloss finish, it is well worth cleaning the whole lot off and replacing it with matt.

'Set' in a cane rod is caused by long use—or misuse—or simply by leaving the rod in one piece resting against a wall. You can attempt to cure it by transferring the rings on the affected joint to the other side, but this is seldom satisfactory. Best thing is to buy a new rod.

Cane rods, and glass ones for that matter, should be kept stored either in the bag, with the flap open and the side ties undone, hanging upright away from the wall in a cool, dry place; or laid in the bag, again with flap open and ties undone, on a shelf or across a series of wall brackets. (A series of wall brackets, not just one at each end.)

Keep everything else away from the rods. It is easy to forget that they are there, and to prop other tackle against them, or dump it on top of them.

Waders and gumboots

Mud, slime and cow dung which is left on to dry will be much more difficult to remove later on. Not only that, cow dung or mud from acid soils can perish the rubber if it is left on. So scrape off as much as possible with a blunt knife, then wash off the rest in lukewarm soapy water. (Not in the sink, please—use a bucket outside if you want to stay popular.)

Waterproof clothing

Outer clothing collects plenty of slime, especially if you have been dealing with bream, tench or eels. Give the clothing a sponge down before hanging it up. Best is to hang it in the bathroom overnight to dry out thoroughly before hanging it in the wardrobe or bundling it up and throwing it in the cupboard.

Odds and ends

Every now and then, and certainly at the end of the season, go through your basket or tackle box and throw away everything which is broken, damaged, frayed or rusted beyond repair. The possibility that a thing may come in handy one day, or may last for another few trips, does not warrant its retention. Be ruthless. Throw away and replace. If you don't, you could find yourself next season wondering why you don't hook so many fish—wondering, too, why you are losing so many that you do hook.

Tackle You Can Make

Throwing stick
A throwing stick for groundbait can be made from an old garden trowel and the bottom joint of an old rod (see Fig. 53).

FIG. 53   Throwing stick.

Throwing tube
A throwing tube for maggots or casters is simply a piece of thick bamboo sawn off about 3 in above a joint. This leaves a hollow which is filled with maggots or casters. With a flick of the wrist the bait can be thrown quite a lot farther than by hand alone.

Spoon
A spoon can be made from . . . a spoon (see Fig. 54):

1   Cut off the bowl of an old spoon and file the cut edge smooth.
2   Drill a hole near each end.
3   Fix a split ring in each of these holes.
4   To the ring at the broad end of the spoon, fix a treble hook. To the ring at the other end, fix a swivel.

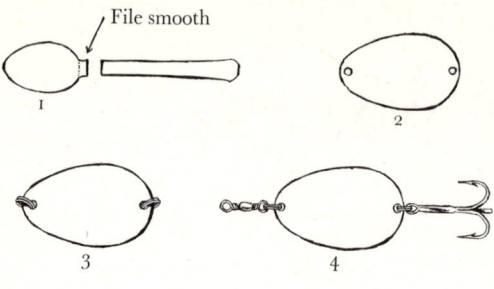

FIG. 54

You can also make a spoon from a sheet of soft metal such as copper. Cut out the shape and smooth down the edges. With a hammer, beat it into the bowl shape. (This also gives one side of the metal a different texture from the other.) Drill the holes and fix the rings, hook and swivel.

Plug

Make a plug from a length of wood (a broom handle will give you enough wood for a dozen or more):

1 Cut the basic shape (see Fig. 55) and sand it down.
2 Cut a slit under the nose and insert a metal or plastic diving vane.

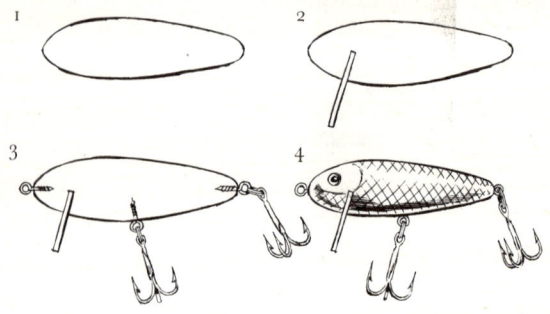

FIG. 55 A plug.

3 Fix the hooks with screw eyes. Use a screw eye in the nose to attach it to the line. Make sure the hooks do not overlap each other.
4 Paint and varnish.

A jointed plug is almost as easy to make. Use a split ring to join the two screw eyes in the centre (see Fig. 56).

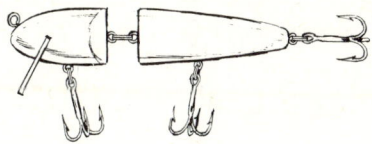

FIG. 56 Two-joint plug.

A slow-sinking leger weight
1 Shape a piece of cork and cut a groove all the way round the body (see Fig. 57). Cut a hole in the bottom big enough to take a swan shot.

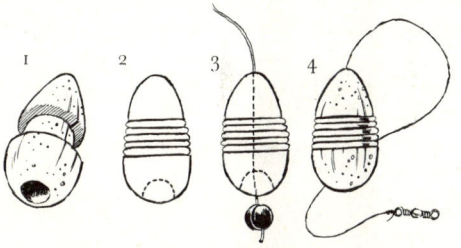

FIG. 57 Slow-sinking leger weight.

2 Wrap lead wire around the groove.
3 Clip a swan shot on to the end of a length of nylon. Thread the nylon through the cork, from bottom to top, so that the swan shot finishes up in the hole in the bottom. Seal in the shot with a mixture of glue and cork dust.

4 At the other end of the nylon length, at a distance of 9 or 12 in from the cork, fix a swivel.

Open-ended swimfeeder

An open-ended swimfeeder can be made from a plastic hair roller and a strip of lead (see Fig. 58):

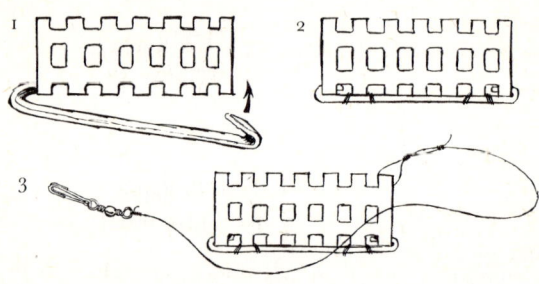

FIG. 58 Open-ended swimfeeder.

1 Bend the ends of the lead strip over to grip each end of the roller.
2 As an additional precaution, tie the strip to the plastic with nylon or fine wire.
3 Tie a link of nylon to the roller. At the other end of the roller, add a snap link swivel.

Bloodworm rake

An aluminium strip about 18 in long is bent at right angles 6 in from one end. The short end is fixed to a 5-ft length of wood.

The rake is drawn through the mud of a pond or ditch with a scythe-like action, collecting the bloodworms on its edge as it goes. The bloodworms are wiped off the blade into a bucket of water and collected by straining through a nylon mesh.

Floats

The simplest is a *quill float* (see Fig. 59):

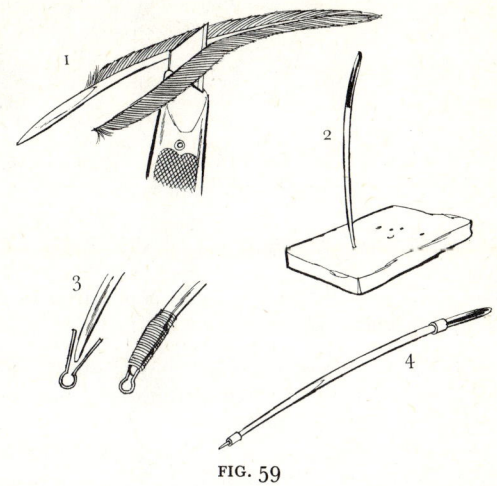

FIG. 59

1. Take a wing or tail feather—anything from a crow to a swan depending on the size you want—and shave off the flights.
2. Paint the top with fluorescent paint (usually over a white undercoat). Stick the other end in a piece of cork, polystyrene or old bread crust, to allow the top to dry. Then repeat the process for painting the other end.
3. If you want one, whip a wire ring to the bottom. Then varnish the whole thing.
4. You may prefer not to have a bottom wire ring, but to use valve tubing both top and bottom.

A *sliding float* can be made by pushing a centre tube—stiff plastic tubing or a ballpoint case—through a bored cork or balsa body (see Fig. 60). The whole thing is then painted and varnished. The float is stopped by a stop knot or split ring on the line above it.

250 *Coarse Angling*

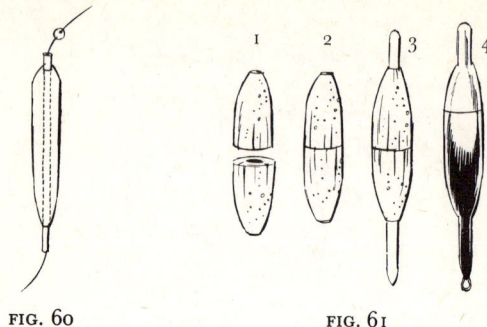

FIG. 60 FIG. 61

A *cork-bodied* or *balsa-bodied float* can be made with a centre stem of cane or reed (see Fig. 61):

1 Two pieces of cork or balsa are shaped and drilled.
2 Glue is squirted down each of the bored holes and the two pieces are glued together.
3 The cane or reed is pushed through the pieces.
4 When the glue is absolutely dry, the body of the float is sanded, the bottom ring whipped on, and the whole thing painted and varnished.

Target board
A target board, for use with a swingtip, needs only a pointed stake, a piece of board and some paint. Nail or screw the board to the stake and then paint on a target pattern.

31

Some Useful Knots

A few simple knots will see you through most freshwater angling situations. Practise them at home with thick string to get used to the sequence of left-over-rights and so on, before you graduate to nylon. It is worth practising until you can do them blindfold, because on a dark day by the bank you may literally be unable to see the nylon you are knotting.

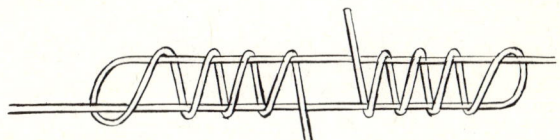

The four-turn blood knot – for joining two lengths of nylon

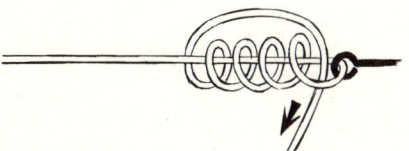

The four-turn half blood knot – for attaching nylon to swivels and eyed hooks

FIG. 62

252 Coarse Angling

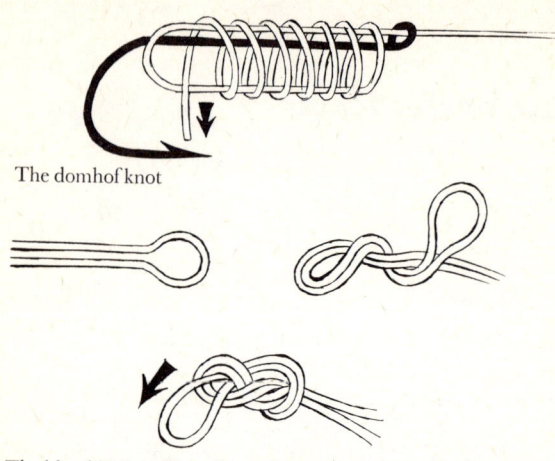

The domhof knot

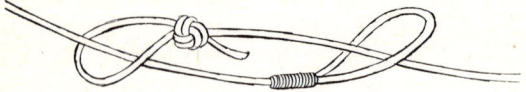

The blood bight – for making a loop on a cast or reel line

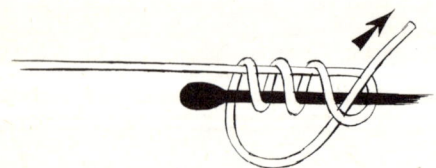

The two-loop knot – for attaching cast to reel line

The spade end knot – for spade end hooks

FIG. 63

Some Useful Knots

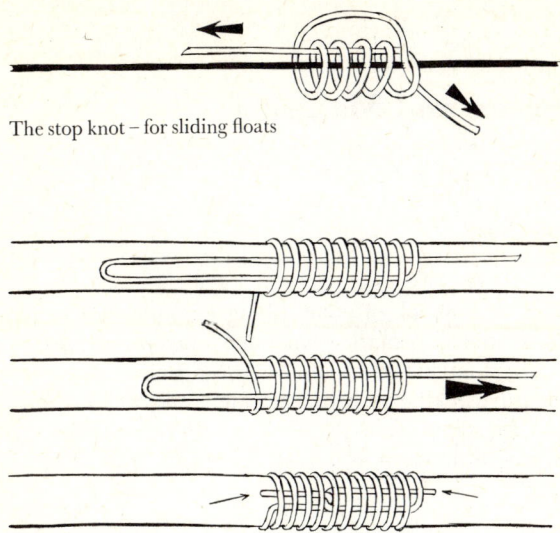

The stop knot – for sliding floats

The whipping knot – for tying rings to rod. (The drawing has been much simplified for clarity. More and tighter turns are needed).

FIG. 64

32

Logging and Mapping

A diary or logbook of your fishing activities comes in very useful as the information on particular waters, particular fish or particular techniques begins to build up.

Record the kind of fish you catch, the weight, location, depth, bait, time of day, state of weather, direction of wind, air temperature and water temperature. You may find a

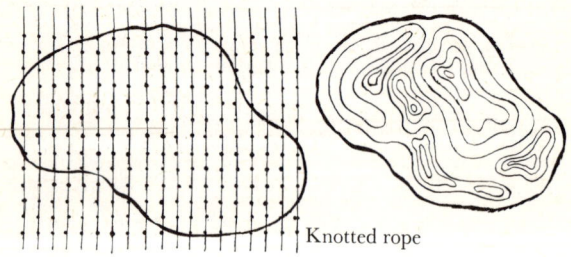

FIG. 65   Charting the bottom with a plumb line. Marks of the same depth are joined up to give an underwater contour map.

pattern beginning to emerge which helps to plan future fishing tactics. Apart from that, it is interesting to look back over a season and remember the triumphs and disasters with more accuracy than your memory can provide.

Mapping your regular waters is well worth while. Note the

position of weedbeds, banks, bars, underwater obstructions, runs under trees and undercut banks.

Take samples of the bottom by smearing a plummet with petroleum jelly. Take samples of weed with a rake, a home-made grapnel, or by running an old spinner or plug through the bed on a heavy line. As well as identifying the weed, sort through it to find out what insect life it contains.

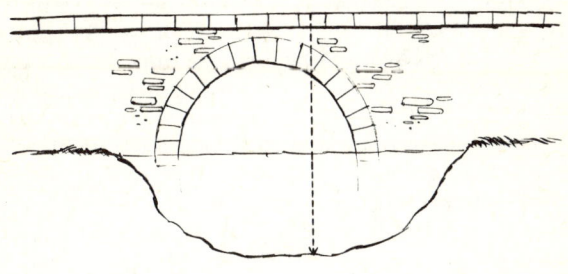

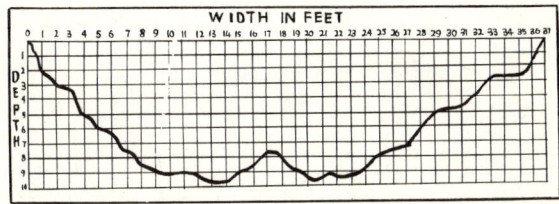

FIG. 66 Measuring depth from bridge. The depth is measured from the top of the bridge at 1-ft intervals. The height of the bridge above the surface is then deducted from the figures to give you the depth chart (below).

You can get a very detailed contour map of the bottom by using a plumb line from a boat. If the water is narrow enough, tie a rope or cord from bank to bank with knots or strips of cloth tied every 2 ft. Take the depth at every knot. By moving the rope 2 ft further down the bank and repeating the operation until you have covered the whole stretch of water, you will have a map in which the depths are marked as dots at 2-ft intervals. Join the dots of the same depth to give you your contour map.

If the water is too wide to allow the use of a rope from bank to bank, put up a marker on the far bank and keep the boat in line with it. The distance between the points at which the depth is taken can be gauged by tying one end of a knotted rope to the near bank and paying it out one knot at a time from the boat. At every knot, take the depth, keeping the boat in line with the marker on the far bank.

When you have run out of rope, and if the depth allows, push a pole into the bottom, tie the rope to that, and start again, always keeping the boat in line with the marker.

If the water is too deep to allow the use of a pole, switch the positions of rope and marker, and start plumbing again from the far bank. With luck, the double length of rope might

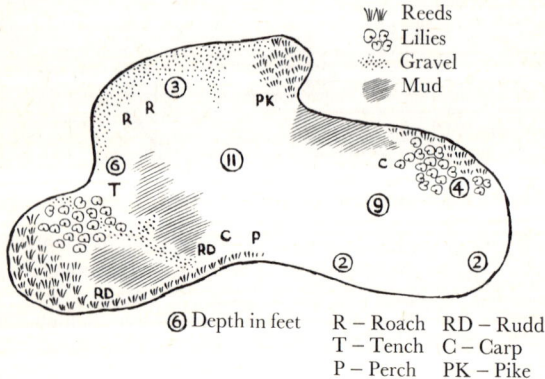

FIG. 67 A useful record of a water is one which gives details of vegetation, bottom conditions, depths and the locations of different species of fish.

Logging and Mapping 257

overlap in the middle. If not, your distance measurements for the remaining stretch of water will be a bit hit and miss.

Taking depth measurements from a bridge is easy. Make chalk marks every foot along the parapet. Plumb the depth of the water from the parapet at every mark. Transfer the depths on to a piece of squared paper, remembering to deduct the height of the parapet.

Another map can show the position of past catches of fish and their weights, with any other information (in symbol form) for which there is room.

The best time for making contour maps is, of course, the close season. Nobody is disturbed by your activities, and the beds of weeds will be well grown (in winter, they all die back).

33

Anglers' Manners

It might seem strange, if not pompous, to have a chapter on manners in a fishing book. But angling has its own codes, as does every other sport.

All manners mean, in any situation, is consideration for others. With the increasing number of anglers, and the decreasing number of fishable waters, this consideration becomes more important with every year that passes.

Let's start with simply getting to the water. Not all that long ago a motor car was a relative rarity. Anglers got to the water on foot or by bicycle, or a group of them would share one car or a coach. Parking was no problem.

Nowadays, scarcely a week passes without some mention in the angling press of friction caused by inconsiderate parking. Farmers or landowners who have allowed a club to use a stretch of water find cars blocking lanes, masking gates, holding up tractors, hemming in herds of cows. If the situation does not change after a few warnings, patience is exhausted and the club finds itself short of a water. One club was banned from a water because a member drove his car clear across a field, flattening the crop in its path and leaving a trail of dirty oil and grease right down to the water's edge. The farmer lost a fair slice of his crop, and several hundred anglers lost the right to fish a very pleasant water because of the thoughtlessness—to put it no worse—of one man.

In spite of continuous propaganda, some town anglers still

seem unaware of, or choose to ignore, the Country Code. (It need be no more than *some*, because the mess or damage caused can be out of all proportion to the numbers causing it.)

So . . .

Close all gates behind you. It is easy enough, and prevents animals from straying on to the road to become a danger to themselves and to traffic.

Keep to the footpaths. The stuff in the field may look like grass, but it may be a field of wheat or barley.

Take your litter home. It soon adds up . . . a bottle here, a tin there, a plastic bag, an empty hook packet, a cigarette packet, a newspaper. All of it is unsightly; some of it is really dangerous. A rusty tin can cut open an animal's leg. A bottle lying in the sunlight can start a fire. A broken bottle hidden in the grass can cut a cow's tongue in half.

The small animals of the waterside can suffer, too. Mice and shrews crawl into bottles and are unable to get out. Birds and small mammals snare themselves in discarded tangles of nylon line.

Do not light fires on the bank, or anywhere come to that. A light breeze, especially in summer, can send even a small fire racing across dry grass, along a hedge and into the nearest haystack.

Leave the farm animals alone, however cute they look. A flock of sheep or a herd of bullocks may stampede, possibly injuring themselves and certainly running off pounds of valuable meat. Bullocks may look docile, and mostly are. But anglers have been injured by bullocks which have turned nasty. If there is a bull in the field, stay right away, even at the expense of your fishing. Anglers have been killed because they took chances with a bull.

Keep your distance from other anglers, both when fishing and when walking to your own swim. A man who has been sitting quietly for several hours, groundbaiting his swim, encouraging the fish and finally getting results, can be excused for being less than polite if someone clumps heavily along the bank behind him, upright against the skyline, or sits a few yards away to reap the benefit of all his patient work.

Even more entitled to fish his swim undisturbed is the man who has spent several days pre-baiting it. You would not, of course, arrive at a water before dawn to get in first at another angler's pre-baited swim, would you? If you were fishing one by accident you would, of course, move on when the other angler turned up and explained things, wouldn't you? You would also bear in mind, should he be a little heated, that he had every right to be.

Don't spin near a bottom fisherman. Your spinner, splashing on to the surface and jiggering away underwater, may scare away the fish he has been patiently collecting around him.

Family fishing outings are becoming more and more popular. But the river bank is not the place for a full-scale picnic, however attractive the setting, when other people are trying to fish.

Keep all noise down, whether from feet, mouth, tackle or transistor radio. In fact, don't take a transistor at all (many clubs ban them, anyway) unless it is one with an earplug. Peace and quiet is a big part of the attraction of angling, and there is nothing so effective as a transistor in shattering it.

Finally, make sure you have a permit for the water you are fishing. Poaching on club waters is not clever or daring. It is just using facilities which other people have paid for—at best, cheating, at worst, stealing.

34

Is This a Record?

It goes without saying that every angler's dream is to catch a record fish. But several times an angler has caught a record weight which did not stand because he did not go about getting it attested and submitted in the proper manner.

The British Record (Rod-Caught) Fish Committee of the National Anglers' Council publishes a list of record fish at frequent intervals. The procedure for registering a possible record is as follows, and is reproduced by permission of the NAC:

Claims must be made in writing to the Secretary stating:

(i) the species of fish and the weight;
(ii) the date and place of capture, and the tackle used; and
(iii) the names and addresses of reliable witnesses both as to the capture by the claimant and the weight, who will be required to sign the forms supporting the claim.

If no witnesses to the capture are available, the claimant must verify his claim by affidavit.

No claim will be accepted unless the Committee is satisfied as to species, method of capture and weight. The Committee reserves the right to reject any claim if not satisfied on any matter which the Committee may think in the particular circumstances to be material.

Identification of species
(a) To ensure correct identification, it is essential that claimants should retain the fish and immediately contact the Secretary

of the Committee who will advise as to production of the fish for inspection on behalf of the Committee.
(b) All carriage costs incurred in production of the fish for inspection by the Committee (if this is required) must be borne by the claimant.

Method of capture

Claims can only be accepted in respect of fish which are caught by fair angling with rod and line. Fair angling is defined by the fish taking the baited hook or lure into its mouth.

Weight

(a) The fish must be weighed as soon as possible on scales or steelyards which can be tested on behalf of the Committee.
(b) The weight must be verified by two independent witnesses who should not be relations of the claimant or a member of his club or party.

Claims can be made for species not included in the Committee's Record Fish List.

The Committee will issue at least once a year its lists of British Record (rod-caught) Fish.

No fish caught out of season shall be accepted as a new record.

A fish for which a record is claimed must be normal and not obviously suffering from any disease by which the weight could be enhanced.

How to photograph your fish

When permission has been granted to submit photographs these must:

1 Be large and in focus.
2 Show as many as possible of the specific characters of the fish. If these are not known consult *Know Your Fish* by Jones and Tombleson (published by Ernest Benn) or any reliable book on fish identification.

The fish should not be held by the head as this distorts the relative lengths of various parts of the body.

Fish should be photographed on a plain background with fins erect so that fin rays can be counted.

It may be necessary to photograph from several angles and also to photograph the teeth.

Some object of known size should be photographed alongside the fish if a measure is not available.

If you catch a record fish
Medium-sized fish can be preserved for considerable periods by refrigeration (deep freeze) or immersion in formalin. If a fish is to be sent by post or rail it is best immersed in a solution of 1 tablespoon of formalin (4% solution of formaldehyde) to 1 pint of water. For despatch, the fish should be wrapped in a cloth wrung out in the solution, placed in a plastic bag and wrapped in stout brown paper: please enclose the name and address of the sender and whether the fish should be returned.

The fish should be weighed as soon as possible after capture and before being placed in preserving liquids.

The claimant should contact the Committee Secretary by telephone, telegram or letter as soon as possible after the capture. Advice will then be given concerning preservation and identification.

Irish record fish
Claims for fish caught in Northern Ireland are dealt with by the British Record (rod-caught) Fish Committee.

Claims for fish caught in Eire should be made to the Irish Specimen Fish Committee, Balnagowan, Mobhi Boreen, Glasnevin, Dublin 9.

The address of the British (rod-caught) Fish Committee is: 17 Queen Street, Peterborough, PE1 1PJ (phone Peterborough 54084 (day) or 252428 (evening)).

Most tackle dealers will gladly weigh any specimen fish brought in to them and will also act as independent witnesses. The *Angling Times* has a large number of Report Stations (often tackle dealers) up and down the country which will make sure that the proper procedure is followed.

35

Some Useful Addresses

Angling and general

Anglers' Cooperative Association, Midland Bank Chambers, Westgate, Grantham

British Association of Fishing Tackle Makers, 145 Oxford Street, London W1R 1TB

British Carp Study Group, P. Mohan, Newhaven, Marsh Lane, Easton-in-Gordano, Bristol, BS20 0NH

Irish Tourist Board, 150 New Bond Street, London W1Y 0AG

National Anglers Council, 17 Queen Street, Peterborough, PE1 1PJ

National Anguilla Club, Brian Crawford, 129 Benland, Bretton, Peterborough, PE3 8EE

National Association of Specimen Groups, G. E. Hodson, 45 Long Croft Road, Dronfield-Woodhouse, Sheffield, S18 5XU

National Federation of Anglers, J. W. Warner, Haig House, 87 Green Lane, Derby

National Water Council, 1 Queen Anne's Gate, London SW1H 9BT

Northern Irish Tourist Board, River House, 48–50 High Street, Belfast, BT1 2DS; and 11 Berkeley Street, London W1X 6BU

Pike Society, G. E. Hodson, 45 Long Croft Road, Dronfield-Woodhouse, Sheffield, S18 5XU

Scottish Tourist Board, 23 Ravelston Terrace, Edinburgh, EH4 3EU

Sports Council, 70 Brompton Road, London SW3 1EX

Water Space Amenity Commission, 1 Queen Anne's Gate, London SW1H 9BT

Regional water authorities
Anglian Water Authority, Diploma House, Grammar School Walk, Huntingdon, PE1 6NZ

Northumbrian Water Authority, Monitor House, Coast Road, Wallsend, Northumberland

North West Water Authority, P.O. Box 261, Dewson House, Great Sankey, Warrington, WA5 3LW

Severn–Trent Water Authority, Abelson House, 2297 Coventry Road, Sheldon, Birmingham, B26 3PR

Southern Water Authority, Eastleigh House, 2 Market Street, Eastleigh, SO5 5WA

South West Water Authority, P.O. Box 22, 3–5 Barnfield Crescent, Exeter, EX1 1RE

Thames Water Authority, Burdett House, 15 Buckingham Street, London WC2

Welsh National Water Development Authority, The Barracks, Brecon

Wessex Water Authority, Techno House, Redcliffe Way, Bristol, BS1 6NY

Yorkshire Water Authority, 21 Park Square South, Leeds, LS1 2QG

Index

Addresses, useful, 264–6

Baits, 40–63
  Groundbaits, 40–2
  Hookbaits, 42–63
  Artificials, 42–3
  Beans, peas and
    sweetcorn, 43–4
  Bloodworms, 44
  Bread, 44–6
  Caddis grubs, 46
  Casters, 46–7
  Caterpillars, 47
  Cheese, 47–8
  Crayfish, 49–50
  Currants and sultanas, 50
  Dock grubs, 50
  Earwigs, 51
  Fish baits, 51
  Fruit, 52
  Hips and haws, 53
  Hempseed, 53–4
  Grasshoppers, 54
  Greaves, 54
  Macaroni, 54
  Maggots, 55–7
  Mealworms, 57
  Meat and fat, 57
  Mussels, 58
  Potatoes, 58
  Shrimps, 58
  Silkweed, 58–9
  Slugs, 59
  Wasp grubs, 59
  Wheat, barley and tares, 60
  Woodlice, 60
  Worms, 60–3
Baits for:
  Barbel, 106–8
  Bream, 115–16
  Carp, Common, 126–8
  Carp, Crucian, 136
  Catfish, 140
  Chub, 143–5
  Dace, 151–2
  Eel, 156–7
  Grayling, 163
  Gudgeon, 166–7
  Perch, 171–2
  Pike, 180–2
  Roach, 198–200

Index

Baits for—*continued*
  Rudd, 210–12
  Tench, 219–20
  Zander, 226
Bait droppers, 38–9
Bank sticks and rod rests, 33–5
Barbel, 9, 104–13
  Baits for, 106–8
  Fishing for, 109–13
  Record weight, 9
  Tackle for, 108–9
Baskets and tackle boxes, 36
Bite indicators, 36–7
  Butt indicator, 37
  Electric bite alarm, 37
  Quivertip, 37
  Swingtip, 36
  Target board, 36–7
    to make, 250
Boating, 230–1
Breaking strain, 24–5
Bream, Common or Bronze, 9, 114–21
  Baits for, 115–16
  Fishing for, 117–21
  Record weight, 9
  Tackle for, 116–17
Bream–roach hybrid, 196
Bream–rudd hybrid, 209
Bream, silver, 9, 114
  Record weight, 9
British Record (rod-caught) Fish Committee, 4, 261–3

Carp, Common, 10, 122–34
  Baits for, 126–8
  Fishing for, 130–4
  Record weight, 10
  Tackle for, 129–30
Carp, Crucian, 10, 135–8
  Baits for, 136
  Fishing for, 137–8
  Record weight, 10
  Tackle for, 136–7
Casting, 69–73
Catch, care of your, 234–8
Catfish, 10, 139–40
  Baits for, 140
  Fishing for, 140
  Record weight, 10
  Tackle for, 140
Chub, 10–11, 141–50
  Baits for, 143–5
  Fishing for, 146–50
  Fishing for in floodwater, 233
  Record weight, 10
  Tackle for, 145
Close season, 1

Dace, 11, 151–3
  Baits for, 151–2
  Fishing for, 152–3
  Fishing for in floodwater, 233
  Record weight, 11
  Tackle for, 152
Dapping, 149–50
Disgorgers, 35

Eel, 11, 154–61
  Baits for, 156–7

Index

Fishing for, 158–61
Record weight, 11
Tackle for, 157–8

Floats, 25–9
  Antenna, 28
  Avon, 28
  Bubble, 29
  Controller, 29
  Ducker, 28
  Quill, 26–8
  Self cocking, 28
  Sliding, 28
  Stick, 28
  Zoomer, 28
Float fishing, 75–84
  Bubble floats and controller floats, 83
  Fishing the swim, 75–9
  Laying on, 81
  Lift method, 82
  Shotting patterns, 79–81
  Sink and draw, 83–4
  Stret pegging, 82–3
  Trotting, 82
Float fishing for:
  Barbel, 111
  Bream, 119–20
  Carp, Common, 132
  Carp, Crucian, 137
  Catfish, 140
  Chub, 146
  Dace, 152–3
  Eel, 158
  Grayling, 164–5
  Gudgeon, 167–8
  Perch, 173–4
  Pike, 187–9
  Roach, 201–3
  Rudd, 214
  Tench, 222–3
Float making, 249–50
Float materials, 29
Floodwater fishing, 232–8
Fly fishing, 100–3
  Tackle, 101
  Casting a fly, 101–2
Fly fishing for:
  Dace, 153
  Grayling, 165
  Roach, 204
  Rudd, 212
Freelining, 92–3
Freelining for:
  Bream, 121
  Carp, Common, 132–3
  Carp, Crucian, 138
  Catfish, 140
  Chub, 147–8
  Dace, 153
  Eels, 159
  Perch, 177
  Pike, 188–9
  Roach, 204
  Rudd, 214–15
  Tench, 224

Gaff, 35, 185, 235
Grayling, 11, 162–5
  Baits for, 163
  Fishing for, 164–5
  Record weight, 11

Grayling—*continued*
  Tackle for, 163–4
Gudgeon, 11, 166–8
  Baits for, 166–7
  Fishing for, 167–8
  Record weight, 11
  Tackle for, 167

Hooks, 21–4
  Barbless, 23
  Crystal, 21
  Eyed, 23
  Longshank, 23
  Model Perfect, 21
  Pennell or New Scale, 21–3
  Redditch Scale, 21
  Round bend, 21
  Snap tackle, 24
  Spade ended, 23
  Treble, 23–4
  Worm tackle, 24
Hooks, care of, 241
Hooks, knots for, 251–2

Keepnet, 33
  How to use, 236–7

Landing net, 33
  How to use, 235
Legering, 85–93
  Float leger, 89
  Freelining, 92–3
  Rolling leger, 92
  Static leger, 89–92
Leger rigs, 86–8
  Link leger, 88
  Running paternoster, 88
  Shot leger, 86
Legering for:
  Barbel, 112–13
  Bream, 120–1
  Carp, Common, 133
  Carp, Crucian, 137–8
  Catfish, 140
  Dace, 152
  Eel, 158–9
  Perch, 176–7
  Pike, 189–90
  Roach, 203
  Rudd, 215
  Tench, 223
  Zander, 226
Lines, 24–5
  Breaking strain, 24–5
Logbooks, keeping, 254–7

Manners, anglers', 258–60
Mapping waters, 254–7

Perch, 12, 169–77
  Baits for, 171–2
  Fishing for, 173–7
  Record weight, 12
  Tackle for, 172–3
Pike, 12, 178–94
  Baits for, 180–2
  Fishing for, 187–94
  Record weight, 12
  Tackle for, 182–7
Pike-perch or zander, 225–7
Pope or ruffe, 169
Priest, 35, 235

Record fish—how to claim, 261–6
Reels, 18–20
  Centre pin, 18–19
  Closed face, 20
  Fixed spool, 18–20
  Multiplying, 20
Reels, care of, 242
Reels, casting with, 69–73
Refraction, 66–7
Roach, 12, 195–207
  Baits for, 198–200
  Fishing for, 201–7
  Fishing for in floodwater, 232
  Record weight, 12
  Tackle for, 200–1
Roach–bream hybrid, 196
Roach–rudd hybrid, 196, 209
Roach pole, 204–7
Rods, 14–17
  Block end, 17
  Carp/specimen, 17
  Leger, 17
  Match, 17
  Pike, 17
  Quivertip, 17
Rods, assembling, 68–9
Rods, care of, 242–3
Rod holdall, 35–6
Rod rests and bank sticks, 33–5
Rudd, 12–13, 208–15
  Baits for, 210–12
  Fishing for, 213–15
  Record weight, 12
  Tackle for, 212–13
Rudd–bream hybrid, 209
Rudd–roach hybrid, 196, 209
Ruffe or pope, 169

Snap tackle, 24
Spinning, 94–9
  Covering the water, 96
  Recovering a snagged lure, 96
  Spinning with deadbaits, 98–9
  Spinning with worms, 99
Spinning for:
  Chub, 150
  Dace, 153
  Perch, 175–6
  Pike, 190–3
  Rudd, 215
  Zander, 226–7
Split rings, 38
Spring balance, 39, 236
Striking and playing a fish, 73–4
Swimfeeders, 38
  To make, 248
Swivels, 37–8

Tackle, care of, 239–44
  Bait containers, 239–40
  Floats, 241
  Hooks, 241
  Landing nets and keepnets, 240
  Lines, 240

Tackle, care of—*continued*
  Plugs, spoons and
    spinners, 241
  Reels, 242
  Rods, 242–3
  Rod rests, 241
  Waders and gumboots,
    244
  Waterproof clothing, 244
Tackle for:
  Barbel, 108–9
  Bream, 116–17
  Carp, Common, 129–30
  Carp, Crucian, 136–7
  Catfish, 140
  Chub, 145
  Dace, 152
  Eels, 157–8
  Grayling, 163–4
  Gudgeon, 167
  Perch, 172–3
  Pike, 182–7
  Roach, 200–1
  Rudd, 212–13
  Tench, 220–1
  Zander, 226
Tackle you can make,
  245–50
  Bloodworm rake, 248
  Floats, 249–50
  Plugs, 246–7
  Slow sinking leger weight,
    247
  Spoon, 245–6
  Swimfeeder, 248
  Target board, 250
  Throwing stick, 245
  Throwing tube, 245
Tackle boxes and baskets, 36
Tench, 13, 216–24
  Baits for, 219–20
  Fishing for, 221–4
  Record weight, 13
  Tackle for, 220–1

Umbrellas, 36

Wading, 228–30
  In floodwater, 233
Weights, 30–2
  Half moon leads, 32
  Lead wire, 31
  Leger leads, 31–2
  Plummets, 32
  Spiral leads, 32
  Split shot, 31
Worm tackle, 24

Zander, 13, 169, 225–7
  Baits for, 226
  Fishing for, 226–7
  Record weight, 13
  Tackle for, 226

LEISURE, DOMESTIC AND GENERAL

Care and Welfare

19503 7	**Alcoholism – A Social Disease** Max Glatt	70p
19501 0	**Caring for the Baby** James W. Partridge	70p
19502 9	**Depression – Understanding a Common Problem** C. A. H. Watts	70p
19504 5	**Schizophrenia – What it Means** A. R. K. Mitchell	70p
05956 7	**Amateur Winemaking and Brewing** Amateur Winemaker Magazine	60p
17886 8	**Analytical Psychology** D. Cox	95p
05933 8	**Antique Furniture** E. Bradford	60p
05510 3	**Archery** M. E. Richardson	50p
05511 1	**Architecture in England** T. W. West	50p
05730 0	**Art, Study** D. Talbot Rice	50p
05963 x	**Assessing Intellectual Ability** B. A. Akhurst	40p
05513 8	**Astrology** Jeff Mayo	50p

15248 6	**Astronomy** D. S. Evans	£1.50
18257 1	**Backpacking** Peter Lumley	60p
20244 0	**Badminton** F. Brundle	£1.00
05520 0	**Bee-keeping** A. N. Schonfield	40p
19082 5	**Billiards and Snooker** R. Holt	70p
16455 7	**British Constitution** R. E. C. Jewell	£1.25
04672 4	**Camping** E. Dominy	60p
05538 3	**Card Games for One** G. F. Hervey	60p
05539 1	**Card Games for Two** K. Konstam	40p
18049 8	**Carpentry** Charles Hayward	40p
05544 8	**Chess** G. Abrahams	40p
20233 5	**Chess Mind, The** G. Abrahams	80p
12493 8	**Codes and Ciphers** F. Higenbottam	60p
05999 0	**Complete Meals** C. Mares	50p
19500 2	**Contract Bridge** E. P. C. Cotter	50p
20379 x	**Creative Crafts** Fredrick Oughton	£1.25
18256 3	**Creative Writing** Victor Jones	50p
17008 5	**Cricket** F. N. S. Creek	50p

05559 6	**Cycling** R. C. Shaw	40p
05978 8	**Crosswords** Alec Robins	£1.25
05562 6	**Drawing** R. Smith	50p
05675 4	**Drawing and Painting** S. A. Knight	40p
05563 4	**Dressmaking** I. Horner	40p
05568 5	**Efficient Reading** C. Mares	40p
15249 4	**Electricity in the House** G. Davidson	70p
19085 x	**Encyclopaedia of Dates and Events**	£1.75
05577 4	**Ethics** A. C. Ewing	70p
05578 2	**Etiquette and Good Manners** W. S. Norman	75p
05960 5	**Exploring our Industrial Past** Kenneth Hudson	£1.75
05583 9	**Express Yourself** R. W. Jepson	40p
05952 4	**Fencing** C. L. de Beaumont	40p
09893 7	**Flower Arrangement** E. Roberts	60p
16310 0	**Flower Arrangement, More** E. Roberts	75p
16677 0	**Fly Fishing** M. Wiggin	50p
05286 4	**Golf** F. G. Jessup and Mark Wilson	50p
12457 1	**Growing Orchids in the Home** Betty Cohen and Eric Roberts	£1.25

Guide to Modern World Literature
Martin Seymour-Smith

19505	3	Volume 1	£2.25
20229	7	Volume 2	£2.25
20230	0	Volume 3	£1.75
20231	9	Volume 4	£1.75

16197 3 **Guitar, The**
Dale Fradd £1.50

05612 6 **Handwriting**
J. le F. Dumpleton 40p

18255 5 **Heraldry and Genealogy**
Leslie Pine 75p

17885 x **History of England**
W. McElwee 50p

05618 5 **Hockey**
Hockey Association 50p

16428 x **Home Heating**
B. J. King and J. E. Beer 40p

05622 3 **Horology**
D. de Carle 40p

05623 1 **Horse Management**
C. E. G. Hope 40p

17661 x **Indoor Aquaria**
D. Latimer-Sayer and Jack Hems 50p

05961 3 **Indoor Plants**
D. M. C. Jones 40p

19497 9 **Into Print**
H. Frayman £1.45

20387 0 **Introducing Hi-Fi**
Peter Turner £1.00

05634 7 **Judo**
E. Dominy 40p

05966 4 **Karate**
E. Dominy 50p

18254 7 **Lapidary**
Del Fairfield 60p

18262 8	**Law**		
	J. Leigh Mellor		75p
05638 x	**Learning, Remembering and Knowing**		
	P. Meredith		40p
05639 8	**Letter Writer**		
	G. S. Humphreys		50p
19820 6	**Local Government**		
	L. Golding		£1.50
05645 2	**Logic**		
	A. A. Luce		50p
19816 8	**Modern Archaeology, Princs and Practise in**		
	David Browne		£1.50
05666 5	**Music**		
	C. King Palmer		60p
05616 9	**Music, History of**		
	A. Percival		60p
05668 1	**Navigation**		
	A. C. Gardner		60p
05673 8	**Orchestration**		
	C. King Palmer		50p
05674 6	**Organ, The**		
	F. Routh		50p
05676 2	**Painting for Pleasure**		
	R. O. Dunlop		40p
19817 6	**Papercraft**		
	Carson Ritchie		£1.25
05681 9	**Philosophy**		
	C. E. M. Joad		50p
05617 7	**Philosophy, History of**		
	J. Lewis		50p
05682 7	**Philosophy of Religion**		
	M. D. Lewis		80p
19084 1	**Photography**		
	Reg Mason		65p

05688 6	**Piano, The** C. King Palmer	50p
12456 3	**Piano, Jazz** Eddie Harvey	95p
05690 8	**Poetry** R. Skelton	40p
17887 6	**Political Thought** C. L. Wayper and C. W. Parkin	50p
16800 5	**Poultry Keeping, Modern** J. Portsmouth	60p
19498 7	**Psychology Today** Ed. Bill Giltham	95p
05699 1	**Public Speaking** P. Westland	40p
19818 4	**Rugby** F. N. S. Creek and Don Rutherford	£1.00
05713 0	**Self-Defence** E. Dominy	50p
05714 9	**Semantics** F. H. George	40p
20377 3	**Shooting** Cogwell and Harrison	£1.25
05717 3	**Singing** C. R. Thorpe	40p
18264 4	**Soccer** F. N. S. Creek	50p
19819 2	**Sociology** J. H. Abraham	75p
05721 1	**Speaker and Debater**	40p
05724 6	**Spelling** K. Baron	50p
17660 1	**Stamp Collecting** F. J. Melville	50p
05729 7	**Study** G. G. Neill Wright	50p

05732	7	**Swimming**	
		F. Waterman	40p
20376	5	**Understanding Social Anthropology**	
		David Pocock	£1.25
18259	8	**Understanding Statistics**	
		Martin Leonard	60p
05992	3	**Violin, The**	
		T. Rowland-Entwistle	50p
05746	7	**Yoga**	
		J. Hewitt	40p
05747	5	**Zen**	
		C. Humphreys	50p

All these books are available at your local bookshop or newsagent, or can be ordered direct from the publisher. Just tick the titles you want and fill in the form below.

Prices and availability subject to change without notice.

TEACH YOURSELF BOOKS, P.O. Box 11, Falmouth, Cornwall.

Please send cheque or postal order, and allow the following for postage and packing:

U.K.—One book 18p plus 8p per copy for each additional book ordered, up to a maximum of 66p.

B.F.P.O. and EIRE—18p for the first book plus 8p per copy for the next 6 books, thereafter 3p per book.

OTHER OVERSEAS CUSTOMERS—20p for the first book and 10p per copy for each additional book.

Name...

Address..

....

....